# HURRICANE

OSPREY
PUBLISHING

# HURRICANE

## HAWKER'S FIGHTER LEGEND

By John Dibbs, Tony Holmes
and Gordon Riley

# DEDICATION

*For the late Air Commodore Pete Brothers and those who flew, fought, maintained and built this magnificent aircraft. You made the Hurricane a truly great machine.*

*And for Liam – Thank you for your unwavering support, smarts and big heart. You are an inspiration.*

John Dibbs

ISBN: 9781472822956
PDF e-book ISBN: 9781472822970
ePub e-book ISBN: 9781472822963

Index by Sandra Shotter
Typeset in Adobe Garamond and Gill Sans
Originated by PDQ Digital Media Solutions, UK
Printed in China through World Print Ltd

17 18 19 20 21   10 9 8 7 6 5 4 3 2 1

## ACKNOWLEDGEMENTS

Air-to-air photography is a 'team sport' and I am sincerely grateful to the
owners, pilots and engineers who worked with me to allow the creation of
the images for this book.
Subject Pilots: Nick Grey, Hoof Proudfoot, Stu Goldspink, Don Sigourney, Paul
Bonhomme, Dave Harvey, John Romain, Bud Granley, Dunc Mason, Alan Walker,
Jan Friso Roozen, Richard Grace, Peter Teichman, Matt Pettit and Johnny Stringer.
Cameraship pilots: Tim Ellison, Norman Lees, Martin Overall, Andy Hill, David
Frasca, Bob Jones and Will Gray.
Owners/Operators: The Fighter Collection, Russell Aviation Group, Historic
Aircraft Collection, Flying Heritage Collection, Jan Friso Roozen, Phillip Lawton,
Peter Teichman and Hangar 11, James Brown from Hurricane Heritage, Peter
Monk, Biggin Hill Heritage Hangar, The Battle of Britain Memorial Flight. Special
thanks to Tim Ellison, Iain Dougall, Brian Denesen, Harry Measures and Kent
Ramsey.

Tony Holmes would like to thank his co-author Gordon Riley, who has supplied
considerable information and many photographs for this volume, as well as fact-
checking the text. Fellow aviation historians Robert Gretzyngier, Phil Jarrett,
Wojtek Matusiak, Rachel Morris, Dave O'Malley, Mark Peapell, Mark Sheppard,
Kari Stenman and Andy Thomas have also provided key photographs and/or
information for the book. Finally, thanks also to John Davies, publisher at Grub
Street, Tom Moulson (author of *The Millionaires' Squadron*) and Nick Thomas
(author of *Hurricane Squadron Ace*) for allowing the use of brief extracts from
their respective books.

## AUTHOR'S NOTE

This book was shot entirely using Canon 35mm equipment:
Camera Bodies:  Canon EOS-1N, EOS 1DS and DX, EOS- 5D II and III.
Lenses:  17-35 mm F4, 28-70 mm f2.8L, 24-70 mm f2.8L, 70-200 mm f2.8L I
and II, 300 mm f2.8L.
Filmstock: Fuji ISO 50 Velvia

## IMAGE ACKNOWLEDGEMENTS

All photographs are by John Dibbs unless otherwise indicated.
Cover, title page and back cover: R4118 with undersides painted in Sky.
Dedication page: Biggin Hill Heritage Hangar's Hurricane XII painted to
represent Flight Lieutenant Pete Brothers' 'Blue Peter.'

Osprey Publishing supports the Woodland Trust, the UK's leading woodland
conservation charity. Between 2014 and 2018 our donations will be spent
on their Centenary Woods project in the UK.

To find out more about our authors and books visit
**www.ospreypublishing.com**. Here you will find extracts, author
interviews, details of forthcoming events and the option to sign up for our
newsletter.

# CONTENTS

The Hawker Hurricane! Now 96 years of age, I seem to have spent half my life flying the Hurricane, fighting in it, teaching others to fly it, writing books about it, talking about it, praising it – and finally (let it be admitted) criticizing it! Like its designer, Sydney Camm, who was born in 1893 and whom I encountered fleetingly in the 1940s and 1950s, I have always regarded both the aircraft and its designer as ever so slightly old-fashioned. But I go too fast.

This official portrait of 20-year-old Pilot Officer Tom Neil was taken shortly after he received the DFC on 8 October 1940. The citation that accompanied this decoration read in part, 'This officer has destroyed six enemy aircraft. He shows great keenness and has displayed dash and courage of a high order.' (John Dibbs)

## A VERY SPECIAL AIRCRAFT

I joined the RAF Volunteer Reserve when I left school at the age of 18 and was trained to fly on various biplanes. These included what were then termed the 'Hart Variants' – the Hawker Hart, Audax, Hector, Hind, Fury and others. These aircraft, beautiful to look at and splendid in every way, were little more than late-1920s versions of the aeroplanes employed in World War 1. Flying steadfastly and unendingly at home and in all corners of the world, they defended Britain and the many nations of the British Empire, all at the breathtaking speed of about 140 mph!

All of Sydney Camm's aircraft were of the same basic design. Fuselages were skeletal metal structures covered in wood and fabric at the back end and inline Rolls-Royce water-cooled Kestrel engines of varying horsepower up front. A radiator was situated underneath each fuselage and a cold and draughty open cockpit contained a scattering of primitive instruments plus a single Vickers or Lewis machine gun, with its associated gunsights. All the various types in the variant range were easy and delightful to fly and were greatly loved.

It was against this sort of background that when rearmament commenced in Britain in 1935, and news of the first new 300 mph monoplane fighters in the form of the Spitfire and Hurricane appeared in the national press, the nation was both startled and ecstatic. The people's ignorance and credulity was further exploited when a Hurricane from No 111 Sqn, based at RAF Northolt and taking advantage of friendly jet streams, was flown between Edinburgh and London in February 1938 at the staggering average ground speed of 408 mph. This was a carefully staged confidence trick, arranged and publicized to bolster the nation's spirits and enhance the reputations of a few of Britain's less famous military aircraft and, of course, that of the RAF and No 111 Sqn!

When, in May 1940, I left Flying Training School as a 19-year-old newly commissioned officer pilot, I could best be described as wildly enthusiastic but entirely lacking in training, experience, wisdom and, not least of all, tact. My description and assessment of the first Spitfires and Hurricanes I flew should, therefore, be judged against the shortcomings I have here described.

Although designated a Hurricane squadron, my new unit, No 249 Sqn, was at first equipped with the Spitfire I. I remember the occasion well. As the first pilot to arrive at RAF Church Fenton and the hangars of No 249 Sqn, I was beside myself with happiness. Having never been near a low-winged aircraft before, and with a mere 158 hours flying in

my logbook, my brand new Spitfire flew like an angel, and everything about it I found absolutely perfect – despite the long nose which blocked my view both on the ground and sometimes in the air; the fact that it tipped up easily if I misused the brakes and got stuck in the mud; the hood, which I always had difficulty in opening and closing in the air; the engine that overheated and boiled given just half a chance because of the aircraft's off-centre radiator; the fact that, having fired 30,000 rounds at a towed target at the Armament Practice Camp, I had not achieved a single hit! All this meant absolutely nothing to me at the time because I was achieving my life's ambition – *I was actually flying a Spitfire!*

Then, on 13 June 1940, I stepped out of the Spitfire that I had flown for 100 hours in a period of four weeks and climbed into a newly arrived Hurricane. The difference was vast. Whereas I had normally *stepped* into my Spitfire, I now had to *climb* into my new fighter, using one outstretched foot and a clutching hand. Where I had formerly sat in a comfy Spitfire cockpit, in my Hurricane,

Flying Officer Neil (left) is seen here with Flying Officer George Barclay, who had also received a DFC in October 1940 following his exploits in the summer of 1940. Both men were already aces by the time this photograph was taken outside No 249 Sqn's dispersal hut during the early spring of 1941. (John Dibbs)

I was now sitting in a bucket seat and suspended in space with a lot of dark 'I didn't know what' underneath my parachuted behind. In fact, exactly as in my old Hawker Hart trainer!

On the other hand, in my new Hurricane, visibility was greatly improved in every direction. The hood could be moved back and forth with one hand and the aircraft be flown with it in the open position – and although everything else (particularly the throttle handle) seemed puny and less well finished, the instruments and other important bits seemed to be more or less the same. Finally, when I taxied my Hurricane away, the undercarriage felt absolutely rock solid and the engine did not show any signs of overheating, even when I was obliged to hang about for five-or-so minutes. Suddenly, it occurred to me: I was in familiar territory. I was back in my old training aircraft, the Hawker Hart – with a much bigger engine, of course, only one wing and a retractable undercarriage. No, my brand new Hurricane, like the chap who designed it, was absolutely splendid – but just a bit old fashioned, even in June 1940!

To move ahead, however, I intercepted my first enemy aircraft on 4 July 1940, a mere ten days after my initial flight in a Hurricane, and in the 16 weeks of the Battle of Britain I flew 157 operational sorties against the Luftwaffe. Later, during the siege of Malta, I flew a further 100 rather unpleasant combat flights, plus a few others in far-away Burma. To all of these may be added the uncounted number I also carried out in other operational areas and during the periods I was instructing at various

HURRICANE

This cigarette card features the prototype Hurricane K5083. (John Dibbs)

Hawker's Chief Test Pilot, Flight Lieutenant P.W.S. 'George' Bulman holds station beneath the camera-aircraft during an early flight in K5083 from Brooklands. It first took to the air on 6 November 1935. (John Dibbs)

Things got a little draughty for the pilot of brand new Kingston-built Hurricane I L1582 during an early pre-delivery test flight from Brooklands in the early spring of 1938 when its 'break-out' emergency exit panel came adrift and jammed itself up inside the canopy. Keen to land as soon as possible, the pilot has already selected fully down for the trailing edge split flaps. (John Dibbs)

Operational Training Units (OTUs). In short, I flew many Hurricanes, many times, in many places!

Even by mid-September 1940, it had become obvious to all those of us who had survived injury in the Battle of Britain that our initial Hurricane I was outclassed when in combat with the Luftwaffe's Bf 109. Also during the battle, we could have done much better against both German bombers and fighters with a faster aircraft firing bigger-calibre guns. We had long been asking for the much-rumoured replacement of the Hurricane I by the Mk II, but the change only occurred for No 249 Sqn during February 1941.

To give a better picture of the advancement of our fighter aircraft during and after the summer of 1940, there were only three marks of Hurricane ever produced, although there were numerous modifications and changes of armament in the Mk II to meet changing wartime needs. By comparison, in the months and years following 1940, there were 24 marks of Spitfire and more than 50 lesser changes incorporated in the basic design until the early 1950s, when the aeroplane ceased to be regarded as a frontline fighter. In short, and to put things properly in perspective, even the Hurricane II had tottered to a standstill by the beginning of 1943, although some were still being used in combat until 1945 and after. The Spitfire, on the other hand, being a more modern design, was capable of much further development, which indeed took place over a number of years.

Finally, whilst it is never my intention to cramp the style of the author of this book writing about the Hurricane, it may be worthwhile making a few additional points of general interest. In my view, in 1940, the Bf 109 was a more effective fighter than either the early Spitfire or the Hurricane. Its Daimler-Benz engine of 39 litres was much bigger than the 27-litre Merlin used in our fighters. It also had a better variable speed supercharger and employed a more modern fuel injection system rather than a carburettor, which, in our aircraft, would always falter when negative 'G' occurred. It also mounted 20 mm cannons plus slightly heavier machine guns with more ammunition. In speed, it could initially outstrip a Spitfire in a zoom climb or

a dive and could always leave a Hurricane standing. On the negative side, however, it was always fighting over 'enemy territory', and had very limited endurance and radius of action. Finally, it was smaller than either of our fighters, and with its splayed-out undercarriage, a little less pleasant to fly in the air and control on the ground.

The belief in Britain that our fighters could always out-turn a Bf 109 in battle was a myth. The German fighter had automatic slats which helped at the point of any stall, and if the pilot chose to reduce speed sufficiently, it could marginally out-turn either of our aircraft. As the Bf 109 always used speed and agility in battle as a tactic, steep turning and dogfights seldom occurred.

There was no heating in either the Spitfire or the Hurricane, and as the Hurricane especially had holes everywhere around the cockpit, the cold was often so intense that, higher than 20,000 ft, the pilot almost ceased to function. This was a difficulty ignored by designers and Air Force hierarchy alike, all of whom seemed to believe that for a period of two hours, a fighter pilot should be expected to cope with almost anything!

The Hurricane was also especially prone to the risk of fire in the air, its 97 gallons of fuel being contained in three tanks, two of which were sited left and right of the pilot's feet. In the Hurricane I, the fuel tanks were not self-sealing and became a well-known target for any German fighter attacking from behind. This became a real problem during the Battle of Britain, and most casualties resulting from fire occurred in the early Hurricane force. The Mk II was better, but fire in the air was always a very nasty problem.

The Hurricane I had no 'rudder bias' so that a pilot could never trim out the foot load. This was a real difficulty during any lengthy full-throttle climb, as the pilot's right leg was fully and often very painfully extended. During a dive at high speed, the left leg was similarly affected. This was rectified in the Mk II, but we all had to suffer in 1940.

The Mk II was better than the Mk I, but only marginally. It had a Merlin 20 engine with a two-speed supercharger, which gave us an extra 20 mph at ground level and enabled us to fight better up to

25,000 ft. There were other marginal improvements but it still had the thick high-lift wing of the Mk I and could never be called a fast aircraft. It also mounted either 20 mm cannons or up to twelve 0.303-in machine guns, which were a help, although we were seldom able to catch the enemy to use them. I remember, too, taking my new Mk II up to 38,000 ft when they first arrived, but it took a long, long time and was a monumental, freezing bore. It was a trip I never repeated.

A final footnote: a facsimile of one of my Hurricanes is now the gate-guardian at RAF North Weald. I flew that particular aircraft 63 times between 3 September and 10 October 1940, on which date it was shot down by a German chap called Mölders and lost. Occasionally, when visiting North Weald, I pause to look at it. I have memories of the many Hurricanes that have passed through my hands over the years, and I am bound to say, not all of them were either fruitful or pleasant.

Thumbing through this fine new volume about the Hurricane I am reminded of the men, the machine and the times in which we fought together. John Dibbs carrying his camera aloft allows the reader to be the wingman on Sir Sydney's stolid design. The beauty and drama of flight are captured in his images. Flight is wonderful, flight in a machine you love is simply magical, and these photographs offer a sense of that. The archive photographs, beautifully restored, blow the dust off distant memories and breathe life into the past. The text, carefully researched and detailed, will allow a new generation to appreciate this uniquely British aircraft, one whose design straddled and affected a pivotal period in history, taking the best of the past and adding a hint of the future to help secure success and ultimately victory.

I have pleasure in recommending this book to anyone who shares a love of flight, history and human adventure.

*Tom Neil*

*249 Sqn*

*Wing Commander Tom Neil, DFC\*, AFC, AE*
*November 2016*

A late British summer sky stretched above the beautiful green grass of the former RAF Bicester airfield in September 2016. Warm air swirled around and the sun bleached sections of my vision.

Walking across the grass with a few minutes to spare before a shoot, I found myself alone looking at the Hawker Hurricane that was parked out on the flightline. Or, rather more accurately, I felt it was looking at me. Standing in front of this iconic machine you get the impression it is challenging you. Its wide-set undercarriage gives it the look of a bulldog, set on it hunched shoulders. It has a bluntness of line that gives it solidity, and its wheels look like closed fists. The tail begrudgingly tapers down to sit on the ground, but the radiator intake set on the centreline and beneath the fuselage gives it a barrel-chested look. This is one very British bulldog – something Churchill would have appreciated, and that he did.

In the mid-1930s to help rearm against Nazi Germany's rising ambition in Europe, British aviation companies were tasked with designing a new fighter. Sir Sydney Camm of Hawker Aircraft Limited hedged his bet, and what a good bet that proved to be. Hawker's design team took a mix of the best of the 1930s technology that they knew so well and added a bit of the future 1940s to keep it cutting edge. The philosophy paid off. The British government liked the conservative approach and the 'Fury Monoplane', due to its technological lineage from the silver Hawker biplanes that twinkled across the skies of the Empire, became the 'Hurricane'.

The Hurricane hit its peak at exactly the right time for the people of the world. Seventy-six years earlier, on summer days similar to the one I found myself admiring Hurricane R4118, that very machine had flown from the same type of airfield I now stood on. Young pilots of the RAF from many different nations flew the Hurricane into battle and claimed more hostile invaders from the Luftwaffe and, belatedly, the *Regia Aeronautica*, than all other types of defenders combined during the Battle of Britain. But the Hurricane's story does not end in the summer of 1940. The aeroplane went on to serve in ever more technologically demanding battles, from duelling in the blazing skies of the Western Desert, to flying from aircraft carriers in defence of convoys in the Mediterranean, attacking ground targets in the heavy, humid, climes of the Far East and engaging enemy fighters over the frozen wastes of Russia and Finland. The bravery of men, their machine a true warrior.

Having grown up in an era where the restoration of warbirds grew exponentially, one of the types that proved challenging to restorers, rather ironically considering its traditional airframe construction, was the Hurricane. Wood and fabric doesn't stand the withering of years passing, and the quirks of British design like hexagonal steel tubing proved hard to replicate. Thanks though to Tony Ditheridge and his determination to see Hurricanes fly again, as well as a handful of historically minded individuals with the means to see this iconic machine sit on the line once more, we are able to see, hear and be inspired by the sight of a Hurricane taking to the same skies it did battle in all those years ago.

It was by no means a perfect machine. There were some terrible design shortcomings, such as the fuel tank that sat in front of the pilot, which, if it ruptured in battle, turned the Hurricane into a flying inferno. Nevertheless, the aeroplane's built-in strength, not to mention its manouevrability, saved pilots countless times.

The many lessons we need to understand are set in our history, and the noise and sound of Hurricanes flying today might act as a trigger for us to look back and understand what went before. A bit like the design philosophy that shaped the Hurricane at such a vital time, let's take what we know for a better future.

*John M. Dibbs*
*Redmond, Washington*
*December 2016*

The Royal Air Force's first monoplane fighter hero of the Battle of Britain, the Hawker Hurricane can trace its lineage back to 1912 and the creation of the Sopwith Aviation Company by leading pioneer aviator Thomas Sopwith. The firm soon established an enviable reputation for itself during World War 1 through the production of aeroplanes such as the Tabloid, Pup, Camel, Dolphin and Snipe. However, immediately post-war, Sopwith was badly affected by the massive reduction in defence spending and the company was forced into liquidation.

Determined to begin again, Sopwith reformed his firm under the name of H. G. Hawker Engineering in recognition of the work done by his Chief Test Pilot, Australian Harry Hawker, during World War 1. The latter was killed in a flying accident whilst practicing for the Hendon Air Display in July 1921. Two years later Sydney Camm joined Hawker as a senior draftsman, and in a relationship that lasted 43 years, he would work on 52 different aeroplane types whose production totalled 26,000 airframes. Camm replaced George Carter as Hawker's Chief Designer in 1925, after which he concentrated his efforts on creating military aeroplanes for the RAF. Undoubtedly his most famous products of the interwar period were the stunningly beautiful Hart two-seat bomber and Fury single-seat fighter, both of which were powered by Rolls-Royce Kestrel inline engines.

In early 1933 Camm began looking at the feasibility of producing a monoplane fighter in order to break the deadlocked biplane formula adhered to by the RAF since World War 1,

although his discussions with the Air Ministry's Directorate of Technical Development at this time failed to secure official support for his proposal. Nevertheless, the Hawker board backed its Chief Designer, giving him approval to press on with the aeroplane – dubbed the Fury Monoplane – as a private venture. This presented Camm with certain problems, however, as Hawker designer Dr Percy Walker recalled:

> As a private venture, the design from the beginning was subject to certain limitations, mainly owing to the need to control costs. The firm was compelled to apply existing design techniques to their monoplane, and make use of existing machine tools and workshop methods. This meant a structure composed mainly of steel tubes covered with fabric. The use of fabric for wing-covering produced a problem which was far from easy to resolve. By the standards of the time, the speed of the Hurricane was very high indeed, much faster than any of its biplane predecessors. Never before had fabric wing-covering been subject to such speeds and loading for any length of time.

Work on the Fury Monoplane commenced in earnest in the spring of 1933, with Camm and his team initially producing a design that essentially paired a Fury fuselage with a single low wing of 38 ft span. The aeroplane, fitted with a fixed, spatted undercarriage, was powered by a Rolls-Royce Goshawk engine of 660 hp. It was estimated that the latter would give the fighter a top speed of 280 mph. The Fury I, by comparison, could achieve 207 mph in level flight.

One in a series of 'roll-out' photographs taken of Hawker Monoplane F 36/34 prototype K5083 shortly after it had been reassembled at Brooklands airfield, in Surrey, in late October 1935. Note the aeroplane's lower hinged wheel doors, strut-braced tailplane and light canopy structure. The aircraft is also devoid of a radio mast, armament and gunsight. (John Dibbs)

Hurricane I L1647 awaits collection, probably from Brooklands, by No 32 Sqn in October 1938. Based at Biggin Hill, the unit received 16 brand new Hurricane Is in place of its Gauntlet biplane fighters during the autumn of 1938. This aeroplane did not last long in the frontline, however, as it was taxied into a tractor and written off at Sutton Bridge on 2 May 1939 during No 32 Sqn's annual aircraft gunnery practice camp. (John Dibbs)

OPPOSITE This dramatic advertisement for the Merlin engine was placed by Rolls-Royce in aviation journals such as *Flight* and *Aeroplane* to coincide with the Hurricane's entry into squadron service with RAF Fighter Command in the summer of 1938. (John Dibbs)

In early 1934 Rolls-Royce announced that it was developing a 12-cylinder, liquid-cooled engine designated the PV 12. Its power-to-weight ratio was significantly better than the company's Goshawk engine, and Rolls-Royce believed that it would produce at least 1,000 hp. Camm quickly realized that the PV 12 had to be incorporated into his monoplane fighter, even though this meant significant changes to the design to the point where the aeroplane's link to the Fury was so tenuous that it was renamed the Hawker Interceptor Monoplane.

In October 1934 Air Ministry officials examined the Hawker design. They were so impressed with what they saw that they in turn issued Specification F 36/34 for a monoplane fighter based on the company project. The following month Hawker's Interceptor Monoplane became the Air Ministry's F 36/34 Single-Seat Fighter – High Speed Monoplane, powered by the Rolls-Royce PV 12. The latter would eventually mature into the mighty Merlin.

On 21 February 1935 the Air Ministry placed an order with Hawker covering the creation of the first prototype of the F 36/34 Single-Seat Fighter – High Speed Monoplane. Although tempted to embrace such cutting-edge techniques as stressed-skin construction when building their new

monoplane fighter, Hawker designers realized that the need to rapidly mass-produce the aircraft meant that they would have to rely on methods that had served them well since World War 1. More modern construction techniques would have required the creation of new jigs and tools on the factory floor, as well as the retraining of the Hawker workforce. Therefore, the F 36/34 Single-Seat Fighter – High Speed Monoplane design was constructed using established concepts that were modified to suit the requirements of the more modern aeroplane.

For example, the steel-tube longerons that formed the backbone of the fuselage were surrounded by a secondary structure of wooden formers and stringers that were in turn covered with fabric from the tail to the cockpit. From the latter forward, the fuselage was covered with light metal panels. The fighter's ailerons were fabric covered, but its split trailing-edge flaps boasted duralumin covering. The PV 12, which was soon to be named the Merlin, was mounted on steel tubes. Initially, the state-of-the art engine drove a simple wooden two-bladed Watts propeller as fitted to the biplane Fury I. Like most monoplane fighter designs of this period, the Hawker aeroplane featured a retractable undercarriage. Crucially, the latter retracted

Four factory-fresh Hurricane Is soak up the sunshine at Brooklands in 1938. All of these aircraft are fitted with early production 'kidney' exhaust stacks, Watts two-bladed wooden propellers, ring and bead gunsights, armour-free windscreens, 'pole' type untapered radio masts (the squared-off top of the radio mast was an identifying feature of the early L-series Hurricanes) and external venturi beneath their cockpits. Early Hurricanes lacked vacuum pumps, which meant a venturi had to be fitted to drive the gyro instruments on the blind flying panel. (John Dibbs)

This detailed view of an anonymous Hurricane I ready for delivery to the RAF shows the trailing edge split flaps in the fully down position, as well as providing a better view of the 'kidney' exhaust stacks and fuselage-mounted venturi. (John Dibbs)

MILITARY - HAWKER HURRICANES - FLYING IN LINE.

This Valentine's postcard of No 111 Sqn Hurricane Is was released shortly after the unit completed its transition to the fighter in early 1938. 'Treble One' suffered heavy attrition during its early operations with the Hurricane, writing off no less than 12 of the 16 aeroplanes it was originally issued with. (John Dibbs)

One of Fighter Command's finest looks up at Hurricane I L1555 as it beats up Northolt upon returning from a training flight. The pilot is wearing a standard issue Type B leather helmet and a Type D oxygen mask, but lacks any form of goggles. His ring for the ring and bead gunsight is mounted on the cockpit coaming ahead of him. Note also that the windscreen lacks a bulletproof armoured glass panel. (John Dibbs)

inwards, thus giving the undercarriage a wider stance when extended and making the fighter better suited to rough field operations.

By October 1935 construction of the prototype, bearing the serial number K5083, was nearing completion at Hawker's Kingston plant. The airframe was duly delivered by road to the company's assembly shed at nearby Brooklands, and at month-end it was rolled out as a complete aeroplane. On 6 November, Hawker Chief Test Pilot Flight Lieutenant P.W.S. 'George' Bulman completed K5083's maiden flight from Brooklands, and three more flights quickly followed. Fellow Hawker test pilot Philip Lucas made one of these early hops, later commenting that 'we found the aeroplane easy to fly, stable in flight and on the ground, and with a much better view than anything we had flown before'.

Following three months of company flight trials, which had seen the aeroplane attain a speed of 325 mph at 16,500 ft, K5083 was transferred to the Aeroplane and Armament Experimental Establishment (A&AEE) at Martlesham Heath in February 1936 for evaluation by RAF test pilots. The report issued at the end of the trials noted,

amongst other things, that the aeroplane had a service ceiling of 35,400 ft. It also confirmed that K5083 was the world's first fighter capable of exceeding 300 mph in level flight.

In the wake of the favourable A&AEE report, Hawker heard rumours that the Air Ministry was likely to recommend that its design be put into volume production. Bert Tagg, who was a member of Hawker's production staff from 1935, recalled:

The Hawker directors demonstrated their confidence in the aeroplane by agreeing in March 1936 that production should be initiated ahead of contract, with a policy to plan tooling and facilities for 1,000 aeroplanes. This early board decision gave a lead of considerable importance in the light of subsequent events.

Historians have since argued that committing the aeroplane to production so early in its development prevented further improvements to the design that could have given the Hurricane a performance comparable with its future adversary, the Bf 109E. However, had the Hawker fighter been delayed for

While the 'erks' fire up the recently delivered Hurricane Is, nine pilots from No 3 Sqn receive last minute instructions from their CO, Squadron Leader H.L.P. Lester (in the black flying helmet with white goggle straps), at Kenley prior to participating in the 1938 Empire Air Day. This event was held at the Surrey fighter station on 28 May 1938, with the Hurricane being just one of 13 RAF types on display. (John Dibbs)

the sake of future development – a fate which initially befell the Spitfire – it is estimated that 600 fewer examples would have been delivered to the RAF by the summer of 1940. This in turn would have almost certainly allowed the Luftwaffe to achieve aerial supremacy on the Western Front, facilitating the invasion of Britain.

On 3 June 1936, the Air Ministry contracted Hawker to build 600 examples of the F 36/34 Single-Seat Fighter – High Speed Monoplane, which was officially named the Hurricane later that same month. In July, K5083 gave the new Hawker fighter its public debut when it participated in the Hendon Air Display. Hawker's Kingston and Brooklands facilities were unable to cope with production on the scale requested by the Air Ministry, but fortunately the company had acquired the Gloster Aircraft Company in 1934, and it was charged with volume Hurricane production from 1938. That same year, Hawker's brand new Langley plant also began delivering Hurricanes, which was just as well as the company received a follow-on contract for 1,000 aeroplanes in November 1938.

By then, problems with the Merlin I engine that had initially plagued K5083 had been well and truly cured. Reliability issues with the Rolls-Royce motor had been so bad that both Hawker and the Air Ministry had decided to wait for the improved Merlin II of 1,030 hp before commencing production of the Hurricane I. The first Mk I,

L1547, made its maiden flight on 12 October 1937. Aside from being fitted with the more powerful Merlin II, this machine differed from K5083 through the fitment of a revised, strengthened, canopy, ejector exhaust stubs and simplified undercarriage doors.

L1548 became the first Hurricane I to be issued to Fighter Command on 15 December 1937 when it was delivered to Gauntlet I/II-equipped No 111 Sqn at RAF Northolt. The unit had replaced all of its Gloster biplane fighters by early 1938. Like the prototype, the first Hurricane Is in service had two-bladed fixed-pitch Watts wooden propellers, but they were subsequently replaced by de Havilland (DH) two-position three-bladed propellers and, finally, DH or Rotol constant-speed units. Watts-equipped aeroplanes saw combat in France in May–June 1940; however, the final examples were not replaced until after Dunkirk.

Another feature of early production Hurricane Is was their fabric-covered wings, which caused some problems for No 111 Sqn in its first months with the fighter. Unit pilot and future 1940 ace Pilot Officer Roy Dutton recalled 'at high speed the wing gun panels sometimes partially blew out and the wing fabric distended like sausages between the ribs'. By 1939 stressed-skin metal wings were being manufactured, and these were considerably lighter, stronger and stiffer in both bending and torsion. Heating units for the guns were also fitted within

To a newcomer, the Hurricane was an immensely powerful but not very demanding aeroplane. Its wide-track undercarriage, stable and responsive flying characteristics and reliable engine and hydraulic system resulted in a general atmosphere of confidence in the squadron, so that the newcomer had no reason to become apprehensive.

Confident in the ability of their Hurricanes to take the fight to Germany, the young men of Fighter Command would subsequently find themselves embroiled in a bitter struggle for aerial supremacy initially over western France and then southern England for much of 1940. Proving that both they and their aeroplanes were more than up to this task, Hurricane pilots would emerge at year end with four-fifths of the aerial kills credited to the RAF in 1940.

From 1941 the Spitfire began to dominate the ranks of Fighter Command. Nevertheless, the Hurricane remained in production until September 1944, by which time 12,780 examples had been built in the UK and 1,451 in Canada under licence. The aeroplane's appearance and performance had altered remarkably little over the intervening seven years, yet the soundness of Sydney Camm's original design had allowed the Hurricane to remain a viable weapon of war through to VJ Day.

The Hurricane I that provides the backdrop for this photograph, taken at Lille-Seclin, in France, in December 1939, is a fabric-winged aeroplane of No 85 Sqn. All early examples of the Hawker fighter were built with fabric-covered outer wings, although production switched to re-stressed metal-covered wings in 1939. (John Dibbs)

the wings themselves, as it had been revealed that at the time of the Munich Agreement in September 1938, Hurricane pilots were unable to fire their weapons above 15,000 ft due to the guns' mechanisms being frozen.

By the time Germany invaded Poland on the morning of 1 September 1939, 497 Hurricane Is had been delivered to 18 squadrons within RAF Fighter Command. Pilots had found the new machine a joy to fly, as 19-year-old future ace Pilot Officer Roland Beamont of No 87 Sqn recalled:

This No 56 Sqn Hurricane I ran out of runway on landing (note its trailing edge split flaps are in the fully down position) at North Weald and ploughed through the perimeter hedge, before eventually coming to a halt on the B181 Epping Road. Schoolboys and groundcrew, and a lone fireman with his limp hose, have assembled to take in this rather unusual sight. (John Dibbs)

# CHAPTER ONE

# BATTLE OF FRANCE SURVIVOR

Hurricane I P3351 cruises along the Channel coast, the White Cliffs near Dover providing an unmistakable backdrop to this veteran fighter of the Battle of France. The aeroplane features authentic markings for this period, with the full rudder stripes that were applied in France in an effort to stop British aircraft from being attacked by fighters from the *Armée de l'Air*. The thin yellow ring was added to the fuselage roundel following an RAF order issued to all Commands on 1 May 1940. Finally, this aeroplane also has a yellow gas detection patch on its port wingtip.

P
resently the sole airworthy Hurricane survivor of the Battle of France, P3351 saw action in the final stages of this ill-fated campaign with No 73 Sqn. By the time the aeroplane joined this unit on the Continent, it had been in France for almost nine months as part of the force sent across the Channel to help defend Western Europe from German occupation. With Britain's declaration of war on 3 September 1939, a long-standing agreement between it and France that would see the former rapidly despatch a substantial armed force to the Continent was invoked. Known as the British Expeditionary Force (BEF), it comprised two distinct elements from an RAF standpoint. The first of these was the Advanced Air Striking Force (AASF), made up of Fairey Battle III medium bombers from Bomber Command's No 1 Group and, eventually, Bristol Blenheim IVs from No 2 Group.

The squadrons from these groups were tasked primarily with strategic bombing operations, and initially had no dedicated fighter cover from Fighter Command – the French *Armée de l'Air* was responsible for protecting AASF assets.

The second element, which was to operate closely with the ground forces of the BEF, comprised the whole of No 22 (Army Co-operation) Group, plus a quartet of Hurricane I squadrons and two ex-No 1 Group Blenheim I units. Emphasizing their close-support mission, the bulk of No 22 Group's squadrons were equipped with Lysander IIs. One of the four Hurricane units sent across the Channel was No 73 Sqn, which became part of No 60 (Fighter) Wing shortly after its arrival at Octeville, near Le Havre, on 9 September 1939. The unit had barely completed a year of flying with the Hurricane at that point, having begun to receive examples of the Hawker fighter as

On 19 April 1940 an RAF photographer by the name of 'Mr Devon' arrived at No 73 Sqn's Reims home to take air-to-air shots of the unit. Seated in the rear gunner's position in a Fairey Battle, the photographer, dubbed 'Glorious' by the irreverent fighter pilots, took a series of memorable images. The three Hurricanes closest to the camera were P2569/'D', P2575/'J' and N2359/'Z'. (John Dibbs)

replacements for its Gloster Gladiator Is at Digby, in Lincolnshire, in July 1938.

The Hurricanes of Nos 1, 73, 85 and 87 Sqns had been the first units within the BEF's RAF Air Component despatched to France in order to cover the disembarkation of troops, and their equipment. Once the BEF was safely on the Continent, No 60 (Fighter) Wing's quartet of Hurricane squadrons commenced their assigned escorting role within the Air Component. However, when Battle units started to suffer losses to German Bf 109s during reconnaissance missions over enemy territory because their French fighter escorts had not proven up to the job, senior RAF commanders were quick to act. Nos 1 and 73 Sqns were transferred to the AASF, forming No 67 (Fighter) Wing. Posted to Rouvres, near Verdun, No 73 Sqn commenced its new role on 10 October.

By then the Hurricane had shown its suitability for operations in France, its wide undercarriage proving more than capable of coping with the undrained and damp airfields that were commonplace in this theatre. During the eight months of the so-called 'Phoney War' (or 'Bore War' as it was christened by the British press), which ended with the launching of the *Blitzkrieg* on 10 May 1940, No 73 Sqn was kept relatively busy during missions on the Franco-German

Flight Lieutenant Reg Lovett, commander of 'A' Flight, leads his section in behind 'Glorious' in his requisitioned Battle over northern France on 19 April. (© IWM C 1288)

border, its pilots being credited with 19 enemy aircraft destroyed and eight probables. This success had come at a high price, however, with five Hurricanes lost to the enemy, two pilots killed in action and two in accidents and three wounded.

During the early hours of 10 May, German forces commenced Operation *Yellow* – the all-out attack on Holland, Belgium and, ultimately, France. British pilots received word of the *Blitzkrieg* at 0410 hrs, and No 73 Sqn was the first RAF unit to engage the enemy. In a day described in the Squadron Diary as one of 'ceaseless activity', its

All Hurricane Is in Fighter Command (including those deployed to France) had three-colour undersurfaces, as seen here on P3351. The underside of the starboard wing was White, the port wing Night and the fuselage Aluminium. Note also that the port wing roundel has the yellow ring added from 1 May 1940.

pilots flew more than 40 sorties and claimed at least four aerial victories. Despite this effort, German advances on the ground forced No 73 Sqn to leave Rouvres on the 10th for an airfield further west near Reims – the first of seven moves as British forces steadily retreated to north-west France.

Between 11 and 19 May, No 73 Sqn fought innumerable battles with the Luftwaffe. Always outnumbered, its pilots nevertheless gave an outstanding account of themselves, being credited with 27 enemy aircraft destroyed. In return, five pilots were killed and one badly burned – the unit had also lost nine Hurricanes in combat. No 73 Sqn was posted out of the frontline to a temporary airfield on farmland at Gaye, north-west of Troyes, on the 19th in order to re-equip with replacement pilots and new aircraft ferried in from Britain.

Back in action five days later, the unit continued to gain victories and sustain losses – admittedly at a reduced rate compared to earlier in the month – through to 1 June.

On this date, Brooklands-built Hurricane I P3351 was one of four replacement aircraft flown in by four new pilots destined to serve with No 73 Sqn. Shortly after its arrival at Gaye, the aeroplane was taken aloft by Pilot Officer Peter Carter, who had also joined the unit in France ten days earlier as an attrition replacement. He had previously served with Nos 1, 43 and 605 Sqns, claiming a share in the destruction of an He 111 off the Scottish coast whilst with the latter unit on 10 April 1940. Carter would fly P3351 on a number of occasions up until he returned to England (in this aeroplane) with the rest of the unit on 18 June. Although it would

P3351 was one of the very last Hurricanes to leave France and return to England during the afternoon of 18 June 1940, flown by Pilot Officer Peter Carter from Nantes to Boscombe Down. 'The flight back to England was the most welcome flight I have ever done, and I greeted these shores more than I had ever thought possible. England and Beauty were in sight', he subsequently recalled in his diary.

Parked in No 1 Sqn's muddy dispersal area on the edge of Vassincourt airfield, in France, Hurricane I N2358 is being refuelled from the unit's Albion three-point bowser whilst its fitter tinkers with the engine. Coded 'Z' by the squadron soon after its arrival at Vassincourt in November 1939 following brief service with No 43 Sqn at Acklington, the fighter retained this marking when it was passed on to No 73 Sqn at Rouvres in early 1940. (Tony Holmes)

No 73 Sqn pilots pose for a press photograph in, on and around the unit's semi-sunken Duty Office at Rouvres on 26 November 1939. At the rear are, from left to right, Sergeant Pilots Fred Perry, 'Humph' Humphris, Bert Speake, Donald Sewell, George Phillips and John Winn, Pilot Officer Henry Hall and Sergeants Ken Campbell and Sid Stuckey. The officers in the front are 'Fanny' Orton, 'Tubs' Perry and Peter Ayerst on the left, George Brotchie and Reg Lovett in the centre and Tommy Tucker, 'Smooth' Holliday and 'Cobber' Kain on the right. (© IWM C 173)

A Hurricane I from No 73 Sqn's 'B' Flight is hastily refuelled and rearmed at Reims-Seclin during the first few days of the Battle of France. A recent delivery to the unit judging by the freshness of its appearance, this aeroplane had just been landed by 'B' Flight commander, Flight Lieutenant Ian Scoular – he is standing in the cockpit of the fighter. (© IWM C 1546)

Another view of Flight Lieutenant Scoular's Hurricane being worked on in the field between sorties. An Albion three-point bowser – capable of refuelling at a rate of 150 Imperial gallons per minute – is being used to replenish the fighter's three fuel tanks. (© IWM C 1551)

appear that he saw no combat in the fighter during this period, Carter had claimed a Bf 110 destroyed on 24 May whilst flying P3274. He described this action in the following diary entry, which was originally published in Ian Brodie's volume *The Alpine Fighter Collection's Hurricane Mk IIA*:

I knew quite a lot about the theory of fighting in the air, but I was not sure how I would react to a dogfight. I soon found out. Ten of us were patrolling at 15,000 ft when we saw about 40 ME 110s approaching from the opposite direction, and it was with mixed feelings that I saw them draw nearer. When we could see their black and white crosses we

positioned ourselves for attack. The MEs, when attacked, always form one big circle, and when they have been round once they half roll, dive full throttle absolutely vertically and come up on the other side.

I was amazed to find that I had no feelings of fear. I eventually got one and was just getting another when I realised that bullets and cannon shells were whizzing past my wing. I at once broke off, and then they started to hit my machine. I sat quite still and watched them, too fascinated to attempt to get out of the way. I saw three bullets pass between my legs and hundreds passing through my wings. How long should I have been content to sit there and watch is a matter of conjecture.

It was not fear that kept me rooted, but an uncanny kind of interest, which may seem extraordinary, but is nevertheless true. My luck lasted out and I was not hit. I did a very realistic dive away. I had an idea, however, that I was on fire and almost baled out, but I found I was mistaken. Suddenly, I realised I was over German territory, so headed south. The instruments were enveloped in steam (as I was), so I steered by the sun. After a few minutes I looked for a field on which to land, and found a beauty. However, instead of landing with my wheels up, I decided to put them down – a very rash thing to do. I made a good approach and a fair landing, but then my troubles started as I hit a soft spot. Suddenly, the tail rose, and I watched my 'prop' chip itself off in the ground. I still felt myself rising, but with a sickening crash she went over on her back, and I literally bit the dust. Again I was lucky, as the softness of the ground – which was the cause of the trouble – allowed me to bury my head three inches in the soil without breaking my neck.

I now felt a very real sense of fear as there was a highly inflammable machine on top of me. I struggled frantically to free my head, and just managed to unearth it before my breath gave out. Help was at hand, however, and some farm labourers rushed to the rescue and hauled me to safety. With the greatest relief, I learned that I was behind the lines and practically unscathed.

Like other No 67 Wing fighter units in France, No 73 Sqn removed the 'TP' code letters from its Hurricanes soon after arriving on the continent – although 'TP-E' was photographed by 'Glorious' on 19 April 1940, this aeroplane perhaps having recently been flown in from England as an attrition replacement. The squadron codes were taken off so as to avoid any confusion by the *Armée de l'Air,* which were not familiar with the use of such letters. Just a single aircraft letter, as seen here, was retained aft of the roundel on both sides of the fuselage.

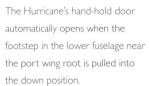

The Hurricane's hand-hold door automatically opens when the footstep in the lower fuselage near the port wing root is pulled into the down position.

New Zealander Pilot Officer E.J. 'Cobber' Kain was a pre-war fighter pilot whose prowess at the controls of a Hurricane had earned him the reputation of being No 73 Sqn's most gifted aviator by time the unit was sent to France. He more than proved this during the 'Phoney War' when he became Fighter Command's first ace with the downing of his fourth and fifth victories (Bf 109Es over Saarlautern) on 26 March 1940. Kain was also the first of No 73 Sqn's pilots to receive the DFC, on 14 January 1940. (John Dibbs)

A No 73 Sqn aeroplane prepares to have its Merlin II changed at Rouvres in the early spring of 1940. With no hangarage facilities at the airfield, all servicing – both minor and, as seen here, major – had to be carried out in the open, with trestles and hoists proving key to jobs such as an engine change. This had not been too bad during the autumn of 1939, but was disastrous during the bitter winter that followed – one of the worst on record. (Tony Holmes)

The engine of this Hurricane I appears to have been partially dismantled so that the rugged-up engine fitters can get at the root of the problem. Nestling between the undercarriage legs is the top half of the Merlin II, and behind it is the fighter's Watts propeller. This aeroplane was one of several flown by No 73 Sqn in France that retained its three-letter squadron code well into 1940. (© IWM C 880)

flying, and having survived two crashes (he destroyed No 73 Sqn's Miles Magister when he lost his bearings during a ferry flight on 5 June and made a forced landing, crashing during the subsequent attempted take-off on boggy ground), Carter wrote about these flights in the following diary entry:

> Our work now lost its former flavour, as we were up at dawn (about 3 o'clock) and were kept at it till dark (about 10 o'clock). Even flying lost its flavour amid such sameness. It was gruelling work, and I wonder that we lasted the time. Our position grew daily worse until one day the Station Commander gathered us together and told us the gravity of the situation. At any moment, he told us, we might expect the enemy, and warned us to make a very careful survey of the aerodrome before landing from patrol, and if we saw signs of the enemy in possession we were to make for England straight away.
>
> Early next afternoon [18 June] we were ordered on patrol, but I refused to let my aircraft [P3351] fly as it was using over a gallon of glycol an hour, and I wanted to keep it serviceable long enough to take me back to England. About an hour after that the look-out phoned us to tell us that the so-and-so Huns were coming, and he was off! The flight back to England was the most welcome flight I have ever done, and I greeted these shores more than I had ever thought possible. England and Beauty were in sight.

Together we inspected the ruins of my Hurricane, and to this day I wonder at my escape. We counted 120 bullet holes and then gave it up as a bad job. Three cannon holes were in evidence in my wings and fuselage. We then looked in the cockpit and were surprised to see that the control column was but an inch off the ground.

Pilot Officer Carter's final flights with P3351 in France came on 18 June, when he completed two patrols in the aeroplane from Nantes as part of Operation *Ariel* – the evacuation of Allied forces and civilians from ports in western France between 15 and 25 June 1940 – before returning in it to England. No 73 Sqn played a key role in this operation, the unit flying myriad sorties from dawn to dusk as it attempted to protect departing troopships from German bombers. Clearly weary after almost a month of near constant operational

No 73 Sqn had been the last RAF unit to leave France. Badly affected by its ordeal on the Continent – the squadron had lost 37 groundcrew during the sinking of the RMS *Lancastria* on 18 June – and short of aircraft, the squadron was sent north to Church Fenton, in North Yorkshire, to rebuild. It was declared operational once again within No 13 Group on 7 July, and both P3351 and Pilot Officer Carter remained with the unit. However, as detailed in Chapter Sixteen: Hurricane Survivors, Sergeant Alf Scott undershot during a night landing on 21 July and the fighter's undercarriage collapsed, tipping P3351 up on its nose. The Hurricane had to be sent away for repairs, never to return to No 73 Sqn.

P3351's beautifully restored cockpit, complete with a Barr & Stroud GM 2 reflector gunsight. No 249 Sqn pilot Tom Neil stated that when he was strapped into a Hurricane he felt like he was 'sitting in space, with lots of darkness below and behind'. This was because the aeroplane had no cockpit floor.

Bathed in warm summer sunshine at Duxford in July 2013, P3351 sits ready for its next flight during the fighter's first visit to England since its restoration to airworthiness more than 13 years earlier. The pilot's footstep is visible in the lowered position just behind the radiator fairing.

Pilot Officer Carter would add two Ju 88s destroyed and a third as a probable to his tally when the unit engaged *Kampfgeschwader* (KG) 30 during its attack on Driffield, in East Yorkshire, on 15 August. Nine days later he was sent to newly formed No 302 'Polish' Sqn at Leconfield. He subsequently saw action with the unit from Duxford and Northolt until his death on 18 October when, during an otherwise uneventful patrol, nine Hurricanes became lost in deteriorating weather over the Surrey Hills and Carter was forced to bail out of his fighter at a height of just 50 ft above Kempton Park Racecourse. The 21-year-old veteran of the battles of France and Britain was killed instantly upon hitting the ground – three Polish pilots also perished.

# CHAPTER TWO

# 'BLUE PETER'

Since October 2014 Hurricane X AE977 has been painted in the colours and markings of Mk I P2921, which was assigned to No 32 Sqn's 'B' Flight commander, Flight Lieutenant Pete Brothers, for much of the Battle of Britain. Recreating history 75 years after the original P2921 had patrolled the Dover coastline from nearby Hawkinge airfield, AE977 of the Biggin Hill Heritage Hangar Collection heads west in the direction of Beachy Head – just as Pete Brothers would have done in his Hurricane on a near-daily basis during July and August of 1940.

No 32 Sqn was one of Fighter Command's most successful units during 1940. Indeed, when it was posted away from Biggin Hill on 28 August after eight straight years at the Kent fighter station, the 'Fighting 32nd Squadron' was one of the top-scoring units in the RAF with 102 victories. Appropriately, today, a Hurricane painted in the colours of No 32 Sqn flies from 'Biggin on the bump' once again. The subject of this chapter, the Biggin Hill Heritage Hangar Collection's AE977 is marked up as P2921 'Blue Peter', which was the aircraft assigned to the commander of 'B' Flight, Flight Lieutenant Pete Brothers. He was one of seven pilots to 'make ace' with No 32 Sqn that year by claiming five or more victories.

A pre-war aviator who had joined No 32 Sqn in October 1936, Brothers had learned his craft flying Gauntlet II biplane fighters for almost two years prior to the unit receiving Hurricanes in the autumn of 1938. He recalled his first flight in the Hawker fighter for a previous volume on the Hurricane published by Osprey in 1995:

The date was 24 September 1938. The place was RAF Biggin Hill. My excitement was intense for today I was to fly Hurricane L1655, the first of No 32 Sqn's long awaited replacements for our Gloster Gauntlet biplanes.

Having studied Pilot's Notes, I climbed into the cockpit and sat for a while, finding my way around the levers and switches, then started up and taxied over the grass – we had no runways – to the boundary of the airfield, turned into wind and took off. The big, two-bladed, wooden propeller [as fitted to the Fury biplane] gave surprisingly rapid acceleration, whilst the throaty roar of the

Merlin and the solid, rugged, feel of the aircraft as it bounced over the uneven surface stimulated and inspired confidence. Retracting the wheels – a novel experience – involved moving the left hand from throttle to stick, selecting wheels up with the right hand and depressing the pump lever until the wheels locked up. As this loss of throttle control made formation take-offs unusually interesting, we later surreptitiously attached a Bowden cable from the stick to the lever to avoid the hand change.

Now airborne, I closed the canopy – another novel experience. Relieved of the head-buffeting slipstream of an open cockpit, I settled down to enjoy myself. Having climbed to a safe height I tried a variety of aerobatics and was delighted by the immediate and smooth response to the controls. When stalling the aircraft, I was interested to note that the right wing dropped – a Sydney Camm characteristic I had found common in other aircraft he had designed. On landing from this 50-minute 'Type experience' flight, I looked forward with exultation to the future, and the opportunity to get to know the Hurricane really well.

So it was on the outbreak of war a year later that I was in the enviable position of thoroughly knowing the Hurricane's advantages and limitations, and was looking forward to the opportunity of testing it in battle. By now we had progressed from the wooden two-bladed Watts propeller, via the de Havilland two-pitch metal propeller, to the constant-speed Rotol, much improving the fighter's performance. Proof that I was by then a Hurricane pilot of experience was available for all to see, for the lower right leg of my trousers bore the customary Hurricane glycol stain.

During the lull in activity after Dunkirk we flew some night patrols, but here the Hurricane was out of its element, for the exhaust flames streaming down each side of the cockpit did not enhance night vision. Moreover, as initially we were allowed no airfield lighting, finding the airfield and landing by use of the aeroplane's landing lamps was fraught with interest. Although adjustable downwards, the beams converged under the nose so the tree through which I flew was totally hidden from view. But this sturdy aircraft,

festooned in branches, merely shuddered, and being of pedigree stock was little damaged.

By then Brothers had already seen action over France from mid-May onwards during the daily rotation of squadrons across the Channel from airfields in Fighter Command's No 11 Group. Sent into action in support of hard-pressed Hurricane units on the Continent, No 32 Sqn would perform a tiresome routine of pre-dawn launches from Biggin Hill that saw pilots making landfall at airfields in France or Belgium at first light. From there, they were given orders to patrol a certain section of the Franco-Belgian border, or perhaps escort a flight of Battles or Blenheims as they attempted to stem the flow of Wehrmacht panzers and troops flooding into the heartland of France. Once their mission had been accomplished, the weary pilots would recover to whatever airfield they could find. Here, they would individually refuel their own Hurricanes using small tins of gasoline and a handpump, with a chamois leather serving admirably as a filter. The pilots then had to help each other with getting their fighters running once again, as Pete Brothers recalled:

The only way to get the Hurricanes started was to have a chap each side winding the [starter] handles, so I'd get into mine and we'd get mine started and then leave it ticking over. Then I'd jump out and wind somebody else's until we'd got them all going. It was pretty ghastly and the French, I'm afraid, were totally demoralised by this time.

The squadron would depart almost as swiftly as it had arrived, returning to a pitch-black Biggin Hill at around 2200 hrs.

It was during one such patrol, on 18 May, that Brothers claimed the first of his eventual 16 victories. His unit had been tasked with escorting Blenheims attacking enemy forces near Douai, but when no bombers materialized, No 32 Sqn pressed on in a north-easterly direction in search of German aircraft. Five miles east of Le Cateau, whilst flying at 14,000 ft, they ran headlong into a formation of 23 Bf 109s from I.(J)/*Lehrgeschwader* (LG) 2.

Few photographs depicting the hectic summer months of 1940 conveyed the seemingly irrepressible spirit of Fighter Command better than this one of Flight Lieutenant Pete Brothers, taken on 29 July – the very day he downed a Bf 109E over Kent to become an ace. It was just one of many shots taken by a Fox Film Unit sent to Hawkinge airfield, near Folkestone. (Tony Holmes)

Above them were Bf 110s, which were in turn escorting bombers. Brothers' Combat Report from this encounter details what happened next:

I saw Green Section engage Me 109s astern of me, so I turned and flew towards them. Three 109s flew over me in line astern, so I turned sharp left as they dived on my tail. They turned away, and as I was turning a 109 flew across my sights. I gave him a short burst and he slowly turned on his back and dived, inverted. I looked round and saw another 109 on my tail. I turned steeply to the left and he opened fire with tracer ammunition. His shooting was hopeless and I saw his tracer pass behind me. I turned onto his tail, but as I was firing he dived into cloud and I lost him. I circled round, but all aircraft appeared to have gone home, so after a few minutes I returned to Merville. The north-west part of Cambrai was burning furiously.

More than 50 years later, Pete Brothers still had vivid memories of his very first aerial success:

I thought, 'Oh those bloody de Havilland propeller oil specks all over the windscreen', but they grew bigger very rapidly. The Bf 109s were flying in the opposite direction and the formations were drawing close. Our reactions were very slow. I remember seeing this thing whizz over my head – I could see oil streaks on the fuselage. I thought 'Good Lord, it's the bloody enemy!' I looked round to see where they'd gone and they were turning around to attack us. He dived on me and I got on his tail. Shot him down.

Throughout the brief chase that lasted just a matter of minutes, Brothers could think of only one thing: a rather incongruous piece of advice given to him and the rest of his intake at RAF Uxbridge some four years earlier by high-scoring World War 1 ace Squadron Leader Ira 'Taffy' Jones, which was made all the more memorable due to the fact that he stuttered quite badly: 'There's going to be a f, f, f, fucking war, and you chaps are going to be in it. I can give you one p, p, p, piece of advice. When you get into your f, f, f, first combat, you will be f, f, f, fucking f, f, f, frightened. Never forget that the chap in the other c, c, c, cockpit is twice as f, f, f, fucking f, f, f, frightened as you are!' Now fighting for his life, just as Jones had predicted, Pete Brothers thought to himself, 'this chap must be having hysterics, so I'd better put him out of his misery'.

By the end of the Battle of France, Flight Lieutenant Brothers had been credited with two victories during the myriad patrols he had flown from mid-May through to early June. One week

The Fox Film Unit photographer has obviously said something to tickle the group's collective fancy. In the background, with a parachute harness draped over the tailplane ready to be strapped onto its pilot's back, is Hurricane I P3522. It was frequently flown by Pilot Officer Rupert Smythe during July and August 1940. The fighter served with No 32 Sqn between 20 May and 18 August, when it was hit by return fire from a Do 17 and force-landed at Tangmere by its pilot, Sergeant Bernard Henson. (John Dibbs)

after the last Allied troops had been plucked from the Dunkirk beaches, No 32 Sqn took delivery of three attrition replacement Hurricanes at Biggin Hill to make good losses suffered in combat over Le Tréport on 9 June. Amongst these aeroplanes was P2921, which quickly became 'GZ-L'. It was allocated to Pete Brothers on 3 July, and he adorned it with a small blue and white marking beneath the cockpit. This personal emblem was based on the international maritime signal flag 'P for Papa', also known as the 'Blue Peter'. P2921 would serve him well for the rest of Brothers' time at Biggin Hill. Indeed, it was the only one of the trio of Hurricanes to survive the Battle of Britain. Always serviceable, the aircraft was never hit by enemy fire whilst in his hands. During the deadliest phase of the campaign, in July and August, Brothers was credited with destroying eight enemy aircraft (six Bf 109Es, a Bf 110C and a Do 17) in P2921.

Perhaps Pete Brothers' most satisfying mission in this aircraft came on 18 August, which was subsequently dubbed 'The Hardest Day' by historians due to the losses suffered by both sides. Fighter Command had 30 Hurricanes and seven Spitfires shot down, but in return its squadrons destroyed 61 Luftwaffe aircraft, including 16 Bf 109Es and no fewer than 17 Ju 87s. No 32 Sqn was heavily involved in the defence of Biggin Hill and nearby Kenley, which were targeted by two separate raids. The first of these, at 1330 hrs, involved more than 50 Do 17s and Ju 88s from KG 76, escorted by Bf 109s and Bf 110s from six units. Leading 'B' Flight into action, Brothers flew directly at the Messerschmitt escorts, before engaging the bombers:

> The original P2921 was allocated to Pete Brothers on 3 July 1940, the aeroplane having joined No 32 Sqn the previous month as one of three Hurricanes supplied to the unit from No 15 MU on 11 June as attrition replacements to make good losses suffered in combat over Le Tréport two days earlier. He adorned it with a small blue and white marking beneath the cockpit, which can clearly be seen in this photograph. Brothers' personal emblem was based on the international maritime signal flag 'P for Papa', also known as the 'Blue Peter'.

A No 32 Sqn Hurricane I has its left wing root tank replenished from an Albion three-point bowser at Hawkinge on the morning of 29 July 1940. Hawkinge was routinely attacked during the Battle of Britain. Indeed, things got so bad in 'Hellfire Corner', as this area of the Kent coast was dubbed, that Press visits such as the one undertaken by the Fox Photo Unit were not repeated during August and September. The pilot has remained strapped into the cockpit, which indicates the presence of enemy aircraft in the vicinity. (Tony Holmes)

The signal to scramble was phoned through to No 32 Sqn's dispersal area soon after the series of relaxed pilot shots had been taken. The various aircrew can be seen preparing for take-off. The pilot of 'GZ-T', furthest to the left, is just doing up his parachute straps, whilst his counterpart at the tail of 'GZ-B' has reached the fighter but is yet to pull on his 'chute. To his right, another pilot strides purposefully towards a Hurricane parked out of shot, whilst a fourth aviator sprints towards 'GZ-K', doing up his helmet straps as he goes. (John Dibbs)

In head-on attacks the question was whether you went over the top of the aircraft or underneath it after firing. I always used to go down, because I thought the bomber pilot would pull up instinctively.

The German aeroplanes blackened the sky, all stacking up with fighters on top and below the vast bomber formation. You thought, 'Where do we start on this lot? You've got to take the leader out,' I decided. It was a bit stupid, because I was trapped in the crossfire. But I got his port engine nicely burning. Bringing down a bomber was really satisfying, particularly if you got it before it dropped

its bombs. Getting them when they were on their way home was better than nothing, but if you caught them before they'd made their drop, it was a real success.

You envied the enemy fighters' their cannon. You also broke the Fighter Command rules stating that your guns were supposed to be toed in to 200 yards' range, where the rounds are gathered together in shot, but you weren't going to get very far like that. The odds were that you toed them in considerably and you got up jolly close – 50 yards if you could – then you really did hammer it.

Brothers claimed a Do 17 destroyed, although he had in fact downed a Ju 88 from 5./KG 76, which crashed into woods at Ide Hill, in Kent.

His second victory of the day came at 1745 hrs near Canterbury when No 32 Sqn was scrambled to intercept a raid that was heading for the No 11 Group airfield at Hornchurch, in Essex. Brothers' Combat Report for the mission read as follows:

At 1745 hrs I was leading Blue Section when I observed about 100 enemy aircraft about five miles north of Herne Bay flying west. They were stepped up, with fighters behind and were too far away to distinguish their type. The fighters, about 20 Me 109s, broke away and attacked us. I saw one behind me and on my right, so I turned sharply onto his tail and put two short bursts into him. He caught fire and dived steeply, so I followed him down and he crashed in a field near Chilham. I circled round low down and observed another aircraft about half-a-mile east of the 109 wreck, also burning on the ground. This aircraft I took to be a Hurricane. As I was circling, Pilot Officer [Boleslaw] Wlasnowalski appeared and joined me in formation. I looked around for more enemy aircraft, but was recalled by wireless ten minutes later.

Brothers also detailed this action in less formal style in his logbook:

We broke formation as they came in and opened fire, and I turned sharply right, onto the tail of an Me 109 as he overtook me. I gave a quick glance behind to ensure that there was not another on my tail, laid my sight on him and fired a short burst. I hit him with another short burst and he caught fire and his dive steepened. I followed him down, he went into a field at a steep angle and a cloud of flame and black smoke erupted, and I flew over it, thinking, 'Jolly good, that's one. Now, where are the rest?'

He had downed a Bf 109E from 7./*Jagdgeschwader* (JG) 26, the aeroplane being flown by five-victory ace Leutnant Gerhard Müller-Dühe.

No 32 Sqn flew its last sorties from Biggin Hill on 28 August, after which it was sent north to Acklington, in Northumberland, for a well-earned rest. Pete Brothers flew north in P2921, noting in his logbook following the 1 hr 50 min flight, 'Bye, Bye Biggin after four years'. Twelve days later he took his beloved 'Blue Peter' aloft for the final

P3522 'GZ-V' was closest to the Fox Photo Unit photographer when No 32 Sqn received the order to scramble on 29 July 1940, and Irishman Pilot Officer Rupert Smythe sprinted to his fighter and clambered aboard with the minimum of fuss. With the starter trolley pulled away and the Hurricane's engine burbling with its familiar throaty growl, Smyth was photographed waiting patiently for the remaining members of 'B' Flight to catch him up, before following Flight Lieutenant Brothers aloft. (John Dibbs)

RIGHT Strapped in and engines running, the pilots open the throttles of their Hurricane Is and start to roll out prior to taking off from their dispersal area. Squadrons based at Hawkinge were only a minute's flying time from the Channel, and 15 minutes away from German fighter airfields in the Pas-de-Calais. This meant that they had to take off as expeditiously as possible so as to avoid being bounced either on the ground or whilst still climbing for height. (John Dibbs)

LEFT P2921 was no ordinary Hurricane, as Pete Brothers modified it with the help of his rigger. 'I took the mirror off the top [clearly visible in this view of AE977] and bought myself a car [rearview] mirror that was curved, and had that mounted inside the windscreen', Brothers recalled many years later. The mirror, gave him both a better view astern and reduced the drag created by the aeroplane. Furthermore, 'when we were sitting on the ground, my rigger and I used to sit on the wing with some sandpaper. The Spitfire was all flush-riveted and the Hurricane was pock-riveted, so we'd file some of the pocks off the top. I reckon we got an extra seven miles per hour out of the aircraft, making "Blue Peter" the fastest Hurricane in the squadron.'

time, having received orders to join No 257 Sqn as the commander of 'A' Flight following the recent loss of the previous incumbent. He wrote the following in his logbook (as noted by Brothers' biographer, Nick Thomas, in his book *Hurricane Squadron Ace*) after the 9 September sortie: 'Last flight in the Fighting 32nd Squadron: break-up starts today. Aerobatics. Goodbye chaps after four years. Bye P2921, old faithful.'

Brothers also added the following extract from the Squadron Diary into his logbook:

It seems incredible to me
To say goodbye to Peter B.
He's been with us here for years and years
He's shared our laughs and shared our tears
And now he's gone – New friends to meet
So long, old pal, we'll miss you, Pete

Having just returned from a successful sortie (note the creases around his mouth from his oxygen mask), Flight Lieutenant Peter Brothers relates details of the mission to No 32 Sqn's 'Spy', Intelligence Officer Pilot Officer R.T. Leighton. The latter would be responsible for writing Intelligence Reports that provided an overall account of the operation just flown by the unit, while pilots making aerial claims filled in their own individual Combat Reports. (John Dibbs)

The original P2921 was assigned to
No 32 Sqn from 11 June 1940
through to 21 February 1941, when
it was transferred to newly-formed
No 315 'Polish' Sqn at Speke, near
Liverpool. Five months later it was
passed on to No 245 Sqn at
Aldergrove, in Northern Ireland.
Placed in storage with a
Maintenance Unit in August 1941,
P2921 was supplied to the Fleet Air
Arm on 31 October that same year
and converted into a Sea Hurricane
IA for use from Catapult Aircraft
Merchantmen by the Merchant Ship
Fighter Unit. According to its service
card, the fighter sailed as far afield
as Ceylon, where it was damaged in
September 1942. The aeroplane
was soon repaired and returned to
Yeovilton, and it was last noted at
St Mawgan in September 1943. Its
final fate remains unrecorded,
however.

# CHAPTER THREE

# 'FIGHTING 56'

Reenacting a scramble from the No 11 Group fighter station at North Weald during the summer of 1940, Canadian-built Hurricane XII 5481 accelerates across the grass at Ed Russell's airfield at Niagara Falls, Ontario. The aeroplane is painted in the colours of No 56 Sqn Hurricane I P2970, which was routinely flown by future ace Pilot Officer Geoffrey Page during the Battle of Britain.

Canadian-built Hurricane XII 5481 was for many years painted in the colours of No 56 Sqn Mk I P2970, which was flown by future ace Pilot Officer Geoffrey Page during the Battle of Britain. Called up when war was declared in September 1939, Page proved to be such a natural pilot that he was initially posted to Training Command to become a flying instructor – 'the last command any self-respecting fighter pilot wanted to end up in', was how he described this news in his autobiography, *Shot Down in Flames*. Fortunately for him, 'Hitler came to the rescue' by launching the *Blitzkrieg* on 10 May 1940 and Page was sent instead to Spitfire-equipped No 66 Sqn. When he joined the unit at Horsham St Faith, near Norwich, on 18 May, he had never previously flown a monoplane aircraft, let alone a modern fighter like the Spitfire. When Page told his new CO, Squadron Leader R.H.A. Leigh, about this, the latter was far from impressed:

'Christ!' he said, and turned his back on me. 'What will they be sending us next? How the hell do they expect me to run a fighter squadron and a training unit at the same time?' he said more to himself than to me. 'Damned disgrace sending along a young boy who's never flown anything more advanced than a Hind. If you get killed,' he added, looking at me severely in the eye, 'it will be Group's fault. I've done my best to warn them.'

Nevertheless, Page successfully made his first solo flight in a monoplane aeroplane when he took a Spitfire aloft the day after he joined No 66 Sqn. After a week of intensive training on the fighter, he was declared operational, only to discover

that he had in fact been sent to the wrong unit due to a clerical error. Page was supposed to have joined No 56 Sqn, rather than No 66 Sqn. 'Good unit, 56', Squadron Leader Leigh told him when he informed the tyro fighter pilot of the mistake. 'You'll like them, Page. They're at North Weald flying Hurricanes'. Page, however, was mortified. 'My depression deepened at the idea of changing over to Hurricanes after flying Spitfires. It was supposed to be a very good aeroplane – that, I knew – but after Spitfires … NO!'

Calling North Weald, in Essex, home from October 1927, No 56 Sqn had been only the third unit in the RAF to transition to the Hurricane – a process that commenced in April 1938. The squadron's first action in World War 2 resulted in two of its aircraft being shot down in error by Spitfires from No 74 Sqn on 6 September 1939 in the 'Battle of Barking Creek'. One pilot was killed. It was not until November that the unit encountered German aircraft for the first time, when pilots damaged two flying-boats

during east coast convoy patrols – its staple mission until the Battle of France commenced in May 1940.

While Geoffrey Page was coming to grips with the Spitfire, No 56 Sqn pilots from 'B' Flight were fighting for their lives during four hectic days of action flying from Vitry-en-Artois. 'A' Flight was also involved in the Battle of France, although it operated by day from Lille and then returned to North Weald in the evening. Between 10 and 31 May, No 56 Sqn was credited with the destruction of 14 German aeroplanes, but it had lost three pilots and five Hurricanes in return. When Page joined the unit on 3 June, No 56 Sqn was at Digby, in Lincolnshire, participating in gunnery training, so he had North Weald effectively to himself. Whilst searching for the squadron offices, he found a pair of brand new Hurricanes that had recently been flown in as attrition replacements parked between two hangars. Page commenced a quick visual inspection of both machines:

Pilot Officer Geoffrey Page christened his Hurricane *LITTLE WILLIE,* this nickname being marked beneath the cockpit on the port side only. He also had Churchill's famous 'V for Victory' gesture applied to the aeroplane, as well as two and one-third swastikas denoting his victories in July 1940 – one and one shared in P2970.

Although the Spitfire and Hurricane were basically alike, inasmuch as they were low-wing, single-seater monoplanes, powered by Rolls-Royce Merlin engines, to the fighter pilot's eye, the similarity ended there. Whereas the Spitfire had all the speed and grace of the greyhound in its sleek appearance, the Hurricane portrayed the excellent qualities of the bulldog, being slower but much more solidly built. To the Spitfire pilot there will be only one machine, and similarly to the man who flew the Hurricane. To the fortunate ones who often took to the skies in both types, there will be an everlasting love for both that borders on sweet-sadness that these aircraft, like human beings, last but a little while and then are gone.

Although he had never even sat in a Hurricane before, Page was ordered to flight-test the newly arrived aircraft:

I was the only available pilot on the station, so despite the fact I'd never previously flown one, I was given the job. After the Spitfire, the first thing I noticed was the added height of the aeroplane off the ground, and the less restricted view directly forward along the nose. The cockpit itself appeared to be roomier, but the individual knobs and levers were not finished with quite the same quality as the other machine. However, I was happy to notice that the undercarriage system was automatically controlled once the position of the wheels had been selected, and the propeller was of the new constant speeding type. The engine-starting procedure was similar to that on Spitfires, with the added advantage that the engine kept cool almost indefinitely owing to the positioning of the radiator between the undercarriage legs.

Despite the strangeness of the aeroplane, I taxied her out confidently to the top end of the airfield, and after doing a thorough cockpit check and receiving the green 'Okay' signal from control, I took off down the hill towards the parked Blenheims. The Hurricane rose gracefully and easily into the air, and I had the immediate sensation that here was a lady with very few vices. Climbing rapidly over the soft Essex countryside, I headed my aircraft eastwards to the North Sea. To the south below the wing tip shimmered the broad reaches of the Thames as they ran their course to meet the distant sea. Contentment filled my soul, and to show my appreciation of the day, I slowly and lazily rolled the Hurricane onto her back. Hanging upside down for a few seconds, I eased the stick back and pulled her vertically downwards with a rush of increasing speed. Far below me along the line of the aircraft's nose moved the tiny speck of a human

Anxious groundcrew look on as No 56 Sqn's 'A' Flight departs for France during the height of the Blitzkrieg in mid-May 1940. 'A' Flight operated by day from Lille and then returned to North Weald in the evening. The pilots of 'B' Flight, meanwhile, were fighting for their lives flying from Vitry-en-Artois – they were overnighting here. (John Dibbs)

being moving across the yard between a farmhouse and a barn. Moving the control column hard over, the responsive machine completed a 180-degree aileron turn vertically downwards, then pulling firmly back on the stick with opening throttle, she climbed swiftly again into the sunlit sky and over into a wide loop. Singing happily to myself, I dived the aeroplane back towards the hangars, no longer sorry that I was going to be flying Hurricanes.

Although Page had had minimal exposure to flying frontline fighter types, he had been thoroughly trained prior to joining No 56 Sqn. The unit also did its best to improve his chances of survival, as pre-war aviator Flying Officer Innes Westmacott recalled:

We gave the new pilots a certain amount of training flying before they went into action, although it was difficult to find time for this, and when they flew operationally they were always put in a section with an experienced leader, at any rate to start with. They learned very quickly – they had to! Here I would point out that there is no substitute for combat experience. An experienced pilot with a lot of hours in his logbook did not necessarily make a good combat pilot straight away. He might become one, but so did many a young man who had only just completed his training.

No 56 Sqn would find itself very much in the thick of the action once the Battle of Britain commenced, flying two or three times a day. Despite his inexperience, Geoffrey Page quickly proved himself to be a tenacious fighter pilot by claiming two and one shared aircraft destroyed between 13 and 25 July – two of these successes coming in his assigned Hurricane I, P2970, which he christened *LITTLE WILLIE*. His first victory, in this aircraft, took the form of a Bf 109 – a type he would duel with on several occasions that summer:

In the Hurricane we knew that the Me 109 could out-dive us, but not out-turn us. With that knowledge, one obviously used the turning manoeuvre rather than trying to beat the man at

the game in which he was clearly superior. With a 109 sitting behind you, you'd stay in a really tight turn, and after a few turns the position would be reversed and you'd be on his tail. In short, I'd say the Hurricane was a magnificent aeroplane to go to war in.

Ironically, it was not a Bf 109 that shot Geoffrey Page down during the evening of 12 August. That day, Fighter Command's coastal airfields had been heavily attacked, and at 1830 hrs 12 Hurricanes from No 56 Sqn were scrambled from Rochford, in Essex, to intercept a force of 30 Do 17s from II. and III./KG 2 escorted by more than 40 Bf 109s of III./JG 54 that was heading for Manston airfield, in Kent. Flying P2970 as No 3 in 'Blue Section', Page followed his Flight Commander, Flight Lieutenant 'Jumbo' Gracie, in to attack the bombers:

In front of us the enemy armada was turning northwards and setting out over the sea. The Hurricanes banked in pursuit as we continued our climb to reach the slender bombers. High above, the Me 109s weaved like hawks waiting to swoop on their victims.

The distance and height between hunter and prey was closing. At last the Hurricanes arrived at the same height as the Dornier bombers, which allowed us to level off and build up some speed. The large enemy aircraft were themselves flying echelon to starboard formation, as were the intercepting fighters.

To my surprise I saw that 'Jumbo' was intending to attack the leading aircraft in the bomber formation. This necessitated flying past the aircraft behind the leader's, and also meant running the gauntlet of their rear gunners' fire.

Slowly, we overhauled the heavy Luftwaffe machines, and I had the impression of an express train overtaking a slower one. There was time to inspect each aircraft before passing onto the next one up the line. Instinctively, I glanced above and behind, but for some strange reason the Me 109s were still sitting aloft. The sweeping movement of my trained eyes showed that Bob [Flying Officer Robert Constable Maxwell] no longer stood

Excess fuel is burned off as Hurricane XII 5481's red block Packard Merlin 28 is coaxed into life by high-time warbird pilot John Romain at Niagara Falls. Once the engine is running smoothly – a quick check of the cockpit instrumentation, and in particular the oil pressure gauge, will confirm this – the pilot sets the 'holding' rpm to 1000 with the throttle and then completes his after-start checks. These are usually completed in seconds, with the flap selector set to neutral and the magnetos individually checked. He is then ready to taxi out for take-off.

ABOVE Pilot Officer Geoffrey Page was forced to bail out of a blazing P2970 ten miles north of Margate after it was hit by return fire from a Do 17 during the evening of 12 August, the badly burned pilot being rescued by a tender and then transferred to the Margate lifeboat. He was subsequently hospitalised for more than two years and underwent plastic surgery on his hands at Queen Victoria Hospital in East Grinstead. (John Dibbs)

between me and the enemy. Momentarily reassured that nothing lethal was sitting behind my aircraft, I settled down to the task of firing at one of the leading machines, although it was still about 600 yards ahead.

Then the enemy rear gunners started firing. Analysing it later, I realised that the firepower of the whole group was obviously controlled by radio instructions from a gunnery officer in one of the bombers. One moment the sky between me and the 30 Dornier 215s [actually Do 17s] was clear, the next it was criss-crossed with streams of white tracer from cannon shells converging on our Hurricanes.

'Jumbo's' machine peeled away from the attack. The distance between the German leader's bomber and my solitary Hurricane was down to 300 yards. Strikes from my Brownings began to flash around the port engine of one of the Dorniers. The mass of fire from the bomber formation closed in as I fired desperately in a race to destroy before being destroyed.

The first bang came as a shock. For an instant I couldn't believe I'd been hit. Two more bangs followed in quick succession, and as if by magic a gaping hole suddenly appeared in my starboard wing. Surprise quickly changed to fear, and as the instinct of self-preservation began to take over, the

fuel tank behind the engine blew up and my cockpit became an inferno. Fear became blind terror, then agonised horror as the bare skin of my hands gripping the throttle and control column shrivelled up like burnt parchment under the intensity of the blast furnace temperature. Screaming at the top of my voice, I threw my head back to keep it away from the searing flames. Instinctively, the tortured right hand groped for the release pin securing the restraining Sutton harness.

'Dear God, save me, save me, dear God,' I cried imploringly. Then, as suddenly as the terror had overtaken me, it vanished with the knowledge that death was no longer to be feared. My fingers kept up their blind and bloody mechanical groping. Some large mechanical dark object disappeared between my legs and cool, relieving fresh air suddenly flowed across my burning face. I tumbled. Sky, sea, sky, over and over as a clearing brain issued instructions to out-flung limbs. 'Pull the ripcord – right hand to the ripcord.' Watering eyes focused on an arm flung out in space with some strange meaty object attached at its end.

More tumbling – more sky and sea and sky, but with a blue-clad arm forming a focal point in the foreground. 'Pull the ripcord, hand,' the brain again commanded. Slowly but obediently the elbow bent

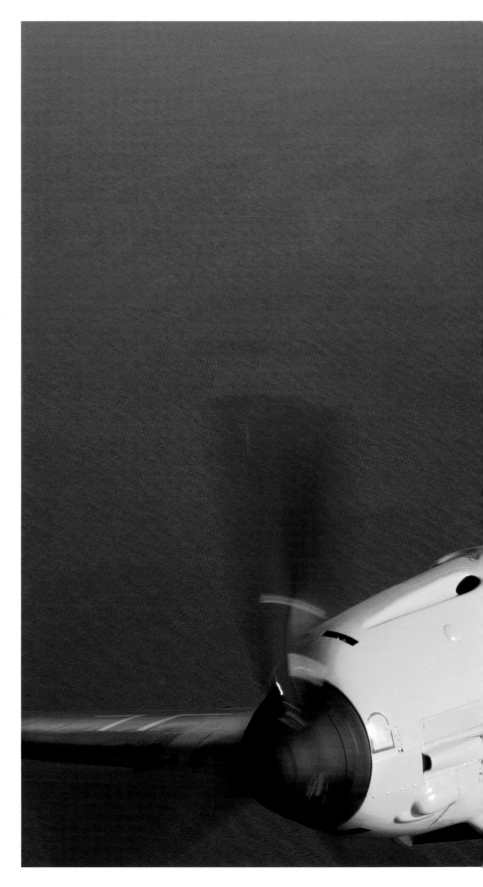

and the hand came across the body to rest on the chromium ring, but bounced away quickly with the agony of contact.

More tumbling at a slower rate now. The weight of the head was beginning to tell.

Realising that pain or no pain, the ripcord had to be pulled, the brain overcame the reaction of the raw nerve endings and forced the mutilated fingers to grasp the ring and pull firmly. It acted immediately. With a jerk, the silken canopy billowed out in the clear summer sky.

Page had bailed out of the flaming P2970 ten miles north of Margate, in Kent, the badly burned pilot being rescued by a tender and then transferred to the Margate lifeboat. He was subsequently hospitalized for more than two years, undergoing plastic surgery on his hands at Queen Victoria Hospital in East Grinstead. Here, he became a founding committee member of the Guinea Pig Club. Geoffrey Page eventually returned to operational flying and was subsequently credited with ten and five shared victories, having finished the war as an acting Wing Commander.

Recreating a scene that took place on 13 July 1940, 'P2970' (Mk XII 5481) closes on the tail of Bf 109E-3 Wk-Nr 3579 when both aircraft were owned by Ed Russell. Geoffrey Page's first victory was a Bf 109E of 4./JG 51, which he erroneously described in his Combat Report as an He 113, that he downed three miles off Calais. 'I was flying in the rear section when we went in to attack the [Ju 87] bombers. I got in two bursts at two of them and chased one down to sea level, but with no visible effect. I then saw a Hurricane being attacked by an He 113, which I attacked. This was at about 500 ft. I attacked from practically dead astern and gave the enemy aircraft three short bursts at about 300 yards, using slight deflection. I could see my tracers all round him. The enemy aircraft turned over on its side and dived rapidly towards the sea.'

The original P2970 was delivered
new to No 56 Sqn at North Weald
on 5 June 1940, shortly after the
unit had returned home following
its brief spell based in France. It
soon became Pilot Officer Geoffrey
Page's aeroplane within 'A' Flight.
Unlike P2970, Mk XII 5481 was
rebuilt without an aerial mast,
although one has recently been
added during the aeroplane's
refurbishment by Luskintyre Aircraft
Restoration in New South Wales.

Battle of Britain Memorial Flight
stalwarts for many years, Hurricane
IIC LF363 leads Spitfire IIA P7350
during a photo-flight in the summer
of 2015. The former has worn the
colours of No 1 Sqn Hurricane I
P3395 since the fighter emerged
from its most recent overhaul in
May 2014, whilst P7350 was
adorned with No 41 Sqn's 'EB-G'
codes in September 2009.

CHAPTER FOUR

# 'IN ALL THINGS FIRST'

During the winter of 2013/14, the Battle of Britain Memorial Flight (BBMF) Hurricane II LF363 underwent a major overhaul at RAF Coningsby, in Lincolnshire, after which it was repainted as Mk I P3395 of No 1 Sqn. The latter machine was assigned to Fight Sergeant Arthur 'Darky' Clowes, a pre-war pilot who saw combat with the unit from September 1939 through to late April 1941. Born in the industrial town of Long Eaton, Derbyshire, in 1912, Clowes was raised by his grandparents after his father was killed during World War 1. He subsequently joined the RAF in 1929 when just 16 years old, becoming a Halton apprentice. He passed out two years later as a metal rigger.

In the mid-1930s Clowes applied for pilot training, after which he was posted to Fury-equipped No 1 Sqn at Tangmere. He transitioned to Hurricanes with the rest of the unit from October 1938, and in September of the following year he flew to France when No 1 Sqn became the first RAF fighter unit to be sent to the Continent in support of the BEF. Clowes achieved early success during the 'Phoney War' when he downed an He 111H from 2.(F)/*Aufklärungsgruppe* 122 that was conducting a reconnaissance mission near Saarbrücken on 23 November 1939 – it was one of six He 111Hs and Do 17Ps destroyed by Hurricanes from Nos 1 and 73 Sqns on this date. Squadron mate Flying Officer Paul Richey wrote about Clowes' victory in his autobiography *Fighter Pilot*:

The Heinkel was brought down near Metz, having been intercepted by 'Blue Section' of 'B' Flight. It was on fire, losing height rapidly, when a bunch of French Moranes came rushing in, all so eager to have a bang that one of them knocked most of

Sgt Clowes' tail off and the pilot had to bale out! Clowes put up a very good show, getting his machine back to the airfield, though he had to land at 120 mph to keep control – he overshot and nosed over. I saw him straight after this little effort and, though he was laughing, he was trembling violently and couldn't talk coherently. I had a good look at his aircraft too – one elevator and half the rudder were completely gone. Anyway, the Heinkel came down all right, but to our disgust we were only credited with one-third of it, as a 73 pilot and the French ack-ack boys also claimed to have shot at it.

Sergeant Clowes added two more victories to his tally on 29 March 1940 when No 1 Sqn claimed the first Bf 110s – from 14.(Z)/LG 1 – destroyed by Allied fighters on the Western Front. This historic encounter was also recalled by Flying Officer Richey:

With [W.H.] Stratton and Clowes, Johnny [Walker] sighted nine Me 110s – the first to appear over France – north of Metz. The Hurricanes climbed to attack. Johnny stuck behind one through some violent manoeuvres and first-class flying – vertical stall-turns and so on. He followed it through cloud, saw it catch fire, and ran out of ammunition. It was later found in pieces, the pilot having parachuted out. Sgt Clowes had a bang at two others, but was uncertain of the results. Stratton attacked another.

Air Marshal [Sir Arthur] 'Ugly' Barratt, who commanded the British Air Forces in France, had a few days previously issued an invitation to dine with him in Paris to the first pilot to shoot down a Messerschmitt 110 on the Western Front. The Air Marshal's personal aircraft, a Percival Q6, collected Johnny, Stratton and Clowes the day after the successful engagement with the 110s. The Air Marshal turned on a slap-up dinner at Maxim's for them – quite rightly I thought.

Clowes missed the first five days of the *Blitzkrieg*, which commenced on 10 May, having been on leave in England. Immediately recalled, 'their train had stopped 15 miles the wrong side of Reims', Richey noted in his book, 'and had been bombed several times but not hit. They were astonished by all they

saw and heard' as they struggled to reach their unit. Clowes soon made up for his early absence, and by the time No 1 Sqn finally returned to England on 18 June, he had increased his tally to six destroyed and one probable. Four days earlier, he had been one of 13 No 1 Sqn pilots to have their names published in *The London Gazette* after they were awarded decorations following their outstanding success in France during the *Blitzkrieg* – 129 aircraft destroyed, 114 of them between 10 and 19 May. The citation that accompanied Clowes' Distinguished Flying Medal (DFM) read as follows:

Sergeant Clowes has displayed courage and determination in many combats against the enemy. He has destroyed at least six enemy aircraft. On 1 June 1940 he led his section in combat against five Messerschmitt 109s and destroyed one. He then observed, above him, three further enemy aircraft and, before they could attack his flight, he engaged them. He succeeded in damaging one and in causing the other two to disperse in the clouds. He has displayed great skill and power of leadership.

He would also be Mentioned in Despatches on 11 July 1940.

No 1 Sqn Hurricanes had their propeller spinners adorned with a thin yellow stripe shortly after the unit returned to England from France on 18 June 1940. Several Hurricane units applied simple identification colours to the spinners of their aircraft during the summer of 1940, while some aeroplanes in Nos 17, 56, 242 and 249 Sqns were painted Sky – No 87 Sqn had a number of Hurricanes with red spinners during the Battle of Britain. Perhaps the most elaborate of them all was the red, white and blue spinner of P3675, flown by No 601 Sqn CO, Squadron Leader Michael Robinson.

Hurricane P3395 was issued to No 1 Sqn at Northolt, in Middlesex, as an attrition replacement shortly after the unit had returned from France. Clowes would not adopt it as his own machine until late August, however, by which time he had claimed two more bombers destroyed over the South Downs on the 16th. Although being scrambled at least twice a day during this critical phase of the Battle of Britain, the veteran NCO still found time to adorn his new mount – which was coded 'JX-B', the 'B' standing for 'Beer' according to its pilot – with a fearsome looking wasp motif on either side of the aircraft's nose beneath its exhaust stubs. Clowes clearly had some artistic abilities, as he painted the insects himself. And with each aerial victory, he added another black stripe to their bodies.

It was at around this time that Clowes had his portrait sketched by prolific war artist Cuthbert Orde, who had been commissioned by Air Commodore Harald Peake of the Air Ministry to visit squadrons all over Britain and spend up to two hours with each pilot sketching their likenesses. According to Orde:

In no case did I choose the sitter myself. He was selected either by Group Headquarters or by the station commander and, generally speaking, four or five in each squadron were chosen, the four or five who were considered the most valuable. So it was for them rather in the nature of a Mention in Despatches, I merely being the scribe who wrote out the despatch.

A pilot in the Royal Flying Corps during World War 1, Orde provided rare insight into Clowes' character. He noted during his brief time with the veteran fighter that he was 'a proper tough guy in his own quiet way, with an inherent toughness apparent in his build and in his walk – an obvious ability to give it or take it both physically and mentally, very cheerful, very much on the ball'.

By early September No 1 Sqn was beginning to feel the strain of near constant combat, its

Aside from being the longest-serving member of the BBMF, LF363 has also appeared in four motion pictures and a BBC television series. One of three Hurricanes to be flown from various locations throughout the summer of 1968 during the making of the *Battle of Britain* film, the aeroplane has subsequently worn the colours and markings of eight RAF squadrons, principally from the Battle of Britain period.

Newly promoted Pilot Officer Arthur 'Darky' Clowes is seen here at Wittering in October 1940 after No 1 Sqn had been posted north out of No 11 Group for a rest. Clowes is standing alongside his Hurricane P3395 'JX-B' (the 'B' standing for 'Beer' according to its pilot). Something of a budding artist, Clowes had painted a wasp motif on either side of the aircraft's nose beneath its exhaust stubs. With each aerial victory he claimed, Clowes added another black stripe to their bodies. (John Dibbs)

Hurricanes struggling with poor serviceability and its pilots – who had been flying at least two operational sorties per day since the *Blitzkrieg* had started in May – suffering from battle fatigue. Nevertheless, during the last two days of August, Clowes had made five claims in P3395, although he had been prevented from confirming the destruction of these aircraft when his own machine had been repeatedly attacked by yet more German fighters. The battle-hardened Flight Sergeant was now one of the most experienced fighter pilots in the RAF, and despite his lowly rank, he had led No 1 Sqn on an afternoon patrol on 6 September when the commanding officer (CO), Squadron Leader D.A. Pemberton, had been left stuck on the ground due to his Hurricane refusing to start. When the unit was subsequently bounced by a gaggle of Bf 109s from above, Clowes and his charges fought an effective defensive action that resulted in them all returning safely to Northolt.

The following day Clowes was credited with his first victory in P3395 when No 1 Sqn engaged a huge raid heading for London. Eleven Hurricanes had been scrambled from Northolt at 1624 hrs, with Yellow Section being headed by Clowes in 'JX-B' – he had already completed two uneventful patrols in the aeroplane earlier in the day. Leading the unit that afternoon was Flight Lieutenant 'Hilly' Brown, who had fought alongside Clowes from the start of the war. They were now the longest serving, and most successful, pilots in No 1 Sqn. The small gaggle of Hurricanes met the German bombers, flanked by as many as 100 Bf 109s and Bf 110s, head-on over the Thames Estuary. The squadron then broke up, Clowes fighting to protect himself from the escorts and avoid colliding with the bombers. He fired several bursts at enemy aircraft as they flew towards Manston.

Finally, having drawn clear of the main formation, he spotted a lone Bf 110 – almost certainly from 6./*Zerstörergeschwader* (ZG) 2 – flying straight and level at 13,000 ft. Clowes fired two bursts at the unsuspecting enemy fighter from above and behind and then watched as it nosed over and flew into the sea off Birchington-on-Sea, in north-east Kent. Out of ammunition and low on fuel, Clowes returned to base. He would be scrambled twice more before the day was out.

On 9 September No 1 Sqn was pulled out of the frontline and sent north to Wittering, in Cambridgeshire, for a rest. Clowes was rewarded with a commission later that month, and he was promoted to flight commander in October. In a little over six weeks he had risen from Sergeant to Flight Lieutenant, without having time to hold the rank of Flying Officer. Clowes would claim his final success (again in P3395) on 24 October when he was credited with sharing in the destruction of a Do 17 engaged east of Banbury.

Clowes' time with No 1 Sqn finally ended on 23 April 1941, and six days later he received a Distinguished Flying Cross (DFC). The citation for this award read: 'This officer has displayed great skill in his engagements against the enemy, and he has destroyed at least 11 of their aircraft. His coolness and judgement on all occasions have been an inspiration to his fellow pilots'. He subsequently spent time both in Training Command as an instructor and with frontline units in command positions in the UK and North Africa. Clowes' flying career came to an abrupt end in November 1943 when he lost his left eye during a party in the Officers' Mess at Uxbridge. He served as a staff officer for the rest of the war, remaining in the RAF until he succumbed to cancer of the liver in December 1949. Clowes was just 37 years old when he died.

OPPOSITE Wearing his spotless white cotton twill overalls, Pilot Officer Clowes climbs into the cockpit of P3395 in its blast pen at Wittering during a visit to the airfield by the Press. Both 'B for Beer' and the anonymous Hurricane in the adjoining revetment have spinners marked with an insignia yellow ring. Issued new to No 1 Sqn in June as an attrition replacement after the unit left a number of its aeroplanes behind in France, P3395 was routinely flown by Clowes over the next five months. Having survived the Battle of Britain unscathed, P3395 was passed on to No 55 OTU on 8 November 1940, before joining No 5 FTS the following year. It was written off on 24 March 1942 when a student pilot from the latter unit landed at Ternhill without first extending the undercarriage, causing the fighter to slew off the grass runway and a hit a nearby gun position. (John Dibbs)

Hurricane X AE977 flies along the Sussex coast soon after being painted in the colours of Mk I P3886 of No 601 'County of London' Sqn. This unit was based at nearby RAF Tangmere for much of the Battle of Britain, seeing considerable action over the Channel convoys in the early stages of the campaign and then playing a key role in the defence of airfields and RDF stations, at some considerable cost in men and machines, during the bloodiest phase of the battle.

# CHAPTER FIVE

# 'COUNTY OF LONDON' SQUADRON

The Biggin Hill Heritage Hangar Collection's Hurricane X AE977 has worn several Battle of Britain-inspired schemes since it was returned to airworthiness in 2000. In 2013 it became Mk I P3886 of No 601 'County of London' Sqn, honouring the memory of American volunteer pilots Flight Lieutenant Carl Davis and Pilot Officer Billy Fiske, both of whom flew the aeroplane in the summer of 1940 prior to being killed during the Battle of Britain.

One of the five units established with the formation of the Royal Auxiliary Air Force in 1925, Hendon-based No 601 Sqn had been staffed from the start by 'well to do' gentlemen from the capital and the surrounding Home Counties. Such was the reputation created by the unit that it soon became known in the RAF as 'The Millionaires' Mob'. Carl Davis joined the squadron in August 1936, by which time it was flying Hawker Hart light bombers. Born in South Africa to American parents, Davis had enjoyed public school education in England that saw him graduate from Trinity College, Cambridge, and then head to Canada to study mining engineering at McGill University, in Montreal. He eventually returned to the UK, where he took up flying and subsequently joined No 601 Sqn.

Life in the pre-war auxiliaries was viewed by most officers as akin to belonging to a uniformed flying club. A squadron mate of Carl Davis at this time was future Battle of France Hurricane ace The Honourable Max Aitken, who had joined No 601 Sqn in 1935. He succinctly described his fellow auxiliaries in the 'County of London' squadron as follows:

My companions there were, as you would expect, a pretty wild and high-spirited gathering, many of whom I already knew from skiing and after-skiing parties at St Anton. They were the sort of young men who had not quite been expelled from their schools, whom mothers warned their daughters against – in vain – who stayed up too late at parties and then, when everyone was half dead with fatigue, went on to other parties. Does that sort of young man still exist? I do not know. But in those days they were quite common. And they clustered in unusual density at the headquarters of No 601 Sqn.

Flying Officer Carl Davis' first taste of combat came at the controls of a Blenheim IF on 27 November 1939 when No 601 Sqn participated in the daring attack on the Borkum seaplane base in the Frisian Islands, off the German North Sea coast. By February of the following year the unit had switched to the Hurricane I, and following the German invasion of the Low Countries in May 1940, elements of both 'A' and 'B' Flights of No 601 Sqn were attached to Hurricane squadrons already based in France. The unit lost 11 Hurricanes and a pilot during the doomed campaign, and P3886 was one of a number of attrition replacement aircraft that was supplied to No 601 Sqn at Tangmere in early June.

Following the fall of France, the unit, like other squadrons in Fighter Command, was kept busy flying several sorties per day in an effort to protect convoys sailing through the increasingly dangerous waters of the English Channel. Being based on the Sussex coast, No 601 Sqn found itself in the thick of the action during this opening phase of the Battle of Britain. Tom Moulson, author of *The Millionaires' Squadron*, described the daily routine observed by Carl Davis in July 1940:

Each pilot flew for two days and then had a day off, a lorry taking him to dispersal on the airfield before dawn and bringing him back after a day's flying and air fighting – unless he was on night readiness – for a pint in the mess and a badly needed night's rest.

The Hurricanes were parked nose-into-wind, their engines run up periodically to keep them

warm between sorties. There were four stages of preparedness: 'Released' – off duty; 'Available' – 15 minutes to get airborne; 'Readiness' – five minutes to get airborne; and 'Standby' – two minutes to get airborne, which meant sitting strapped in the aircraft. The different categories of preparedness in themselves introduced an element of strain, an invisible tether of varying radius broken only by the end of the day or the febrile bustle of a 'scramble'. 'Available' was the bugbear of them all; there was no time to remove the cumbersome flying

The original P3886 was flown by a number of No 601 Sqn pilots during its time with the unit, many of whom enjoyed some success with the fighter when engaging the enemy. Amongst those to fly the aeroplane was 'Billy' Fiske, who was described by his flight commander, Flight Lieutenant Sir Archibald Hope, as 'the best pilot I've ever known. It was unbelievable how good he was. He picked it up so fast, it wasn't true. He'd flown a bit before, but he was a natural as a fighter pilot. He was also terribly nice and extraordinarily modest. He fitted in to the squadron very well.'

clothes or go very far, although one would spend hours inactively, and one of the fighter pilot's greatest anxieties was the possibility of being scrambled whilst on the lavatory.

Having failed to open his account against the Luftwaffe during the fighting in France, Carl Davis claimed his first victory within 48 hours of the Battle of Britain officially starting when he was credited with downing a Bf 110 from 9./ZG 76 off The Needles, at the western end of the Isle of Wight, during the late afternoon of 11 July. No 601 Sqn was still making good losses in both men and machinery at this time, and the following day a second American arrived at the unit in the form of Pilot Officer William Meade Lindsley Fiske III, known universally as 'Billy'. A colourful character, his background was described in *Over-Paid, Over-Sexed and Over-Here*, written by Lieutenant-Colonel James A. Goodson and Norman Franks:

Although an American [born in Chicago in 1911], he was the son of an international New York millionaire stockbroker living in Paris. Despite his American citizenship, Billy Fiske was very much an Anglophile, for he had been educated at Trinity College, Cambridge, and later joined the London office of his father's company. In his spare time he had become a well-known racing car driver and bobsleigh champion, a first-rate shot, played golf and sailed a yacht. In fact he held a record for the Cresta Run at St Moritz and captained the US Olympic team that won the bobsleigh event in 1932. He also drove in the 24-hour Le Mans race in a Stutz at just 19.

Billy married Rose, the former Countess of Warwick, in 1939. He was the Golden Boy – good looks, wealth, charm, intelligence. He had it all. He excelled in most sports and was good in business. He was very American, but completely international at the same time. The English loved him, and he loved them.

It was not surprising that someone like Billy should also want to fly, and in September 1939 he joined the RAF. In August he had been at the New York office, but returned to England on the *Aquitania* on the 30th. With his background it was natural that he 'got fighters', and that he managed to get himself posted to No 601 Sqn.

According to Moulson's volume on No 601 Sqn, 'Billy Fiske arrived at Tangmere with no pretensions or illusions. The leading members of 601, many of whom had some American blood in their veins, had urged him to join the Legion. His reputation was already high and he was welcomed with open arms.' One of those to greet Fiske was Flight Lieutenant Sir Archibald Hope, who had led 'A' Flight since the start of the war. His view on the 'polished man of the world' is most revealing:

Unquestionably Billy Fiske was the best pilot I've ever known. It was unbelievable how good he was. He picked it up so fast, it wasn't true. He'd flown a bit before, but he was a natural as a fighter pilot. He was also terribly nice and extraordinarily modest. He fitted in to the squadron very well.

Sadly, Billy Fiske would survive in the frontline for just a matter of weeks.

After a hectic July, No 601 Sqn was to enjoy no respite come August. In fact, its operational tempo increased markedly as the month wore on, the enemy switching its tactics from bombing convoys and naval bases to striking directly at fighter airfields in Nos 10 and 11 Groups, as well as the all-important radar stations along the south coast. Flying Officer Davis and Pilot Officer Fiske had been involved in most of the interceptions flown by the unit in the weeks since the latter had arrived at Tangmere. Although both 29 years old and from wealthy families, in terms of actual flying experience the two men were poles apart. Davis had served with No 601 Sqn since 1936 and had more than 1,500 flying hours in his logbook (400 on Hurricanes alone). Fiske had learned to fly in early 1940 and had arrived at the unit having never even sat in a Hurricane! Having clocked up 11 hours on the Hawker fighter at Tangmere, he flew his first operational sortie on 20 July, and never looked back from there.

By 16 August Carl Davis had downed four Bf 110s (including three the previous day), claimed

The charred remains of Flight Lieutenant Carl Davis's Hurricane I P3363 sit in the back garden of Canterbury Cottage in the village of Matfield, near Brenchley in Kent, on the morning of 6 September 1940. Eyewitness reports state that the flaming fighter broke in two soon after being bounced from above by a Bf 109, the forward section hitting the ground inverted and then flipping over and eventually skidding to a halt right side up. (John Dibbs)

three more as probables and damaged a further two. He had also downed a Ju 88 to 'make ace', shared in the probable destruction of a second and damaged a third, as well as a Bf 109. Fiske, too had proven his worth as a fighter pilot during this period, having damaged a Bf 110 whilst leading a section on 11 August, followed by a Ju 88 confirmed destroyed and a second as a probable 24 hours later. On the 13th he was credited with two Bf 110s probably destroyed and a further two damaged.

Tangmere had been targeted for the first time on 16 August, and Davis was credited with downing another Ju 88 whilst defending the airfield. During the same mission Billy Fiske, according to the Squadron Diary, had succeeded in manoeuvring a straggling Ju 88 into the Portsmouth balloon barrage after he had exhausted his ammunition. Two days later the airfield was struck a devastating blow by close to 50 Ju 87s of *Sturzkampfgeschwader* (StG) 2 that managed to penetrate No 11 Group's fighter screen and attack Tangmere unmolested. No 601 Sqn was circling over Bembridge at 20,000 ft at the time, providing top cover for another squadron awaiting the arrival of a massive raid heading for the south coast. The fighter station was badly bombed, with buildings and hangars destroyed, 14 aircraft written off and ten RAF personnel and three civilians killed.

The Luftwaffe paid a high price for this success, however, with No 601 Sqn getting amongst the fleeing Ju 87s and their Bf 109 escorts. Amongst those to claim victories was Flying Officer Davis at the controls of P3886 – he claimed a Bf 109 and a Ju 87 destroyed, and was credited with sharing in the destruction of a second Stuka. Extracts from his Combat Report for this mission reveal that he was leading Yellow Section during the engagement, and that No 601 Sqn dived from 20,000 ft down to 2,000 ft to effect an interception. The Stukas had dropped their bombs and were heading south for the nearby Sussex coast by the time the Hurricanes caught up with them, Davis quickly singling one out and pressing home his attack:

I closed with one Ju 87 and after several bursts he went down under control and landed between Pagham and Bognor, crashing through some trees in a hedge. No one got out. Heavy fire, fairly accurate, and violent evasive action were employed by the Ju 87. My aircraft was hit in the radiator so I returned to Tangmere and landed at 1305 hrs. I fired 30 rounds per gun.

Billy Fiske had also tangled with the main Ju 87 force over Bognor Regis, and whilst seeking out a

P3886 was issued to No 601 Sqn at Tangmere as an attrition replacement at the very start of the Battle of Britain. It is seen here four months later being serviced on the eastern fringe of the perimeter dispersal at Exeter Airport. This aircraft enjoyed success whilst being flown by No 601 Sqn aces Sergeant L.N. Guy (a Ju 88 shared on 15 August) and Flying Officer C.R. Davis (one and one shared Ju 87 and a Bf 109 on 18 August, followed by a Bf 110 probable on 31 August) – both pilots had been killed in action by the time this photograph was taken. (John Dibbs)

target his Hurricane had been struck in the reserve tank immediately forward of the cockpit. This had exploded, causing his fighter to burn fiercely. Instructed by his fighter controller to bail out, Fiske replied calmly, 'No, I think I can save the kite. I'm coming in'. His decision appeared to be the right one, for the fire quickly burnt itself out and Fiske glided in over the airfield boundary with nothing more than a thin ribbon of smoke emanating from the engine to denote his predicament. The Hurricane touched down and rolled along the grass runway, and all seemed fine until its pilot failed to spot a fresh bomb crater in his path. The fighter crashed heavily into the hole and blew up.

Fuel and ammunition exhausted, 'Archie' Hope landed back at the shattered fighter station minutes later, and he rushed to Fiske's burning Hurricane:

As I came down I saw one of our aircraft on its belly, belching smoke. It must have got a bullet in its engine. I taxied up to it and got out. There were two ambulancemen there. They had got Billy Fiske out of the cockpit. He was lying on the ground there. The ambulancemen didn't know how to take his parachute off, so I showed them. Billy was burnt about the hands and ankles, so I told them to put on Tanafax, the stuff we were supposed to apply to burns. I am told now it's one of the worst things you could put on a burn. I told Billy, 'Don't worry. You'll be alright,' got back into my aeroplane and taxied back to the squadron. Our adjutant went to see him in hospital that night. Billy was

sitting up in bed, perky as hell. The next we heard, he was dead. Died of shock.

The first American to die in the Battle of Britain was subsequently honoured with a bronze tablet in the crypt of St Paul's Cathedral, which was unveiled by the Secretary of State for Air, Sir Archibald Sinclair, on Independence Day in July 1941. The memorial plaque was inscribed with the words, 'An American citizen who died that England might live'.

Following the raid on Tangmere, No 601 Sqn was temporarily posted to Debden, in Essex, whilst the Sussex fighter station was repaired. The unit operated from here for two weeks from 19 August, Flying Officer Davis being kept busy for the remainder of the month by flying two or three times per day. On the 28th he wrote a brief note to his brother, John:

Thank you very much for your letter, which arrived here today. I am glad you are getting some shooting.

AE977's repaint as P3886 was perfect in every detail, bar the excessive wearing of the paint following several months of near-constant combat operations. The original aeroplane had suffered an engine failure on 26 July 1940, and when changing Merlins the fitters had also replaced the camouflaged cowling over its propeller reduction gearbox with a natural metal one – hence the unpainted example on AE977.

One of the things that annoys me about the war is that I have not been able to get up to Scotland this year, although the shooting down here is quite good just now!

For your ear only, I have now shot down ten German aeroplanes that I have actually seen crash and two or three others that should have crashed, but which I hadn't the time to watch. The sorts I have met are Ju 87s, Ju 88s, Me 109s and Me 110s. I have not yet met any Dorniers or Heinkels, but I expect that will happen in time.

Being in a fighter squadron is really a very odd business, as half the time you are bored stiff and the other half scared stiff! But having such wonderful aeroplanes makes a great difference, and you always feel that you can outfly and outshoot any German you meet when you are in them. Our Squadron has Hurricanes, and mine is now the old warrior of the flight with quite a few bullet holes in it. The only bullet that did any harm though was one through the radiator. That was done by a Ju 87 dive-bomber, but I shot him down and managed to get back to the aerodrome afterwards, so no harm came of it.

Davis was awarded a well-earned DFC two days after he posted this letter, the citation for the decoration reading as follows:

Flg Off Davis has been engaged on operational flying since 3 September 1939. He has taken part in nearly all patrols and interceptions carried out by his squadron. He has been a section leader for the last two months, and on several occasions has led his flight. Flg Off Davis has personally destroyed six enemy aircraft and severely damaged several others. He has shown great keenness and courage.

No 601 Sqn returned to Tangmere on 2 September, and 48 hours later Davis downed a Bf 110 from *Stab* III./ZG 76 over Worthing. This proved to be his final success, taking his tally to nine and one shared destroyed, four and one shared probables and four damaged. Five of his victims had been Bf 110s.

On 5 September, No 601 Sqn was informed that it was at last to receive a proper spell of rest, having been instructed to depart Tangmere on the

7th for Exeter, in No 10 Group. On the morning of the 6th, its pilots scrambled for the final time from the Sussex airfield that had primarily been their home since the end of December 1939, an incoming raid of substantial size having been detected. However, on this occasion, the 'County of London' squadron was 'bounced' well short of the bombers by a large formation of Bf 109s (possibly from JG 27) over the Tunbridge Wells area. For some reason the squadron 'weaver' failed to spot the enemy fighters diving from above, and in a matter of seconds four Hurricanes were hurtling earthward in flames. Two wounded pilots succeeded in baling out of their stricken fighters, but the remaining pair slammed into the ground still strapped into their respective aircraft.

One of the latter was newly promoted Flight Lieutenant Carl Davis, whose Hurricane hit the ground inverted in the back garden of Canterbury Cottage in the village of Matfield, near Brenchley, at 0930 hrs. His pre-war squadron mate, and fellow ace, Flight Lieutenant W.H. 'Willie' Rhodes-Moorhouse crashed in a high-speed dive near High Brooms Viaduct, in Southborough, seconds later. Like Davis, Rhodes-Moorhouse had participated in the Borkum raid, earned a DFC and been promoted to Flight Lieutenant on the same day (3 September) as the American.

Davis had been shot down in Hurricane I P3363, which he had used to claim all five of his Bf 110 victories. P3886 was subsequently flown to Exeter the following day.

Following service with No 601 Sqn, the original P3886 joined No 1 Sqn at Kenley in early January 1941, although its stay with the unit was only brief as new Hurricane IIAs started to arrive at the Surrey fighter station the following month. P3886 was then passed on to No 59 OTU, prior to being transferred to the Fleet Air Arm and conversion into a Sea Hurricane IA for the Merchant Ship Fighter Unit. The veteran fighter would end its days in India, where it was struck off charge on 28 September 1944.

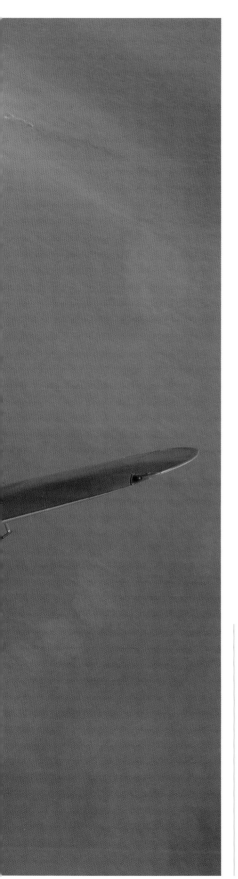

When Hurricane X AE977 was returned to airworthiness during the early summer of 2000, the aeroplane was marked up in the colours of a No 242 Sqn aircraft as flown by legendary ace Squadron Leader Douglas Bader during the Battle of Britain. The legless pilot had flown three Hurricane Is between July 1940 and March 1941. Bader's radio call-sign during this period was 'Dogsbody' after the 'D' in the fighter's 'LE-D' squadron code – two of three Hurricanes flown by him were marked accordingly.

# CHAPTER SIX

# BADER'S 'DOGSBODY'

When Hurricane X AE977 returned to the skies during the early summer of 2000, the aeroplane was painted in the colours of the No 242 Sqn aircraft flown by legendary ace Squadron Leader Douglas Bader during the Battle of Britain. He had at least three Hurricane Is (all coded 'LE-D', with the 'D' giving rise to his radio call-sign, 'Dogsbody') assigned to him between July 1940 and March 1941, when he became Wing Commander Flying at Tangmere.

Already a legendary figure within Fighter Command by the summer of 1940, Bader had returned to the cockpit in October 1939, eight years after he had lost both legs in a flying accident whilst at the controls of a Bulldog of No 23 Sqn. Posted initially to No 19 Sqn and then on to No 222 Sqn (both flying Spitfire Is from Duxford) as a flight commander, Bader claimed his first victory on 1 June 1940 with the latter unit when he downed a Bf 109 near Dunkirk. Promoted to acting Squadron Leader shortly thereafter, he was given command of Hurricane I-equipped No 242 Sqn at Coltishall, in Norfolk.

This unit had formed at Church Fenton in October 1939 with predominantly Canadian personnel, many of whom had joined the RAF during its pre-war expansion. Like most Fighter Command Hurricane squadrons, it was involved in the Battle of France, having been posted south to Biggin Hill on 21 May 1940. Despite suffering heavy losses while trying to protect the Dunkirk beaches, No 242 Sqn became the last RAF unit posted to France on 8 June to provide rear-guard cover for British forces as they were pushed towards the Atlantic coast. The unit went with them, moving three times in the ten days it was on the Continent. Pilots were forced to carry out their own servicing, with the remnants of No 242 Sqn finally fleeing the

The tough, but inspirational, Squadron Leader Douglas Bader sits on the cockpit sill of one of his Hurricane Is at Coltishall in September 1940. Obscured by his legs is the squadron leader's pennant, which Bader had applied to all three of his fighters. (John Dibbs)

country on 18 June. By then the unit had had ten Hurricanes shot down (and a handful more abandoned in France) and seven pilots killed, two captured and one wounded.

What remained of the squadron was sent to Coltishall, where it was joined by newly promoted Squadron Leader Bader in late June. He had his work cut out for him, as the unit was 'demoralised, shot through with reverses and utterly deranged', according to Bader's biographer, fellow fighter pilot and ace Laddie Lucas. Nevertheless, he more than proved up to the task at hand, as Lucas described in his volume *Flying Colours – The Epic Story of Douglas Bader*:

Douglas now applied all his skills and flair to pulling the squadron together in the air. It was a relentless, dynamic application. The effect was dramatic and deep. According to Denis Crowley-Milling (a future ace and air marshal), who was then a 21-year-old pilot officer who had joined the unit at the same time as Douglas after briefly seeing action in France with No 615 Sqn, the new CO had an immediate impact. Apart from his own flying and his leadership in the air, it was the age gap between him and the young members of the squadron which set him apart. It was a sort of head-of-the-school/new-boy divide. Douglas communicated with the squadron all the time – in the air, on the ground, on duty and off; but it didn't stop the young pilots holding him in real awe. He was on a different plane altogether. In a word, he was God.

Two immediate demands were placed upon the pilots. From them, there could be no escape. As few in the squadron had more than 200 hours flying in their logbooks at the time, the effect was sharp and positive. Each man was exhorted to get in the habit of chucking his aircraft about the sky. Stand it on its tail; fly it upside down; twist it about on its fore-and-aft axis; loop it, spin it, roll it off the top, do anything – but don't go about flying straight and level. There was another thing. Practise combat. Get on the other man's tail and stay there – *stay there*: never let him out of your sights. If he goes through the most violent evasive manoeuvres, stick there; never allow him to shake you off. Cling to him. Down, round, underneath, upside down, over the top, skidding one way then the other, spinning off … Keep your grip on him.

The pilot of AE977 performs a smart breakaway from the cameraship over the Kent coast, revealing the fighter's underside. The neatly retracted undercarriage and ventral fairing for the radiator and oil cooler dominate the centre fuselage area – note also the three circular identification lights immediately aft of the ventral fairing. The four small rectangular cut-outs clustered together beneath each wing are the chutes through which expended cartridges, and their links, from the Browning 0.303-in machine guns would fall when the weapons were being fired.

The ability to thrive on aerial contortions was an essential part of a fighter pilot's make-up. There must be absolute mastery over the aircraft. There could be no question of being timid or hesitant with an aeroplane, of worrying about falling out of the sky or getting in some unnatural attitude. Every man must know the extremes of his aircraft. All this had to be practised and repeated and practised again until it became second nature.

There was one man in 242 when Douglas arrived who had never slow-rolled, let alone spun, a Hurricane before. It could hardly be credited. For him it was quite an awakening. Even for the rest, who were not given to such stability, the regimen came as a rude and revealing disturbance. Hurricane Bader blew one or two of them irrevocably off course. They did not return to the fold.

He made the squadron go through as many manoeuvres as he could *together*. One aim was to

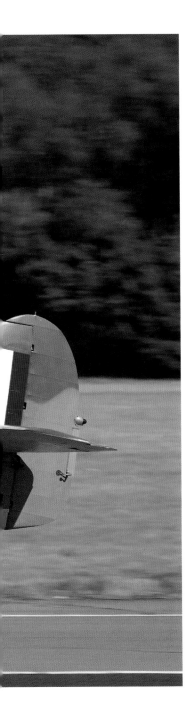

make the pilots feel that they were as one, not a dozen individualists. The other was to instil tightness, discipline and control into the flying. Putting ten or twelve aeroplanes in line astern, Douglas would loop the lot in formation. It was all right for those in front; for those at the back it was a tortuous exercise. Crowley-Milling was usually in the last aircraft; his seniority in the squadron normally ensured it. It was the hell of a job, he recalls, for 'Plt Off Prune' at the rear to get over the top of the loop without losing too much speed and falling out of it. It was an unsettling experience. Pilots didn't take much to falling about out of control. If one of them failed to make it and plummeted earthwards like a crumpled high pheasant, hit right up in the neck, Douglas would put the squadron through it again; and again. The further back you were the less chance you usually had of succeeding. It came as a great relief to Tail-End Charlie, by now soaked through with perspiration, when the leader elected to switch to some easier exercise.

It was all part of the accepted routine in those days of power. Douglas wanted the squadron to have cohesion in the air; he gave expression to his wish by insisting that its formation flying be very tight. Bader tended to fly 242 tighter than the rest, even up to the moment of opening an attack on a cluster of bombers. Vics of three aircraft – really tight vics of three, keeping close station – was the order.

Between 27 June and 3 July 1940 – seven days – he had 242 up nine times for squadron formations;

ten hours and twenty gruelling minutes of it. There was no more demanding form of flying for pilots with a couple of hundred hours under their belts – no matter how 'operational' they thought they might be. It required an exceptional output of concentration, and it was hardly the kind of work most calculated to commend itself to a bunch of Canadians, pulverised by the fiasco in France. And yet, as with so much discipline, it worked wonders for spirit, confidence and bearing. Bader's First Hundred Days were packed, of necessity, into a fortnight. Their impact was breath-taking, the effect decisive.

Being based at Coltishall, however, meant that No 242 Sqn only played a peripheral part in the early stages of the Battle of Britain, much to Squadron Leader Bader's increasing frustration. Despite his drilling of the unit to act as a team when in the air, he claimed his first victory with No 242 Sqn when airborne by himself. A weather reconnaissance Do 17 from *Wettererkundungsstaffel (Wekusta)* 26 had been detected on radar shortly after dawn flying north up the Norfolk coast. The squadron was alerted to its presence by a Coltishall fighter controller, and he asked if a section could be scrambled to intercept it. The weather was poor, and Bader decided not to risk the lives of his pilots in such conditions, choosing instead to take off alone. No 242 Sqn's Intelligence Report from the mission read as follows:

At 0539 hrs a single aircraft – Leader 242 Sqn – was ordered to intercept Raid 22. The enemy, a Do 17, was encountered at 0600 hrs at half-a-mile off the coast from Cromer. At first a head-on attack was made by the pilot for approximately two seconds, then he made a stern attack of approximately six seconds. He fired all ammunition and had two stoppages about 20 rounds from the end of the belt. Visibility was extremely bad, with heavy rain and low cloud. The bad weather conditions prevented the pilot from observing enemy aircraft markings. The pilot saw his tracer hitting the enemy aircraft, and one short burst came from the rear gunner. The pilot did not see the result of his combat because of poor visibility, which caused him to lose sight of the enemy

The inner workings of AE977 are revealed following the removal of one of the outer fuselage panels. Sections of the fighter's 1930s-era tubular-framed fuselage can be clearly seen, whilst in the foreground is silver-painted pipework for the oil and coolant systems (the larger pipes), as well as various hydraulic and pneumatic lines. The hydraulics raise and lower the flaps, whilst the pneumatics operate the wheel brakes and, on wartime Hurricanes, the guns. In the centre of the photograph is the elevator trim wheel sprocket and chain. To the left of the hand hold is the back of the aeroplane's electrical system.

LEFT The distinctive No 242 Sqn 'giving Hitler the boot' motif that was adopted by the unit shortly after Squadron Leader Bader's arrival as CO. The marking was devised by Canadian Pilot Officer Norris Hart, who claimed four victories with the squadron prior to his death in combat off Sheerness on 5 November 1940. His sketches for the emblem were applied to a number of aircraft by LAC Thompson, with Bader's P3061 almost certainly being the first to feature the motif.

AE977, like Bader's original 'D for Dogsbody', is marked up with a 35-inch diameter Type A 1 fuselage roundel as per Fighter Command regulations for the summer of 1940. No 242 Sqn used code letters that were 30 inches high, which was the norm in most Hurricane units during the Battle of Britain.

in a particularly dense rain cloud. It is confirmed as conclusive by the Observer Corps (Norwich), who reported that a Do 17 crashed into the sea off Cromer at the time the attack was delivered.

Bader would dramatically increase his score between 21 August and 27 September 1940, claiming ten victories in 'D for Dogsbody' as his controversial 'Big Wing' theory – a tactic whereby incoming bomber raids were met by a wing-sized formation of three to five squadrons, rather than just one 12-aeroplane unit as was commonplace in Fighter Command during the Battle of Britain – began to gain traction in No 12 Group. Although still based at Coltishall, the unit would routinely fly down to Duxford, in Cambridgeshire, shortly after dawn and operate from here during the day, before returning to the Norfolk fighter station in the evening. One of the more successful 'Big Wing' engagements took place on 7 September when Bader and No 242 Sqn led Czech-manned No 310 Sqn and Spitfire-equipped No 19 Sqn into battle in defence of North Weald on the day the Luftwaffe deliberately targeted London for the first time. The Form 'F' Combat Report submitted by Flight Lieutenant G. Maybaum, who was the Sector Intelligence Officer (IO) at Coltishall, detailed Bader's success in this engagement, which saw No 242 Sqn claim no fewer than ten victories, two probables and three damaged for the loss of one pilot and his Hurricane:

Squadron 242 was ordered off from Duxford at approximately 1645 hrs to patrol North Weald at 10,000 ft. Arriving at North Weald at 15,000 ft, the squadron noticed AA fire to the east and saw a number of enemy aircraft at 20,000 ft. The enemy was about 70 to 90 strong. The bombers were flying in tight box formation, with Me 110s circling round and Me 109s flying 5,000 ft higher. On sighting the enemy the leader, Sqn Ldr Bader, advised Duxford and obtained permission to engage. The squadron was at an initial disadvantage, being below the enemy and having to give full throttle to climb and get level with the enemy formation, thereby eliminating the element of surprise. When climbing up to make a stern attack, enemy fire was very heavy but not effective.

During 242's steep climb to attack, the squadron formation straggled out so that full weight could not be pressed home. In this first attack 242 Squadron was supported by 19 and 310 Squadrons. 242 Squadron, now being spread out, started a dogfight with the enemy, picking out individual bombers, at the same time avoiding the enemy fighters – Me 109s – that came down from their position above. Red Section was leading and the first to attack the enemy aircraft, which were proceeding north over the Thames Estuary. During the whole period of combat, weather was fine and visibility excellent.

Red 1 (Sqn Ldr D.R.S. Bader), on sighting enemy aircraft, opened throttle and boost and

Bader is flanked by 'A' Flight commander Flight Lieutenant George Ball (left) and high-scoring Canadian ace Pilot Officer 'Willie' McKnight in front of the newly-applied squadron emblem on the CO's P3061. (John Dibbs)

Only recently returned from four years as a PoW, Wing Commander Douglas Bader converses with Air Chief Marshal Lord Dowding (centre) at North Weald prior to leading the first Battle of Britain flypast over London on 15 September 1945. Bader is surrounded by serving officers who participated in the campaign five years earlier, including Wing Commander Pete Brothers (far right). The flypast, led by 300 fighters from 25 squadrons, took a full 90 minutes to fly over London. (John Dibbs)

climbed and turned left to cut off the enemy. He arrived with Red 2 only, on the beam slightly in front. Sqn Ldr Bader gave a very short beam burst at about 100 yards at the enemy Me 110s who were then flying in a section of three line astern in a large rectangle. Then, accompanied by Red 2, he fired short bursts at the middle enemy aircraft in the rear section. The enemy aircraft started smoking, preparatory to catching fire. Sqn Ldr Bader did not notice the result, which later was confirmed by Plt Off [Stan] Turner as diving down in flames from the back of the bomber formation.

At the time of Sqn Ldr Bader's attack on the Me 110, a yellow-nosed Me 109 was noticed reflected in his mirror, and he turned to avoid the enemy aircraft. A big bang was then heard by Sqn Ldr Bader in the cockpit of his Hurricane, a bullet (explosive) having come through the right hand side of the fuselage, touching the map case, knocking the corner off the undercarriage selector quadrant and finishing up against the petrol priming pump.

Sqn Ldr Bader executed a quick, steep diving turn and found a lone Me 110 below him, which he attacked from straight astern and above him and saw the enemy aircraft go into a steepish straight dive, finishing up in flames in a field just north of the railway line west of Wickford and due north of Thameshaven.

Late on the morning of 15 September 1940 – a date that would later officially become Battle of Britain Day – the largest bomber formation of the campaign to date headed for London. It was eventually broken up by more than 300 RAF fighters, including Squadron Leader Douglas Bader in his Hurricane V7467 'LE-D' at the head of the Duxford 'Big Wing'. He claimed a Do 17 destroyed and two more damaged, these being his first successes in this particular aircraft. Bader's Form 'F' Combat Report read as follows:

Patrolled south of Thames (approximately Gravesend area) at 25,000 ft. Saw two squadrons pass underneath us in formation travelling north-west in purposeful manner. Then saw AA bursts, so turned wing and saw enemy aircraft 3,000 ft below to the north-west. Managed perfect approach with two other squadrons between our Hurricanes and sun and enemy aircraft below and down sun. Arrived over enemy aircraft formation of 20 to 40 Do 17s: noticed Me 109s dive out of sun and warned our Spitfires to look out – Me 109s broke away and climbed south-east.

Was about to attack enemy aircraft which were turning left-handed – i.e. to west and south – when I noticed Spitfires and Hurricanes engaging them. Was compelled to wait for risk of collisions.

OPPOSITE Following its lengthy spell with No 242 Sqn, V7467 was passed on to No 111 Sqn when the Canadian unit started to receive Hurricane IIBs in March 1941. The aeroplane's tenure with 'Treble One' lasted only a matter of weeks, however, as the RAF's first Hurricane squadron unceremoniously switched to Spitfire Is at Dyce in April. Remaining in Scotland, V7467 was posted to No 59 OTU at Turnhouse, in Edinburgh. It was destroyed in a crash when a student pilot lost control in cloud near Dumfries on 1 September 1941.

However, warned wing to watch for other friendly fighters and dived down with leading section in formation onto last section of five enemy aircraft. Plt Off [Norman] Campbell took left-hand Do 17, I took middle one and Sub-Lt [Dickie] Cork took right-hand one, which had lost ground on outside of turn. Opened fire at 100 yards in steep dive and saw a large flash behind starboard motor of Dornier as wing caught fire: must have hit petrol pipe or tank; overshot and pulled up steeply.

Then carried on and attacked another Do 17, but had to break away to avoid Spitfire. The sky was full of Spitfires and Hurricanes queuing up and pushing each other out of the way to get at Dorniers, which for once were outnumbered. I squirted at odd Dorniers at close range as they came into my sights, but could not hold them in my sights for fear of collision with other Spitfires and Hurricanes. Saw collision between Spitfire and Do 17, which wrecked both aeroplanes. Finally ran out of ammunition chasing crippled and smoking Do 17 into cloud. It was the finest shambles I've been in, since for once we had position, height and numbers. Enemy aircraft were a dirty looking collection.

Bader would claim three more victories and a probable by month-end, these proving to be his final successes in a Hurricane. With his score then standing at 12 victories (11 of them with No 242 Sqn), he received a Distinguished Service Order (DSO) on 1 October for 'gallantry and leadership of the highest order. During three recent engagements he has led his squadron with such skill and ability that 33 enemy aircraft have been destroyed. In the course of these engagements Sqn Ldr Bader has added to his previous successes by destroying six enemy aircraft'. The way Bader had transformed No 242 Sqn from an 'utterly deranged' outfit into a crack fighter unit (that claimed 71 victories and suffered just six losses between 1 July and 31 October 1940) in only a matter of weeks was nothing short of miraculous.

The first of Bader's Hurricanes with No 242 Sqn was P3061, which joined the unit as an attrition replacement at the same time as its new CO. He proceeded to destroy six aircraft with the Hurricane before it was severely damaged during the first 'Big Wing' operation on 7 September – the fighter was hit in the cockpit by an exploding cannon shell fired from a Bf 109. It was subsequently repaired and sent to No 17 Sqn, before ending up with No 52 OTU. Like many 1940-period Hurricanes, P3061 was passed on to the Fleet Air Arm in 1942. Bader selected the newly arrived V7467 (it reached Coltishall on 11 September) as his next 'Dogsbody'.

O f all the Hurricanes featured in this volume, the subject of this chapter is the only one to have seen combat in the Battle of Britain. Gloster-built R4118 joined No 605 'County of Warwick' Sqn on 17 August 1940, the unit having received its first Hurricanes in June of the previous year – it operated a handful of these machines alongside Gladiators at Tangmere until November 1939, when re-equipment was at last completed.

No 605 Sqn's first taste of action came in April 1940 after it had been posted north to Wick, in Scotland, to defend the naval base at Scapa Flow. It returned south again on 21 May when the unit was sent to Hawkinge, in Kent. From here No 605 Sqn was thrown into action over France in support of Operation *Dynamo* – the evacuation of the BEF from Dunkirk. During a week of hectic action, the unit claimed 12 victories and six unconfirmed for the loss of nine aircraft and four pilots (including the CO, Squadron Leader G.V. Perry), with two more captured and one wounded. The unit was sent north once again following its operations over France, receiving new aircraft and replacement pilots at Drem, in East Lothian. It was here that R4118 joined No 605 Sqn on 17 August, having only been delivered to the RAF three weeks earlier.

Forty-eight hours before the aeroplane's arrival, No 605 Sqn had been one of eight fighter units from No 13 Group involved in the massacre of He 111s, Ju 88s and Bf 110s from *Luftflotte* V that had attacked targets in north-eastern England from airfields in Scandinavia. The squadron claimed eight He 111s (from KG 26) destroyed, three probables and two damaged off the coast of Newcastle, with two Hurricanes force-landing in return. R4118 was a replacement for one of these machines.

Currently the world's only airworthy Hurricane to have served in the Battle of Britain, Mk I R4118 is a fitting tribute to the craftsmanship of the employees of Hawker Restorations Ltd (HRL), who restored the fighter over a three-and-a-half-year period.

Following its restoration, R4118 was accurately painted in the camouflage and markings it wore whilst serving with No 605 'County of Warwick' Sqn between 17 August and 22 October 1940. Being a Glosters-built Hurricane, R4118 had had its roundels and fin flash originally applied in pre-war bright colours for the red and blue. Hurricanes constructed by Hawker from late 1939, and those being overhauled or repaired (both at MUs and at squadron level) once the conflict had started had dull wartime national insignia applied. As can be seen here, HRL went with the bright colours too.

ABOVE R4118 first fired its guns in anger – against a lone Ju 88 – on 13 September whilst being flown by future ace, Pilot Officer Bob Foster. He had joined No 605 Sqn at Drem as an attrition replacement in early July, and would fly the fighter nine times during the Battle of Britain. Almost 65 years later, Foster was guest of honour when R4118 performed its second post-restoration air test from Cambridge Airport. (John Dibbs)

On 7 September, No 605 Sqn was posted to Croydon to join No 11 Group in place of battle-weary No 111 Sqn, R4118 being flown south by unit CO and Battle of France ace (with No 3 Sqn), Squadron Leader Walter Churchill. He subsequently gave the fighter its combat debut on the 9th when he led the squadron into battle near Farnborough. It appears that R4118 first fired its guns in anger on 13 September whilst being flown by future ace Pilot Officer Bob Foster. He had joined No 605 Sqn at Drem as an attrition replacement in early July, and would fly the fighter nine times during the Battle of Britain. The Form 'F' Combat Report for this encounter, compiled by No 605 Sqn's IO, Flying Officer D.H. Price, read as follows:

Two Hurricanes (Red 1 [Sergeant Ricky Wright] and Red 2 [Pilot Officer Bob Foster] of 605 Squadron left Croydon at 1410 hrs. After various vectors and while flying north-northwest at 10,000 ft, they saw a Ju 88 near Tunbridge Wells at 15,000 ft just under ten-tenths cloud flying east. They turned onto a course parallel with the enemy aircraft and climbed to attack. The enemy aircraft, however, dived into a lower layer of broken cloud at 8,000 ft, Red 1 and Red 2, in line astern, making an astern attack upon it. Red 1 fired a four seconds burst before the enemy aircraft disappeared into the clouds. Red 2 lost the enemy aircraft in the clouds and did not see it again.

The enemy aircraft, going very fast, emerged on the same course on the other side of the cloud, and Red 1 did a diving beam attack from starboard, giving a two seconds burst from 400 yards, closing to 100 yards, before the enemy aircraft again entered cloud. The enemy aircraft again emerged from the clouds on the same course, and Red 1 did another diving beam attack from port, giving a two seconds burst from 250 yards, closing to 50 yards, and saw pieces falling from the enemy aircraft. After this, the top rear gunner ceased firing. The enemy aircraft again emerged from the cloud on the same course, and Red 1 was able to fire a five seconds burst from astern from about 400 yards until it disappeared into the clouds once more near Hastings, and Red 1's ammunition was exhausted.

Cloud base was about 5,000 ft, clear between 8,000 ft and 15,000 ft and ten-tenths above 15,000 ft. Red 1 returned to Croydon at 1445 hrs and Red 2 at 1505 hrs.

Bob Foster gave brief details about this interception in his autobiography *TALLY-HO!*:

On the 13th there was little hostile activity. The weather wasn't too bad – bright intervals with showers, but there was rain over the Channel. The summer of 1940 was not all 'wall-to-wall' sunshine as some people seem to remember. Ricky Wright was credited with damaging a lone recce Ju 88 between Tunbridge Wells and Hastings that afternoon. I was with him and got in a few shots at the fleeting machine, and I must have believed I had it for I noted 'one Ju 88 damaged' in my logbook. Then I found myself in cloud and lost sight of Ricky as he continued the pursuit. According to Luftwaffe records there was a Ju 88 from III./LG 1 that was severely damaged over southern England and returned to its base with one wounded crew member, although I believe 238 Squadron had a similar claim. The Junkers was, in the event, so badly hit that it had to be written off.

Although R4118 was not assigned to one pilot in particular, it was flown most frequently – 14 times in fact – by Pilot Officer I.J. 'Jock' Muirhead. According to squadron mate Bob Foster:

[He] came from East London and had been accepted into the RAF as a 16-year-old apprentice in 1929. Like so many boy-entrants, 'Jock' managed to get himself accepted for a flying course, his first squadron being 151, but then moved to 605 in April 1940. He had claimed some scalps over France and Dunkirk, although he was himself shot down on 26 May during a fight with some Me 110s. He baled out safely and got home by ship. 'Jock' became the first member of 605 Squadron to win the DFC for these recent actions, the award being announced in *The London Gazette* on 28 June 1940 with the following citation:

Bob Foster's logbook entry for the last day of September and the first 11 days of October 1940 reveal that he made four flights in R4118 during this final phase of the Battle of Britain. He flew the fighter twice on 1 October, claiming a share in the destruction of a Ju 88 during the first of these sorties.

| 1940 | | AIRCRAFT | | PILOT, OR 1ST PILOT | 2ND PILOT, PUPIL OR PASSENGER | D (INCLUDING RESU |
| MONTH | DATE | Type | No. | | | |
|---|---|---|---|---|---|---|
| T | 30 | HURRICANE | V6786 | SELF | — | PATROL |
| | 30 | HURRICANE | R4118 | SELF | · | PATROL |

C.A. Curran,
OC 'A' FLT.

W.Kellett.
OC 605 SQDN.

<table>
<tr><td colspan="7">SUMMARY FOR .. SEPTEMBER ............... 1940</td></tr>
<tr><td colspan="4">UNIT .. 605 SQDN ...... AIRCRAFT</td><td>1. HURRICA</td></tr>
<tr><td colspan="4">DATE .. 1-10-40 ...... TYPES</td><td>2.</td></tr>
<tr><td colspan="4">SIGNATURE .. R.W.Hart .........</td><td>3.</td></tr>
<tr><td colspan="4"></td><td>4.</td></tr>
</table>

| | | | | | | |
|---|---|---|---|---|---|---|
| | HURRICANE | R4118 | SELF | | | |
| | HURRICANE | R4118 | " | · | PATROL & COMBAT (1.HUR. |
| | HURRICANE | R4118 | " | · | PATROL. |
| | HURRICANE | V6783 | " | · | PATROL. |
| | HURRICANE | V6783 | " | · | PATROL |
| | HURRICANE | V6783 | " | · | PATROL |
| | HURRICANE | V6783 | · | · | PATROL |
| | HURRICANE | V6783 | · | · | PATROL & COMBAT. |
| | HURRICANE | V6783 | · | · | PATROL & COMBAT. (1. ME10 |
| | HURRICANE | V6193 | · | · | PATROL & COMBAT. |
| | HURRICANE | V6783 | · | · | PATROL |
| | HURRICANE | V6783 | · | · | PATROL |
| | HURRICANE | V6783 | · | · | PATROL |
| | HURRICANE | V6786 | · | · | PATROL |
| | HURRICANE | V6788 | · | · | PATROL |

R4118 cruises over cloud during a late summer photoshoot arranged specially for this volume. Owned by Peter Vacher after he secured its recovery from India, the aeroplane was sold to software entrepreneur James Brown in September 2015 to form the centrepiece of new organisation, Hurricane Heritage.

'This officer had shot down five enemy aircraft and has shown outstanding skill, coolness and daring in carrying out eight patrols in five days over northwest France and Belgium. During the last patrol he was forced to escape by parachute and after surmounting many difficulties succeeded in reaching his unit'.

Muirhead's solitary victory claim in R4118 came during his 14th, and last, mission in the fighter on 24 September – this was his third sortie in the aeroplane that day, having flown it three times on the 23rd and four times on the 18th. Muirhead was flying with Polish Pilot Officer Witold Glowacki as his wingman at the time, the latter being lost during this engagement. No 605 Sqn's IO, Flying Officer D.H. Price, detailed the action in the Form 'F' Fighter Command Combat Report he typed up after interviewing Pilot Officer Muirhead upon his return to Croydon:

Two Hurricanes (Yellow Section) from 605 Squadron left Croydon at 1541 hrs on 24 September 1940 with orders to patrol Beachy Head, angels 10 [10,000 ft]. While flying east near Beachy Head at angels 12, they saw a Do 215 [actually a Do 17 of 2./KG 76] at angels 14, in cloud, also flying east. These clouds were more in the nature of mist down to 12,000 ft, with

The pilot gently pushes the throttle forward and R4118 commences its take-off run from Old Warden. 'When taking off, the view from the Hurricane is considerably better than the Gauntlet and better than the Demon, both individually and in formation', Squadron Leader Gillan of No III Sqn explained in his report, which he wrote just four weeks after his unit had received its first examples of the new fighter at RAF Northolt in December 1937. 'Taking off in formation is simple, but immediately after leaving the ground when pilots retract their undercarriages and flaps aircraft cannot keep good formation as undercarriage and flaps retract at different speeds in each aircraft. It is recommended, therefore, that take-off should be done individually in succession.'

visibility of about 1,000 yards. Yellow 1 [Pilot Officer Muirhead] and Yellow 2 [Pilot Officer Glowacki] climbed and overhauled the Do 215 rapidly, Yellow 1 attacking with a three-second burst from the starboard quarter astern from underneath, but observed no result. The enemy aircraft then turned left and Yellow 2 made a beam attack, after which both of its engines were on fire, it lost height and Yellow 2 made a further attack while the enemy aircraft was losing height. Yellow 1 and Yellow 2 followed it down just below the cloud base, which in mid-Channel was 1,000 ft, and saw it crash into the sea five miles southwest of Cap Gris Nez.

At this moment four Me 109s appeared overhead, so Yellow 1 and Yellow 2 dropped down to sea level and crossed the French coast at Albermuse [sic]. After this, Yellow 1 did not see Yellow 2. The Me 109s attacked Yellow 1 over land, so he hedge-hopped east for 15–20 miles, then turned southwest, shook off the Me 109s and crossed the coast again between Boulogne and Le Touquet, climbing into cloud at 12,000 ft, and returned to Croydon at 1725 hrs.

Yellow 1 saw five ambulances along the Boulogne–Le Touquet road, painted grey with a white circle and red cross in the middle, very similar to RAF ambulances. Along the same road there were only a few hundred scattered troops. Yellow 1 saw six lines of two boats abreast moving very fast northwards three miles off the coast between Boulogne and Le Touquet, practically no boats inside the mile at Boulogne, and only a few offshore

from Le Touquet, which he thought were barges. It appeared that there was no serious attempt at invasion from this quarter.

Pilot Officer Glowacki had fallen victim to future ace Oberleutnant Michael Sonner of 3./JG 51, the Pole crash-landing at high speed and suffering a head injury in the process. He passed away in a German hospital later that day, possibly due to an allergic reaction to a tetanus injection that he was given as part of his treatment. Muirhead was himself shot down by a Bf 109 on 7 October, but survived, only to be killed eight days later in a major dogfight over Maidstone – he crashed to his death near Gillingham, having been bounced by Bf 109s from 1./JG 26 moments after No 605 Sqn had intercepted another formation of Messerschmitt fighters.

Following Muirhead's final sortie in R4118 on 24 September, the fighter was flown by Canadian Pilot Officer J.A. Archie Milne five times in three days. A private pilot pre-war who had also served in the Royal Canadian Air Force (RCAF) as an aero engine fitter prior to joining the RAF in the summer of 1939, Milne had been posted to No 605 Sqn, via No 72 Sqn, as an attrition replacement in mid-June 1940. On the morning of 27 September he took off with the rest of the squadron from Croydon and headed south. Milne compiled the following Combat Report in the wake of this flight:

Took off at 0925 hrs. The squadron climbed to 18,000 ft, circling round some Me 110s which were

R4118 has been based at Old Warden airfield, home of the Shuttleworth Collection, since it was acquired by Hurricane Heritage in September 2015; the aeroplane was previously flown from Kidlington Airport, in Oxfordshire. The wide track of the Hurricane's undercarriage is obvious from this angle.

being engaged by fighters. The squadron went into line astern. As we closed with the Me 110s one of them broke left away from his formation and I delivered a full beam attack at 300 yards with a five-second burst. He began to spiral down in left- and right-hand turns and I delivered two more attacks of three-second bursts from astern. Both engines were smoking after my first attack, and his port engine burst into flames at 3,000 ft just east of Dorking (approximately). I then returned to base.

The following afternoon Pilot Officer Foster again saw action in R4118 (which he flew four times that day, with a fifth sortie being undertaken by Pilot Officer Milne), as he briefly recounted in *TALLY-HO!*:

Ricky Wright and I were sent off after a 'bogey', along with Archie Milne, but Archie became separated from us in cloud. Off Beachy Head we ran into a Ju 88 that was attempting to bomb some shipping. We both attacked and scored hits on the raider before it too became lost in cloud.

During the early afternoon of 1 October Pilot Officer Foster claimed R4118's final success in combat when he shared in the destruction of a Ju 88, although the details of this particular engagement are lacking. Indeed, it is only noted in his logbook. This proved to be the last time that R4118 would fire its guns in anger, despite it performing a further 17 operational flights with seven different pilot through to 22 October. At 1411 hrs on the 22nd, the aeroplane was one of twelve Hurricanes scrambled from Croydon and ordered to patrol between Kenley and Biggin Hill at

The Hurricane's unique shape, form and construction is evident in this sunset image as Stu Goldspink patrols an English autumn sky in Hurricane R4118, just as this machine did in 1940. Hurricane Heritage's Mk I has been restored in the markings it wore when flown by No 605 Sqn's Pilot Officer Bob Foster, amongst others.

R4118 is camouflaged in standard RAF Dark Earth and Dark Green in the B scheme as per Hawker factory drawing No 116520. The latter actually shows the A Scheme, which is a mirror image of the B Scheme, but without a yellow gas detector patch on the left wing. It also features Type B upper wing roundels, applied in pre-war bright colours.

20,000 ft. According to Flying Officer D.H. Price's Form 'F' Fighter Command Combat Report, 'the squadron was flying in flights abreast pairs astern, with one aircraft weaving below the squadron'. R4118, being flown by Flying Officer Derek Forde, was Yellow 1 in 'A' Flight, while the 'weaver' mentioned by Flying Officer Price was Pilot Officer Ricky Wright (Yellow 2). The latter would claim a Bf 109 damaged, as detailed in his Combat Report:

When patrolling in pairs by Flights at 22,000 ft (I was weaving underneath the rear of the squadron), two Me 109s, followed by three more, passed us on the port side going the opposite way, and flew round behind us into the sun. As the squadron turned right towards them, the three made a feint attack, while the other two came out of the sun into the last pair of 'A' Flight. I endeavoured to climb up towards the two Me 109s which had broken up our last pair and were now attacking the next two of 'A' Flight [including R4118]. One of them saw me coming and broke away right, and climbed. I gave him a 1.5-ring deflection from 200 yards three-second burst. His Perspex hood seemed to come off, he turned onto his back and went into a vertical dive. I followed him down to 5,000 ft, firing at 200 yards range from astern, but increasing to 400–500 yards (two four-second bursts). Pieces

came off the tail end of the aircraft, but did not affect his flying ability. He continued in a shallow dive, going south-east, and I lost him in haze at 3,000 ft towards Dungeness.

Flying Officer Forde, who had previously experienced combat with No 145 Sqn in France (he had been shot down over Dunkirk) and during the early stages of the Battle of Britain, managed to nurse the badly shot-up R4118 back to Croydon, where it was found to be Cat II (damaged beyond repair at site). His squadron mate Pilot Officer Milne was not so lucky, being forced to crash-land his Hurricane near Dorking. Wounded in the initial attack, he then fractured his hip on landing. It appears that No 605 Sqn had been bounced out of the sun by high-scoring Luftwaffe ace Major Werner Mölders of *Stab./*JG 51. At the controls of a brand new Bf 109F, he claimed three Hurricanes destroyed north-west of Maidstone to take his tally to 62 victories.

R4118's time with No 605 Sqn was now over. In less than two months it had been flown on 49 sorties by 11 pilots. The day after it had been shot up by Major Mölders, the fighter was transported to the workshops of the Service Aircraft Section of the Austin Motor Company at Longbridge for repair. Details of its subsequent service can be found in Chapter Sixteen: Hurricane Survivors.

OPPOSITE On 24 September 1940 R4118 was being flown by Pilot Officer I.J. 'Jock' Muirhead when he and Polish Pilot Officer Witold Glowacki (pictured) chased a lone Do 17 back across the Channel towards France. Although the bomber was reportedly destroyed, the two Hurricanes were attacked by four Bf 109s and Glowacki (in P3832 'UP-P') was forced down. He suffered a head injury as his fighter crash-landed at high speed, and he is seen here standing near the wreckage with a rudimentary bandage over the deep gash. (Robert Gretzyngier)

OPPOSITE FAR RIGHT The destruction wrought on Glowacki's Hurricane is graphically revealed in this photograph, the aeroplane's rear fuselage section and tailplane being bent back over the cockpit. The pilot passed away several hours later, having possibly suffered an allergic reaction to a tetanus injection. (Robert Gretzyngier)

Although this photograph is of Hurricane Is of No 85 Sqn (there are next to no shots of No 607 Sqn aeroplanes during the summer of 1940), R4118 participated in similar patrols during its time with the 'County of Warwick' squadron in the Battle of Britain. These aircraft are seen in tight Battle Formation over Kent. The rigid adherence to such unwieldy tactics by Fighter Command throughout 1940 resulted in Hurricane and Spitfire units sustaining heavy losses to both Bf 109Es and Bf 110s conducting their favoured 'dive and zoom' attacks from a superior altitude to their British opponents. (John Dibbs)

Stu Goldspink holds close formation with the camership on a flight from Bicester airfield during the filming of *Spitfire – The Feature Documentary* on 28 September 2016. Along with The Fighter Collection's Chief Pilot Pete Kynsey, Stu Goldspink carried out R4118's early test flights leading up to it being issued with a CAA Permit to Fly. His flying experience is truly vast, ranging from Chipmunk glider tugs and Pawnee crop-sprayers through to Boeing 767s. He has also flown numerous restored military types, including half of the world's population of airworthy Hurricanes.

LEFT Stu Goldspink pulls R4118 up and away from the cameraship, prior to rolling the aeroplane over onto its back and diving away through a break in the cloud cover below. 'The Hurricane was a thoroughly war-like machine, rock solid as a platform for its eight Browning machine guns, highly manoeuvrable despite its large proportions and with an excellent view from the cockpit', noted Battle of Britain ace Group Captain Peter Townsend.

BELOW By the time R4118 was delivered to the RAF on 23 July 1940 all new Hurricanes and Spitfires were having their undersides painted in Sky as per an Air Ministry Order dated 6 June 1940. This distinctive colour had first been used operationally on Blenheim bombers in November 1939, and it was adopted by Fighter Command in place of the 'black and white' scheme that had been in widespread use since the start of the war.

OPPOSITE When No 605 Sqn was posted south to No 11 Group to replace battle-weary No 111 Sqn, R4118 was flown from Drem to Croydon – with a refuelling stop at Abingdon – on Saturday, 7 September 1940 by future ace Pilot Officer C.F. 'Bunny' Currant. He was a real fan of the Hurricane, noting. 'I flew this fighter for just short of three years, from December 1938 until August 1941. The Hurricane was a magnificent warhorse, with its unsurpassed gun platform in the leading-edge of the wings, which had a deadly promise. It had no vices whatsoever, with superb reliability, and was so easy to fly in any weather conditions. Totally trustworthy in every respect. A confidence-giving aeroplane, loved by all who flew it.'

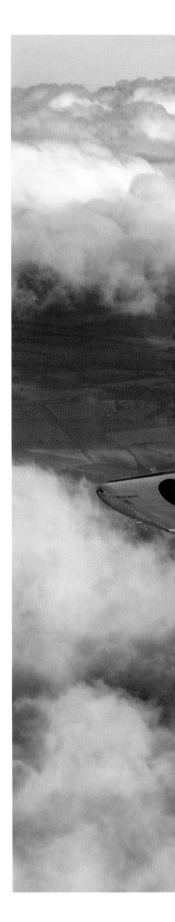

# CHAPTER EIGHT

# 'WARSAW-KOSCIUSZKO' HURRICANE

During the Battle of Britain only two units claimed more than 100 victories, and both were equipped with Hurricanes. No 501 'County of Gloucester' Sqn was credited with 101 victories in the 35 days it was engaged – the longest duration of any Fighter Command unit – although it lost 41 Hurricanes in the process (more than any other RAF fighter squadron). The leading unit in terms of aerial successes was No 303 'Warsaw-Kosciuszko' Sqn with 121 victories, which it achieved in just 17 days of action at a cost of 17 aeroplanes. In early 2015, in honour of the Polish pilots from this unit who participated in the Battle of Britain, the Historic Aircraft Collection (HAC) repainted its Hurricane XII as P3700 'RF-E', which was amongst the first 16 Hawker fighters issued to the unit in August 1940.

O f the 3,080 aircrew who fought in the Battle of Britain, about 20 per cent of them were not British – 537 pilots from 13 different nations saw combat with Fighter Command. Hundreds of men were from countries in Europe that had fallen under Nazi domination, while volunteers from across the British Empire also made their way to Britain to join the air war. The latter would duly fight alongside a number of Australian, Canadian, New Zealand and South African pilots already serving as short commission officers in Fighter Command when the war commenced.

No fewer than 147 Poles flew with the RAF in 1940, and they made the greatest contribution to Fighter Command of any foreign nation during the campaign. They deeply resented the fact that their air force had been wiped out within the first few days of the German invasion in September 1939. Noted military historian and novelist Len Deighton described them as 'homeless men, motivated often by a hatred bordering upon despair, who fought with a terrible and merciless dedication'. In the main, the Polish aviators were more highly trained than British pilots of the period, although they had no experience of high-performance monoplanes. They were, however, crack marksmen. Most Polish pilots spoke no English, so they were initially given British squadron and flight commanders to lead them alongside their own officers.

Finally declared operational on 30 August 1940 due to Fighter Command's growing shortage of pilots, their scoring rate proved to be phenomenal. Indeed, No 303 'Warsaw-Kosciuszko' Sqn achieved the highest victory tally – 121 – in

The original P3700 is given a wash between sorties at a sunny Northolt in late August 1940. The airman scrubbing its fuselage is fitter AC1 Ryszard Kwiatkowski, whose grandson Jacek Mainka (an Airbus A320 pilot) suggested to HAC that its Hurricane could be repainted in this scheme. (Robert Gretzyngier)

Three sergeant pilots from No 303 Sqn pose for the camera during a photo session staged at Leconfield, in East Riding, in November 1940, several weeks after the unit had been posted north to No 13 Group for a rest. They had all seen action, and made claims, flying P.XIs with the Polish Air Force prior to reaching Britain. On the left is Sergeant Eugeniusz Szaposznikow, who was credited with eight victories and one probable during the Battle of Britain to add to his previous successes in Poland and France – he survived the war. In the middle is Sergeant Stanislaw Karubin, who was credited with six victories after claiming one kill in Poland – he was killed in a flying accident on 12 August 1941. To the right is Sergeant Kazimierz Wünsche, who claimed four and two shared destroyed with the RAF after sharing an aerial victory in Poland – he too survived the war. (Robert Gretzyngier)

Fighter Command during the Battle of Britain. Overall, this unit, and Polish-manned No 302 Sqn, contributed 7.5 per cent of Fighter Command's entire total of enemy aircraft destroyed despite missing the first seven weeks of the campaign. The Poles had 'swung into the fight with a dash and enthusiasm which is beyond praise', wrote Air Chief Marshal Sir Hugh Dowding, the Commander-in-Chief of Fighter Command. 'They were inspired by a burning hatred of the Germans, which made them deadly opponents'.

Amongst the Hurricane Is supplied to No 303 Sqn was Brooklands-built P3700, which was transferred to the unit at Northolt from No 238 Sqn on 14 August 1940 when the latter was posted out of the frontline. It had lost nine pilots and

12 aircraft in just six days flying from the No 10 Group airfields at Warmwell, in Dorset, and Middle Wallop, in Hampshire. In the spring of 2015, to honour the sacrifice of the Polish pilots in the late summer and autumn of 1940, the Historic Aircraft Collection's Hurricane XII 5711 was repainted as P3700 'RF-E'.

During the final two weeks of August 1940, No 303 Sqn worked hard to attain operational status by flying myriad training sorties – P3700 was heavily involved in these flights. Formation flying, interception practice, gunnery training and, of course, English language lessons, filled the pilots' days. On 30 August No 303 Sqn was declared operational, and the following day the unit flew its first patrol at full strength – 13 Hurricanes,

The original P3700 was a Brooklands-built Hurricane that was transferred to No 303 Sqn at Northolt from No 238 Sqn on 14 August 1940 when the latter was posted out of the frontline. It was one of 16 Hawker fighters supplied to the newly formed unit at Northolt, where the Polish pilots initially struggled with them, as future Hurricane ace Pilot Officer Jan Zumbach recalled. 'The cockpit drill had us baffled at first. By comparison with every other type of plane we'd ever flown, everything here was back to front. In Poland and France when you wanted to open the throttle you pulled; here, you pushed. We had to reverse all our reflexes.'

The HAC Hurricane was repainted in the early spring of 2015, making its public debut at the RAF Northolt Open Day on 13 June that year. The extra doped fabric patches on the aircraft's wing leading edges confirm that the aeroplane is a Mk XII Hurricane that was originally fitted with twelve 0.303-in machine guns.

although P3700 was not involved in this historic mission. It would have to wait until the late afternoon of 2 September before engaging the enemy, future ace Pilot Officer Jan Zumbach being scrambled with the rest of the unit to engage a raid approaching Ashford, in Kent. Zumbach, a Swiss national with a Polish father, had been a pre-war fighter pilot in the Polish Air Force and then fought with the *Armée de l'Air* during the Battle of France – he was credited with the shared destruction of a Bf 109 during this campaign. Part of 'A' Flight on the 2nd, Zumbach failed to add to his tally when the unit tangled with Bf 109s from JG 3 and JG 77 near Dover.

Four days later, P3700 was one of nine aircraft from No 303 Sqn that were scrambled from Northolt at 0840 hrs with orders to patrol west Kent. Future ace Pilot Officer Miroslaw Ferić – also a former Polish Air Force pilot, who had claimed two victories flying PZL P.XIcs in September 1939 – was at the controls of 'RF-E'. Squadron Leader Ronald Kellett, joint CO of No 303 Sqn, led the unit aloft. He subsequently wrote in his Combat Report:

This was the biggest formation I have seen. It covered an area 20 miles by 5 miles. There were many big aeroplanes, Dorniers, He 111s and some four-engined. There were the usual Me 110s among them, and formations of Me 109s up to 25,000 ft – fully 300 to 400 aircraft.

Ferić was flying as Yellow 3, his section being led by the unit's joint CO, Squadron Leader Zdzislaw Krasnodebski, who described what happened next in the Squadron Diary:

We are flying towards the Channel. On our way we come across other squadrons. They are flying in the same zone. German bombers going to London show on the horizon. Our position is coming out of the sun, convenient to attack. I turn to see if there are any 109s behind. Looking up at the sun is difficult, but I can see no enemy machines, so full throttle and on to the Jerries. My whole attention had moved forward now, to go as quickly as possible

and aim as accurately as possible. The will of victory is so great that you forget everything that happens around you – you can only see the enemy.

Suddenly, the glass of the clocks shatters, the tank riddled with bullets – burning petrol pouring out. The whole cockpit is filled with fire. I want to bail out as quickly as possible, but cannot unfasten my harness. A short moment of surrender. But the will to live wins. Finally, I unfasten the belts, open the cockpit, the door and bail out. Remembering the sad experience from Poland, I do not open my parachute to leave the combat area as fast as possible and not to be a target. After a while I decide to open the parachute, but here is another problem – when abandoning the machine my parachute has shifted and I cannot find the ripcord, and the ground is coming fast. At last I find the ripcord and pull. Strong jolt – sudden peace and quiet, only the sounds of battle coming from above. After a moment I heard a machine approaching, and thought of history repeating itself [Krasnodebski had bailed out over Poland in September 1939 and then been shot at by a German pilot]. Fortunately, it was a Hurricane, which protected me down to the ground. I later learned that it was Witold Urbanowicz [Yellow 2], who at first took me for a German and intended to reverse the direction of my journey.

Coming to the ground, I thought that would be the end of my adventures, but it was not, as silhouettes of Homeguardians, with their guns ready to fire, started to emerge out of houses and bushes, looking to have some sport with a German paratrooper, but the calm Englishmen kept their nerves and did not fire.

Krasnodebski had been badly burned prior to getting out of his Hurricane, and he would remain off operations for two years while undergoing long and painful treatment in the Queen Victoria Hospital in East Grinstead.

No 303 Sqn's replacement 'RF-E', P3901 (from No 615 Sqn), is refuelled and rearmed at Northolt during late September 1940. Its high-scoring pilot, Squadron Leader Witold Urbanowicz, can be seen climbing back into the cockpit of the aeroplane. Between 26 and 30 September Urbanowicz would claim nine victories in P3901, which later served with No 253 Sqn. (Robert Gretzyngier)

The Polish Embassy in London co-financed the repainting of the HAC Hurricane XII in No 303 Sqn colours. 'The contribution made by 145 Polish fighter pilots to the Battle of Britain, who fought in 302 and 303 Polish Squadrons, as well as in British units is a source of immense pride for Poland and the Polish community in the UK', explained Polish ambassador Witold Sobków when the fighter was unveiled.

Like most No 303 Sqn Hurricanes from the Battle of Britain, P3700 was adorned with the distinctive unit badge that consisted of the US 'star and stripes' with a Polish peasant's hat and scythes superimposed over the top. Originally devised in 1920 by an American volunteer unit that had participated in the Polish-Bolshevik war of that year, the badge was far more prevalent on No 303 Sqn Hurricanes in 1940 than was the Polish Air Force insignia.

Flying Officer Urbanowicz and Pilot Officer Ferić enjoyed better luck than their leader, however, both men claiming Bf 109s destroyed. The latter's brief Combat Report detailed how he despatched his quarry in P3700:

> Flying to the south of Farnborough I noticed 20–30 enemy bombers to the right of my course at a height of about 20,000 ft, and about 60 enemy fighters about 3,000 ft above the bombers. Yellow Leader changed his course and prepared to attack. In the meantime, enemy aircraft dived and attacked us. I found myself engaged in a dogfight in which Spitfires were also taking part. Suddenly a Me 109 painted white from his nose to the end of the cockpit zoomed up. I caught him head-on and fired three short bursts at 200–250 yards. He burst into flames and fell to the ground.

No 303 Sqn was hit hard during this action, having three Hurricanes shot down and two seriously damaged and three pilots badly burned. According to the Form 'F' Fighter Command Combat Report compiled by No 303 Sqn IO, Flying Officer E.M. Hedwin, these losses were caused by a 'lack of height forcing the pilots to attack whilst still climbing, and at only 140 mph. This contributed very largely to our heavy casualties'. The unit's acting CO, Flight Lieutenant Johnny Kent, noted in his post-war memoirs:

> By the evening the squadron was reduced to three serviceable aeroplanes, and – this was just when No 12 Group was trying to force its 'Big Wing' philosophy onto No 11 Group – the Northolt 'Wing' was scrambled with myself leading all three squadrons with a grand total of nine aeroplanes, all that were left on the airfield.

Pilot Officer Ferić, who was also the diarist for No 303 Sqn, summarized the unit's combat on 6 September as follows:

> The raid was enormous, and we were few, as apart from us I saw a squadron of Spitfires, so in this whole upheaval we had to avoid the enemy, numbering some 100 aeroplanes, and think more of our own safety than fighting according to rules. I am certain that the Englishmen are too moderate in sending more squadrons to completely annihilate the enemy, and even more to create chaos in his lines.

I noticed new tactics by the Jerries – from the Channel into England, along the path of the bombers, the fighters form a sort of path, or rather bridge, or lucky chain, up to the spot of bombing, and under this cover of circling squadrons, bombers fly in peace and quiet, and it is really difficult to get at them.

Having survived the fierce fighting of 6 September, P3700 would fall in combat with Bf 109s three days later. At 1800 hrs, Flight Lieutenant Kent led 12 Hurricanes against a large formation of 40 Ju 88s and He 111s, escorted by Bf 109 and Bf 110s, over Beachy Head. The aeroplanes had already attacked targets in London, and were escaping south towards the Channel at great speed as they lost height. When they were initially spotted, the German aircraft were 1,000 ft above the Hurricanes, and they were engaged by the leading fighters in the formation at about 13,500 ft. Only Kent, Flying Officer Zumbach and Sergeant Josef Frantisek succeeded in firing at the enemy aircraft, claiming four victories between them. Kent later recalled:

They were in a shallow dive and moving fast, so I picked on a Ju 88 and gave chase. It took a little time to accelerate, so I pulled the boost override plug and opened the throttle wide. Very slowly I began to gain on the German, but, at the same time, I could see one of the 109 escort fighters diving down after me. I kept on in the hope of catching the Junkers before the 109 caught me, but it looked very much like I was going to lose the race. I was on the point of

P3700 was flown by both of these pilots during its brief service with No 303 Sqn, Pilot Officer Jan Zumbach (left) and Pilot Officer Miroslaw Ferić (right). Both men were aces by the time this photograph was taken at Leconfield in November 1940. (Robert Gretzyngier)

breaking away as the 109 was getting uncomfortably close when a Hurricane flashed across in front of the 109 and forced its pilot to pull up.

While Flight Lieutenant Kent was pursuing his Ju 88, Sergeant Frantisek (who would claim no fewer than 17 victories with No 303 Sqn prior to his death on 8 October 1940) possibly witnessed the demise of P3700, as he noted in his Combat Report:

When we arrived in sight of the Germans, swarms of Me 109s dived from a great height to attack us. I saw one Me 109 going in to attack a Hurricane in front of me. I attacked it, starboard beam, firing at 150–100 yards at the engine, which began to burn. The pilot tried to escape by climbing, and I saw him open the cockpit preparatory to jumping. I shot at the cockpit and the pilot collapsed. The enemy aircraft fell in flames to the ground (Horsham area). I then saw a Hurricane in flames [probably P3700, as it was No 303 Sqn's sole loss that day] and the pilot jumped. A Spitfire came down to circle around the pilot.

I went for a He 111, and two Me 109s attacked me. I hid in a cloud at about 17,000 ft for seven minutes – I played hide and seek with them in the cloud. During a right turn I came out of the cloud, and saw in front of me, ten yards away, also coming out of the cloud, a He 111. I very nearly collided with it, and fired at the front of the fuselage at an angle of 45 degrees from above and behind. The front of the enemy aircraft fell to pieces, with cockpit and both engines in flames. I do not know if this enemy aircraft fell on the ground or in the sea, owing to the clouds.

As I broke away one Me 109 attacked me from above and another from below. I hid again in the clouds and flew towards France to keep under cover. Over the Channel, I climbed out of cloud and was hit by four Me shells – one in the port wing, one through the left tank, which did not catch fire, and one through the radiator. It is only owing to the armour plating behind me that the fourth shell did not kill me. Two Spitfires came to my rescue and shot down the Me 109, which was apparently the one which had hit me. I saw the damage which had been done, and was obliged to find a landing place as the engine temperature was mounting dangerously.

G5/41H/130643
GX

In September 2016 'P3700' was flown from England to Konstancin-Obory airfield in Poland to participate in the filming of *Dywizjon 303* (Squadron 303). The script for this motion picture is based on the book of the same name written by Polish explorer and writer Arkady Fiedler shortly after the Battle of Britain and published in 1942. During the war it was secretly published in four editions in occupied Poland and translated into French, Portuguese and Dutch. The film is being co-produced by Polish and British companies, with some roles being played by British actors.

On a little hill north-east of Brighton, I found a field of cabbages and made an excellent landing. The police came immediately – not only did they not make any difficulty, they were very kind to me. They anchored the Hurricane, shut off the petrol and oxygen and left the aeroplane guarded by a policeman. They took me by car to Brighton, and I returned to Northolt by train. Sgt Wünsche's parachute was at the police station. I brought mine back. At the railway station the people were very kind to me, girls gave me chocolate and people photographed me. I am very grateful for the kindness which was shown to me by everybody.

The 'Sgt Wünsche' mentioned in Frantisek's account was Sergeant Kazimierz Wünsche, pilot of P3700, who was forced to bail out of his fighter with burns to his back and both arms after the aeroplane was bounced and set on fire over Beachy Head – he had probably fallen victim to a Bf 109 from either II. or III./JG 53, which were escorting the bombers attacked by No 303 Sqn. He landed near Devil's Dyke, north of Brighton, and was admitted to Hove Hospital. Like many of his compatriots, Wünsche had seen combat in P.XIcs during the German invasion of Poland, and he later served with the *Armée de l'Air* prior to making his way to England and joining the RAF. He had claimed three Bf 109s destroyed (to add to the Hs 126 he had downed in Poland) by the time he was shot down, and he was credited with three more victories with No 303 Sqn in 1941–42.

Having lasted less than four weeks at Northolt, P3700 was one of 16 Hurricanes destroyed whilst serving with No 303 Sqn during the Battle of Britain.

Arguably the best known photograph of No 303 Sqn pilots in 1940, this shot of ten airmen walking towards the camera was taken at Leconfield in November 1940. They are, from left to right, Pilot Officer M. Ferić, Flight Lieutenant J.A. Kent, Flying Officer B. Grzeszczak, Sergeant J. Radomski, Pilot Officer J.E.L. Zumbach, Pilot Officer W. Łokuciewski, unknown, Flying Officer Z.K. Henneberg, Pilot Officer J.K.M. Daszewski and Sergeant E. Szaposznikow. All bar two of these pilots (Grzeszczak and Daszewski) achieved ace status. (Robert Gretzyngier)

HAC's Hurricane XII 5711 has worn several guises since it was returned to airworthiness in 1989, when its original owners, The Fighter Collection (TFC), marked it up as Hurricane IIA Z3781 of No 71 'Eagle' Sqn. This scheme was primarily chosen because no photography of the original aircraft in Canadian use has ever come to light, despite the fighter having spent time with Nos 123 (F), 127 (F) and 129 (F) Sqns between 1942 and 1944.

# 'EAGLE SQUADRON'

The Historic Aircraft Collection's Hurricane XII 5711 has worn several guises since it was returned to airworthiness in 1989, its original owners, The Fighter Collection, marking it up as Hurricane IIA Z3781 of No 71 'Eagle' Sqn. The latter unit was the first of three such squadrons within Fighter Command manned by American citizens prior to their country being dragged into World War 2. These early volunteers had travelled to the UK despite the US government having issued a presidential proclamation in September 1939 specifically banning the recruiting of men for the armed forces of foreign countries from within the USA and its territories. The early arrivals joined four pre-war Americans already serving with Fighter Command, being sent to frontline units defending Britain from attack by the Luftwaffe in the summer of 1940.

The RAF's triumph in the Battle of Britain acted as a spur for many more idealistic young Americans to volunteer for combat. They were helped in their quest by anglophile Charles Sweeny, a wealthy businessman who had lived in London for a number of years. He had initially recruited men to fly in the *Armée de l'Air*, but with the fall of France in June 1940 his volunteers became part of the RAF instead. Sweeny's would-be fighter pilots had originally joined the RCAF, before heading to the UK. His contact in Canada was World War 1 ace Billy Bishop, while in America Sweeny worked with artist Clayton Knight to form the Clayton Knight Committee. By the time the United States entered the war in December 1941, the committee had processed and approved 6,700 applications from Americans to join the RCAF or RAF. Sweeny, along with his various wealthy contacts on both sides of the Atlantic, bore the cost (more than $100,000) of processing and bringing the US recruits to the UK for training.

ABOVE Having coped with poor weather, poor aircraft and a near incessant stream of visiting VIPs and members of the press since the formation of No 71 'Eagle' Sqn in October 1940, the unit's American volunteer pilots were itching for action by the time this group shot was taken at Kirton-in-Lindsey by an Air Ministry photographer on 17 March 1941. All the pilots are wearing 1930 pattern Sidcot flying suits, bar Squadron Leader Bill Taylor and Pilot Officer 'Red' Tobin. Five of these men would not survive the war; two were killed in action and three died on active service. (John Dibbs)

Initially, the volunteers were sent to regular units within RAF Fighter Command as attrition replacements. However, in the autumn of 1940, the RAF created the first of three 'Eagle' squadrons that would be manned exclusively by 'Sweeney recruits'. Although at first frustrated by a lack of equipment, No 71 Sqn (followed by Nos 121 and 133 Sqns) would eventually find itself in the thick of the action once the RAF went on the offensive over occupied Europe from early 1941.

The unit received its first war-weary Hurricane Is at Church Fenton in November 1940, although it was subsequently issued with brand new Mk IIAs following its move to Kirton-in-Lindsey, in north Lincolnshire, later that same month. Amongst the Hurricane IIAs was Z3781, which was built by Hawker in the spring of 1941. At about this time, the aeroplane's most successful future pilot was checking in to No 71 Sqn following its recent move to Martlesham Heath after at last being declared operational. Formerly a soldier in the US Army, Pilot Officer Bill Dunn from Minneapolis, Minnesota, had joined the RAF via the Canadian Army after his attempts to reach the UK via the RCAF were thwarted. He saw action with the Seaforth Highlanders of Canada during the Battle of France and was credited with downing two Ju 87s using a Lewis machine gun on 16 August 1940 when Borden military camp, in Hampshire, was attacked.

With the formation of the 'Eagle Squadron', Dunn volunteered for the RAF as a pilot and was sent to No 5 Service Flying Training School (SFTS) in February 1941. He was posted directly to No 71 Sqn in mid-April, having not attended an OTU and having never even sat in a Hurricane. Although this had occasionally happened during the height of the Battle of Britain, it was rare for a new pilot to miss the OTU altogether. Dunn wrote about this in his autobiography, *Fighter Pilot – The First American Ace of World War II*:

I had entered No 57 Course [at No 5 SFTS] a couple of weeks after it had begun, and here I was leaving the course several weeks before it was to graduate, with only 56 hours of Miles Master flying time. I asked, 'What about my OTU training and getting checked out in a Hurricane fighter?' Flt Lt Lord [Dunn's flight commander] said that my fighter squadron people would get me checked out, that there was no OTU vacancy for me at that time, and that I had been rated by the SFTS as an 'above average' pilot. The last bit was good to know, but I certainly wasn't overly enthusiastic at being sent directly to an operational unit with so little flying time and no OTU training at all. I could only assume that somebody at the Air Ministry knew what the hell was going on (which, of course, was a gross error on my part).

Once at Martlesham Heath, Dunn was told by his CO, Squadron Leader Bill Taylor, that No 71 Sqn was too busy on operations to train him, and he had managed to get him a place in the Hurricane OTU at Debden. Here, Dunn was fortunate enough to be briefly trained by one of the RAF's leading Hurricane aces, Flight Lieutenant Frank Carey – his tally at that time stood at 18 and three shared victories, four unconfirmed destroyed, four probables and five damaged, all flying Hurricanes.

Following a crash course on the fighter that lasted four days and saw the American log 4 hr 40 min of flying time in the Hawker fighter, he was suddenly posted back to No 71 Sqn. Dunn recalled:

Why I wasn't permitted to complete the six-week course, no one at the OTU knew. I'd only had an hour of simulated dogfighting in the Hurricane. So, all in all, my total RAF flying time when I went operational was about 64 hours. Frank Carey came to see me as I was checking out of the Officers' Mess. 'I'm sorry Bill,' he said. 'We both know you need a hell of a lot more Hurricane time before you'll be ready for combat. That's a crazy outfit you're being assigned to. They all lack proper training. One word about gunnery before you go. Don't waste ammo on long range firing. If an enemy kite fills your whole windscreen, the range is right and the deflection is nil. Give him a good squirt and you've got him. Take care Bill, and don't get your arse shot off by some bloody Hun bastard. Keep your eyes open and your head on a swivel. Good luck to you, Yank.'

FAR LEFT The first three 'Eagles' pose for the camera at Church Fenton in early October 1940. Pilot Officers 'Red' Tobin, 'Shorty' Keough and 'Andy' Mamedoff had all been pulled out of Spitfire-equipped No 609 Sqn the previous month, having fought with the unit during the Battle of Britain. Mamedoff is holding a newly created 'Eagle' squadron patch in place on Keough's sleeve, the badges having only just arrived at the station. (John Dibbs)

BELOW LEFT Pilot Officers 'Red' Tobin, 'Shorty' Keough and 'Andy' Mamedoff pose with a Hurricane during the photoshoot at Church Fenton in October 1940. The exact identity of the fighter remains a mystery, as does the unit it was assigned to. The Polish Air Force marking on the nose offers a clue, but neither Nos 302 or 303 Sqns were based at Church Fenton – the latter unit was not too far away at Leconfield, however. (John Dibbs)

'Z3781' departs Duxford at the
start of a display during the spring
of 1994. The aeroplane has called
the Cambridgeshire airfield home
since its delivery to TFC's HQ from
Coningsby in January 1988. The
fighter has remained here ever
since, moving from the TFC's
Hangar 2 to Hangar 4 in August
2002 after it was acquired by HAC.

When the Air Ministry photographer visited No 71 Sqn at Kirton-in-Lindsey in March 1941, he covered all aspects of the unit's daily routine. Recreating a typical scramble for the camera, a quartet of 'Eagles' dash along the worn perimeter track to their awaiting Hurricanes. Leading the sprint is Pilot Officer 'Red' Tobin, who seems to be finding the pantomime rather amusing – perhaps that is because he is the only one not wearing a bulky 'Sidcot' suit. The three men chasing Tobin are, from left to right, Pilot Officers Peter Provenzano (killed on active service flying a P-47 Thunderbolt in Alaska in 1942), Sam Mauriello (killed in a civil aircraft accident in 1950) and Luke Allen. (John Dibbs)

Dunn duly learned his craft and built up his hours on Hurricanes under the tutelage of his flight commander, Flight Lieutenant George Brown – a pre-war pilot who had experience over France in Spitfires with No 66 Sqn and then seen action in the Battle of Britain with Hurricane-equipped No 253 Sqn until he was shot down. Dunn credited Brown with his survival in combat, stating in his autobiography, 'Too bad every new boy in a fighter squadron didn't get a George Brown for his flight commander'. By mid-June Dunn had been made a section leader, although he had seen very little combat up to that point as No 71 Sqn had spent most of its time performing mundane convoy patrols along the east coast of England. This would all change for him on 2 July 1941, whilst at the controls of Z3781:

My first big day came when our squadron formed part of the fighter escort for 12 Blenheim bombers on Circus 29 (the code name for a daylight bomber raid) to bomb the Lille electric power station in occupied France. Just before reaching Lille we were attacked by two enemy squadrons of Me 109Es and 109Fs. Their attacks continued during the bombers' run to the target and for about 30 minutes after, until the French coast was crossed near Gravelines. Since we were flying Hurricanes, we formed the close escort for the Blenheims. High cover escort was provided by the faster Spitfires of our fighter wing.

I was flying the Red 2 position, with Sqn Ldr Paddy Woodhouse leading, when I saw an Me 109E diving through the bomber formation at about 6,000 ft, squirting at the Blenheims as he dove. The 109 pilot made his break to port, right in front of me, maybe 75 or 100 yards away. I jammed the throttle wide open and, attacking the Me 109 from the port quarter, fired one burst of four seconds and three bursts of two seconds each. At about 50 yards range (the Hun kite filled my whole windscreen) I could see my machine gun bullets striking all over

One of the Hurricane Is sent aloft for the Air Ministry photoshoot was V7608, seen here in the process of being started. The fighter's underside is painted in the short-lived Black and Sky scheme, which was introduced by Fighter Command on 27 November 1940. Harking back to the black and white scheme of the first months of the war, the revised finish was adopted after pilots stated that they found split underside colours the best way to locate the position of friendly fighters above them. (John Dibbs)

the German's fuselage and wingroot. Then he began to smoke. I continued my attack down to 3,500 ft, again firing at point-blank range. Now the 109 began burning furiously and dived straight down to the ground, where it crashed with a hell of an explosion near a crossroad. Scrub one Squarehead!

Both Dunn and squadron mate Pilot Officer Gus Daymond were credited with victories following this mission, these being the first aerial successes claimed by No 71 Sqn. Four days later Dunn claimed a Bf 109F as a shared probable whilst at the controls of Z3267, and he was back in Z3781 on

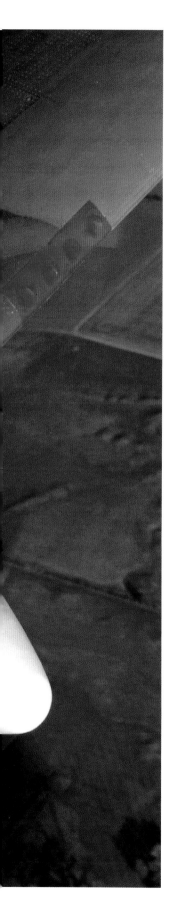

OPPOSITE Stu Goldspink has pushed the canopy hood back so that he can get a better look at the photographer during an air-to-air sortie from Duxford in the early 1990s. 'The hood could be moved back and forth with one hand and the aircraft flown with it in the open position', noted Battle of Britain veteran Tom Neil. Indeed, the canopy can be locked in the open position but not locked shut. All Hurricanes have a small gap between the windscreen and the edge of the canopy that creates considerable wind noise in flight. Rain also manages to enter through this gap, leaving the pilot rather damp.

BELOW The contours of fabric and metal that comprise a Hurricane are accentuated in this view of 'Z3781' in the evening light at Duxford. The tautness of the doped Irish linen over the stringers and formers built around the steel and duralumin girder fuselage gives the Hawker fighter a solid look that belies its predominantly wooden secondary structure.

the morning of 21 July when he achieved his second victory – and last in this aeroplane:

On Circus 54 we were again given the role of close escort, this time for Stirling bombers attacking the Lille steel factories – I was leading White Section. Enemy 88 mm flak guns had been banging away at us continuously ever since we'd crossed the French coast, some of the ugly black bursts coming close enough for us to hear the crack of the exploding shells. Most of the shells, however, burst behind and slightly below our Circus formation, causing little or no damage. Over the target area flak increased in accuracy and intensity, which was an indication that enemy fighters were not yet in position to attack us. Late scramble no doubt.

Shortly after the Stirlings had dropped their bombs and we were leaving the Lille target area in a shambles of bomb bursts, shock waves, billowing dust, smoke and debris, I spotted two Me 109Fs climbing up fast behind our formation to attack the bombers from below. The time was about 0835 hrs and we were flying at 16,000 ft. I pulled my Hurricane around in a steep turn, with White 2, Tommy McGerty, flying just off my starboard wing. One Squarehead saw us coming in to attack, took violent evasive action, and breaking away went into a fast, steep dive. We couldn't hope to catch him with our slower Hurricanes. We fared well enough against the Me 109Es, but the newer 109Fs were just too fast for us. Spitfires would have gotten him.

The second Kraut took no evasive action other than a shallow climbing turn. I attacked him from the port beam at 50 or 60 yards, firing two bursts from my eight machine guns into him. The 109's rudder and port elevator were completely shot off, and its starboard elevator was ripped to shreds by my blast of bullets. At first the Hun went into a gentle dive, which soon steepened until the 109 was falling fast on its back. The pilot jettisoned his hood, bailing out at a very high speed, his chute undoubtedly giving him a hell of a jerk when it popped open. At least the SOB got out of his busted kite. I didn't actually see the Me 109 go in, but there could be no doubt about that, pilotless, it did hit the deck some 14,000 ft below – another confirmed kill. My gun-camera filmed the whole episode.

LEFT The forward section of the fuselage, by contrast, is covered in the main by detachable duralumin panels that are secured via quick-release fasteners. Plywood panels surround the cockpit, however.

BELOW TFC had a Merlin 29 installed when it was restored, the zero-timed engine having been acquired with the airframe. It was checked over in California by Merlin specialist Jack Hovey prior to the engine being shipped to England and fitted to the fighter in mid-1988. The unpainted, detachable, tubular steel engine mountings are clearly visible, as are the early-style Rolls-Royce exhaust stubs.

Bill Dunn would claim another Bf 109E destroyed on 9 August, flying Z3267, after which he and No 71 Sqn transitioned to the Spitfire IIA. He would subsequently become one of the first 'Eagle Squadron' aces – possibly *the* first, although there is some contention over this – and later enjoy more aerial success flying P-47 Thunderbolts with the USAAF's Ninth Air Force over France in 1944.

Hurricane II Z3781 was transferred to No 133 'Eagle' Sqn at Coltishall upon its formation in August 1941, and the aeroplane was lost on 8 October that same year. Its pilot, Battle of Britain

veteran Pilot Officer Andrew Mamedoff, was killed, having become lost in thick cloud whilst flying from Fowlmere, in Cambridgeshire, to the unit's new home at Eglinton, in Northern Ireland. Having refuelled at Sealand en route, 15 Hurricanes from No 133 Sqn then headed for Andreas, on the Isle of Man, prior to pressing on to Eglinton. Four failed to arrive, one of which was Z3781. The wreckage of the fighter, and its pilot, were found shortly thereafter on Ballaskeig Moor, near Ramsey, just south of Andreas.

FAR RIGHT The boxing eagle motif adopted by No 71 Sqn was one of the most famous emblems of World War 2, subsequently adorning a number of the Spitfires flown by the unit. It also became the emblem of the USAAF's 4th Fighter Group, which formed in September 1942 when the three 'Eagle' squadrons were transferred to the Eighth Air Force.

RIGHT Former North Dakota cowboy Pilot Officer Bill Dunn poses with his Hurricane II Z3781 at Martlesham Heath shortly after claiming his second Bf 109 in it on 21 July 1941. The remaining two victory markings were for a pair of Ju 87s that he claimed to have shot down with a Lewis gun whilst serving with the Seaforth Highlanders of Canada. He would duly become one of the first 'Eagle Squadron' aces. (Tony Holmes)

BOTTOM RIGHT The Sky fighter band and propeller spinner were also introduced at the same time as the all-black port wing seen on V7608 earlier in this chapter, and such was the immediacy with which all squadrons had to comply with this Air Ministry order that serials on fighters across the country were either partially or completely obliterated. Hurricane I 'XR-Z' (with its codes applied in non-standard Sky, rather than regulation Medium Sea Grey) has had its serial totally covered, although squadron records indicate that this aircraft was actually V7816. (John Dibbs)

Nick Grey holds station with the Harvard camership as the latter goes into a gentle banking turn high over a cloudy Cambridgeshire. When flying at medium altitudes at a cruising speed in the region of 200 mph, the Merlin engine is set at 1900 rpm with zero boost, the associated fuel consumption in Auto or weak mixture being about 40 gallons per hour. However, for formation work like this, the pilot will have to reduce the speed to about 150 mph and crank up the revs to 2600 rpm. He may also switch the fuel mixture to rich, depending on the type of Merlin installed in the fighter, although engine boost is likely to remain at zero in order to conserve fuel. A small amount of flap may also be selected to allow the pilot to get in close to the camership without compromising his levels of control over the aircraft.

# CHAPTER TEN

# MALTA DEFENDER

The Historic Aircraft Collection's Hurricane XII 5711 became No 126 Sqn's Z5140 'HA-C' upon the completion of an 18-month-long overhaul at Duxford in the spring of 2004. As detailed in Chapter Sixteen: Hurricane Survivors, the fighter was the first Hurricane to return to Malta since World War 2 when in September 2005 it flew there along with the Historic Aircraft Collection's Spitfire VB BM597 as part of the 'Merlins Over Malta' project.

The original Z5140, built by Gloster in the early spring of 1941, was one of 43 brand new Hurricane IIs that were sent from England to Gibraltar aboard the carrier HMS *Argus*. Assigned to No 46 Sqn, the aeroplane was then loaded on board HMS *Ark Royal* for delivery to Malta on 6 June 1941 as part of Operation *Rocket*. Coming increasingly under attack by Axis forces as the Allies suffered a series of reversals in both the Eastern Mediterranean and North Africa, Malta's importance as a 'strategic redoubt' was now becoming glaringly obvious to both sides. Its previously poor aerial defences clearly needed improving if the islands were not to fall to the Axis powers, as Crete had just done, and although the Spitfire was the obvious fighter to protect 'Fortress Malta', none could be spared in 1941. This vital mission would instead be performed for almost two years by fewer than 200 Hurricanes flown by seven units manned in the main by Battle of Britain veterans and pilots from the Commonwealth. Amongst the No 46 Sqn pilots flying Hurricanes to Malta from *Ark Royal* was Flying Officer John Carpenter, who had previously seen combat in Norway in Gladiators of No 263 Sqn and then claimed three victories flying Spitfires with No 222 Sqn during the Battle of Britain:

HAC acquired Hurricane XII 5711 from TFC in August 2002 in exchange for Hawker Nimrod I S1581. After almost two years of ownership, it decided to change the markings on Hurricane XII 5711, which became No 126 Sqn's Z5140 'HA-C' upon the completion of an 18-month-long overhaul at Duxford in the spring of 2004.

Hurricane XII 5711 was not completely resprayed following its overhaul in 2003–04, but instead its scheme was suitably modified to allow it to become 'Z5140' through the application of new fuselage codes and an appropriate serial number. Although some Hurricanes had reached Malta camouflaged in the RAF's desert scheme of Dark Earth and Middle Stone, with Azure undersides, these were aircraft that had originally been intended for Egypt. Many more had looked just like 'Z5140' in north-west European temperate camouflage, as Malta squadrons were desperate to receive aircraft regardless of colour.

No 46 Sqn took off from the carrier some 200 miles south of Sicily and flew at 500 ft all the way to Malta. It was not comfortable – we had 500-gallon drop tanks, and all our kit was stuffed in empty spaces. We could only fly straight and level, anxious not to be seen or intercepted by enemy aircraft in this position. Thank goodness for the Merlin engine – not a cough or splutter, it ran like a sewing machine. Next day the air raids started, mainly by the Italian air force, so we had a breathing space.

The aircraft flown in from *Ark Royal* would be assigned to No 46 Sqn until the unit became No 126 Sqn on 28 June, the fighters swapping their 'PO' for 'HA' codes at this time. The CO of No 46 Sqn, Battle of Britain ace Squadron Leader Sandy 'Ragbags' Rabagliati, and his pilots remained on Malta with the 'new' unit. He had quickly added to his seven victories from 1940, claiming three and one shared kills in the weeks prior to the redesignation of his squadron. Fortunately for the handful of Hurricane squadrons on Malta during this period, their principal opposition in the skies over the besieged islands was the *Regia Aeronautica*, rather than the Luftwaffe – the latter was busy elsewhere supporting the *Afrika Korps*' advance in North Africa or the new offensive on the Eastern Front. The Hurricane IIs proved to be more than a match for the Savoia-Marchetti S.79 bombers and their Macchi C.200 and Fiat CR.42 fighter escorts that were mounting ever larger raids on Malta.

One of the units flying alongside No 126 Sqn at Ta Kali airfield at this time was No 249 Sqn, which had enjoyed great success over southern England a

LEFT No 261 Sqn's 'C' Flight became No 185 Sqn at Hal Far, on Malta, in mid-May 1941 when more aircraft and pilots began to reach the islands, allowing the battle-weary No 261 Sqn to disband – it reformed at Habbaniyah, in Iraq, two months later. Hurricane IIB Z2961 was among the aeroplanes flown by No 185 Sqn, having previously served with the Malta Night Fighter Unit and then No 249 Sqn. Flown by several aces during 1941–42, Z2961 was assigned to No 605 Sqn in early 1942, before returning to No 185 Sqn. (Andy Thomas)

year earlier. Included in its ranks was ace Flying Officer Tom Neil, who had flown in to Malta with the rest of the unit from *Ark Royal* on 21 May 1941. Like No 126 Sqn, his unit also had some Hurricane IIs, but primarily tropicalized Mk Is. Conditions in-theatre were harsh at the best of times, and the Hurricane IIs, lacking any kind of dust filters to prevent grit from getting into the moving parts of the aircrafts' Merlin XX engines, suffered terrible

ABOVE The original Z5140, built by Gloster in the early spring of 1941, was one of 43 brand new Hurricane IIs sent from England to Gibraltar aboard the carrier HMS *Argus*. Assigned to No 46 Sqn, the aeroplane was then loaded on board HMS *Ark Royal* for delivery to Malta on 6 June 1941 as part of Operation *Rocket*.

reliability problems as a result. Neil alluded to this in his autobiography *Onward to Malta*:

After three weeks on Malta, the best we could muster on average was about ten aircraft – eight Mk Is and a couple of Mk IIs. Most of the Mk Is were tropicalised but the Mk IIs were not, their open air-intakes, situated under the engine and between the undercarriage legs, ideally placed to suck in every particle of dust and filth whipped up by our whirling airscrews during take-off and landing, and even taxiing. Mr Sydney Camm, in his moments of inspiration when designing the Hurricane, clearly did not have deserts in mind – nor Malta!

Leading No 126 Sqn by example, 'Ragbags' Rabagliati made a series of claims prior to being promoted to Wing Commander Ta Kali in October 1941. However, his first challenge as CO of the 'new' unit was to raise the morale of his men, as Tom Neil explained:

When the pilots of No 46 Sqn learned that they were to forfeit their squadron number and be known henceforth as No 126 Sqn they were stunned – absolutely – as were the rest of us. *What* a thing to do! Here they were, one of the oldest squadrons in the Air Force and among the most famous, being instructed at a moment's notice to lose their identity. There was near mutiny. Even I was horrified; to me 'Rags' Rabagliati, Pete LeFevre, and all the rest, colleagues throughout the Battle of Britain and after, *were* 46, as were their illustrious forebears.

Unperturbed, Rabagliati subsequently waged an almost one-man war against the *Regia Aeronautica*'s flying boat force during the mid-summer of 1941, targeting them initially in their base at Syracuse, on the island of Sicily, on 9 July. Four Hurricane pilots claimed six CANT flying boats destroyed and four damaged on the water. On 10 August Rabagliati was out on an evening air test when he spotted another Italian flying boat, but this time it was in the air:

Since acquiring 5711, HAC has gone to great lengths to reintroduce authentic equipment to the airframe. The cockpit of the fighter certainly shows this, with the various dials and gauges installed when the aeroplane was originally restored having been replaced with period examples laid out more in keeping with a Hurricane II from World War 2. The aircraft also has an original Barr & Stroud GM 2 reflector gunsight fitted onto the cockpit coaming. (Harry Measures)

When at 5,000 ft I sighted a single enemy machine (seaplane) flying just over the water, two miles off shore. I closed and recognised it as a CANT Z.506. From astern, two very short bursts were delivered and the aircraft landed with its port wing on fire. Four men got out and the port wing subsequently fell off and the enemy aircraft sank.

BELOW Although better known for his Spitfire, Buchón and Blenheim flying, high-time warbird pilot John Romain also has a number of hours in his logbook on the Hurricane, principally HAC's 5711.

Rabagliati led a second strafing attack on Syracuse on the 17th that netted him another Z.506B on the water, and on the 20th he and three other pilots from No 126 Sqn strafed the harbour at Augusta, again on the Sicilian coast:

Attacked diving from 9,000 ft from the east. Four aircraft detailed to attack [barrage] balloons. Two cannon-armed aircraft detailed to attack petrol storage tanks on mole. I gave two two-second bursts on one storage tank and observed explosive shells hitting it and bursting, but apparently with no effect. Dived between balloon cables and attacked a CANT Z.506 on water, but with no result. Three

Framed by the clouds, and with the fertile fields of Cambridgeshire below, 5711 keeps in close formation with the cameraship. All Canadian-built Hurricanes had metal wings, with the 'A' wings being fitted with eight 0.303-in machine guns as per all British-built Mk Is and some Mk IIs. 'B' wings, like 5711's, boasted twelve 0.303-in weapons, of which eight were sited conventionally in a grouped layout just wide of the propeller arc, and a further two per wing were installed outboard of the landing lights to avoid the structural stresses associated with two banks of six guns.

LEFT This was one of two No 249 Sqn Hurricane IIs destroyed in a strafing attack on Ta Kali airfield by Bf 109Es from 7./JG 26 during the afternoon of 25 May 1941. Three more fighters were damaged in the surprise raid, which came just four days after the squadron had flown in to Malta from HMS *Ark Royal*. (Phil Jarrett)

Hurricane XII 5711 has been parked into wind, facing the unmistakable Duxford skyline on the south side of the airfield. The aeroplane has been a familiar sight at the former RAF fighter station for almost 30 years.

cannons failed during this attack. Sgt Mayall shot down one balloon in flames and attacked a seaplane. Strikes observed but no other effect. Three balloons were observed on fire. AA fairly intense but poor direction. AA opened up at Syracuse in barrage over harbour when aircraft were ten miles away.

Rabagliati switched to C.200s for his final two victories with No 126 Sqn, targeting Italian fighters that were flying sweeps off the Maltese coast. His Combat Report for the engagement with Macchis from 7° *Gruppo CT* during the late afternoon of 26 August read as follows:

About 10–15 miles south of Sampieri, after the controller had informed us that the enemy aircraft were three miles south of us, the whole formation orbited to port and I sighted six Macchis about 5,000 ft below, and a further formation of three Macchis at the same height. We were at 23,000 ft and dived to attack. I badly overshot in my first attack and climbed steeply. Saw one enemy aircraft diving towards Sicily, and I chased him along the beach, giving it a short burst whenever possible. Eventually, after the third two-second burst, his starboard wing caught fire and he crashed in flames. Controlling and information were excellent.

At 1130 hrs on 4 September, 12 Hurricanes from No 126 Sqn and nine from No 185 Sqn clashed with 19 C.200s from *10° Gruppo CT* that had sortied from Comiso, in southern Sicily, in search

One of the final two victories credited to the Hurricane whilst flying from Malta – on 8 May 1942 – was claimed by seven-kill Australian ace Flight Sergeant Gordon Tweedale in a No 126 Sqn aeroplane. The following day, in his first sortie in one of 62 newly-arrived Spitfires, the 24-year-old former stockman from Queensland was shot down and killed. (Andy Thomas)

of an Allied ship that Italian Ju 87 crews had claimed to have sunk the previous night. The RAF fighters had been scrambled when the Macchis were detected by Malta-based radar, Rabagliati leading the interception:

When at 25,000 ft, sighted six enemy aircraft 10–15 miles south of us [in the Grand Harbour area]. Dived to 22,500 ft, which was their level, and engaged from behind. One pulled up and appeared to have been hit. I pulled up after him and gave a short burst. Strikes were observed and he half-rolled and disappeared with black smoke coming out and streaks of white. I did a steep turn to the left and almost immediately observed three parachutes in the sky, although at the time it was not obvious whether they were enemy. One Macchi dived in, out of control. Sgt Simpson confirms seeing the enemy aircraft I fired at going down on fire and out of control, but did not see it hit the sea.

Although the Hurricane units on Malta had managed to effectively protect the islands from attacks by Italian aircraft for much of 1941, Luftwaffe units began returning to Sicily in December after an absence of more than six months. Ju 88s quickly started to appear over Malta, escorted by Bf 109Fs from JG 53, and by the end of December ten Hurricane pilots had been killed – four of them on the 29th alone. Nevertheless, No 126 Sqn still claimed the odd success over German bombers if its pilots managed to avoid being intercepted by the fighter escorts. Amongst those to achieve a rare kill during this period of increasing hardship was Flight Lieutenant 'Chips' Carpenter, who downed a Ju 88 from *Stab* II./KG 77 to become a Malta Hurricane ace on 27 December:

While leading Wing at 24,000 ft for 40 minutes we were given a vector of 045 degrees. The cloud was ten-tenths at 7,000 ft, and we spotted aircraft against it flying at around 16,000 ft. There were four or five Ju 88s in loose formation, with some

109s a little above them. I dived down on the last bomber and opened fired at 300 yards from a beam attack, turning to line astern. I closed right up till there was a risk of collision and broke away down and to the left. In the quarter attack that followed, an engine was hit by de Wilde [incendiary ammunition] and began smoking. The Ju 88 kept on a straight course during the attacks, but turned around soon after. He dived for cloud cover and I managed to get in another two attacks from astern before he got to it. His engine was on fire and I did not get any return fire from the rear gunners.

By February 1942 the rate of attrition amongst the fighter units on Malta was so bad that all airworthy Hurricanes had to be consolidated within one unit, with squadrons at Ta Kali or Hal Far flying them on alternate days. February ended with Nos 242 and 605 Sqns being absorbed into Nos 126 and 185 Sqns, respectively. The bad situation for the depleted Hurricane units got immeasurably worse in March, as Malta's battering at the hands of superior Axis forces continued unabated. Amongst the seven Hurricane pilots killed in action that month was Australian Sergeant John Mayall of No 126 Sqn, who was shot down in combat-weary Z5140 on 10 March. Records suggest that he was the 19th, and last, victim of Battle of Britain ace Hauptmann Karl-Heinz Krahl, *Kommandeur* of Bf 109F-equipped II./JG 3. Krahl himself perished exactly five weeks later when he fell victim to an AA battery whilst strafing Luqa airfield.

Three days prior to Z5140's demise, the first Spitfires had at last reached Malta. More and more of them would be flown in from carriers in the Western Mediterranean during the course of 1942, allowing the few surviving Hurricanes to be quietly retired. Fittingly, one of the final two victories credited to the Hawker fighter whilst flying from Malta – on 8 May 1942 – was claimed by seven-kill Australian ace Flight Sergeant Gordon Tweedale in a No 126 Sqn aeroplane. The following day 62 Spitfires arrived on Malta, and that evening, in his first sortie in one of these new fighters, the 24-year-old former stockman from Queensland was shot down and killed.

The real Z5140 had been flown
to Malta from HMS *Ark Royal* on
6 June 1941 as part of Operation
*Rocket*, the fighter being one of
43 brand new Hurricane IIs that
had been shipped out from England.
Astonishingly, considering the high
rate of attrition amongst RAF
fighters flying in the defence
of Malta, Z5140 survived until
10 March 1942, when it became
the nineteenth, and last, victim
of Battle of Britain ace Hauptmann
Karl-Heinz Krahl, *Kommandeur*
of Bf 109F-equipped II./JG 3.

# CHAPTER ELEVEN
# HURRICANE WITH A HOOK

Despite the RAF's No 46 Sqn proving during the ill-fated Norwegian campaign of April 1940 that the Hurricane could take off and land from a carrier, the first dedicated Sea Hurricanes did not reach the Fleet Air Arm until early 1941. In fact the first examples of the Hawker fighter to be embarked aboard ships were the 50 war-weary 'Hurricats' that were converted for use on board Catapult Armed Merchant Ships. Developed to counter the threat posed to Atlantic convoys by long-range Fw 200 Condors, these aircraft, once launched, either had to land ashore or ditch into the sea upon the completion of their mission.

The pressing need for more modern fighters for the conventional Fleet Air Arm resulted in a number of ex-RAF aircraft being converted into Sea Hurricane IBs at around the same time, the standard land-based airframe simply being fitted with slinging points, catapult spools and an arrester hook, together with general strengthening to absorb the stresses put onto the fuselage during a catapult launch. Later variants featured the engine and airframe of the Mk I combined with the Mk IIC's cannon armament, whilst the final naval Sea Hurricane (the Mk IIC) was identical to its RAF equivalent, boasting a four-cannon wing and Merlin XX engine. Sea Hurricanes eventually equipped 38 Fleet Air Arm units between 1941 and 1944, and saw action over the Mediterranean Sea and the Arctic Ocean from the flightdecks of fleet and escort carriers, as well as from land bases on Malta and along the North African coast.

Despite its widespread service, the Sea Hurricane was very much a stopgap naval fighter until better machines could be either built in Britain or acquired from the USA. Its land-based heritage duly provided naval aviators with quite a challenge

The Shuttleworth Collection's Canadian-built Sea Hurricane IB Z7015 was originally delivered to the RAF as a Mk X in March 1941. It was subsequently one of 400 Mk Is and Xs converted into Sea Hurricane configuration by General Aircraft Ltd through the fitment of slinging points, catapult spools and an arrester hook – the airframe was also generally strengthened in order to better withstand the rigours of carrier operations.

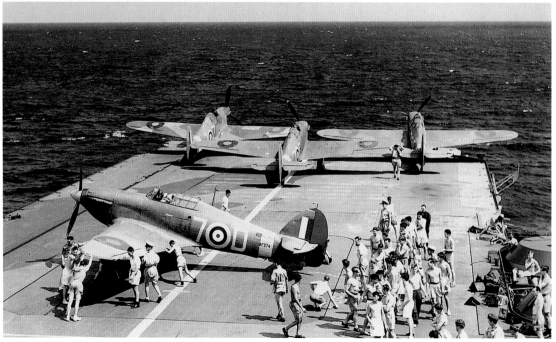

**LEFT** With the pilot still strapped into the cockpit, Sea Hurricane IB AF974 '7-D' of 880 NAS is positioned on HMS *Indomitable*'s forward lift prior to being taken down to the hangar deck after landing back aboard the carrier during flight operations in the western Mediterranean in 1942. Forward of the fighter, the Sea Hurricane lashed to the flightdeck near the port bow is BD721 '7-Z', which was flown several times by 880 NAS's senior pilot and Battle of Britain Hurricane ace, Lieutenant Dickie Cork. (Andy Thomas)

when the Sea Hurricane was sent to sea for operations from a pitching carrier flightdeck, as Captain Eric 'Winkle' Brown, arguably the greatest Fleet Air Arm pilot of them all, recalled:

Short in range, with the ditching propensities of a submarine, harsh stalling characteristics, a very mediocre view for deck landing and an undercarriage that was as likely as not to bounce it over the arrester wires. What less likely a candidate for deployment aboard aircraft carriers as a naval single-seat fighter than the Hurricane could have been imagined. Yet, legacy of parsimony, expediency and shortsightedness inflicted on British naval aviation it undoubtedly was, the Hurricane was to take to the nautical environment extraordinarily well. The Sea Hurricane was, thus, like the Seafire that was to follow it aboard British carrier flightdecks, very much a product of desperation, albeit a product that, despite its inevitable shortcomings, was very welcome indeed as it was, for a year, to reign as the fastest fighter in the FAA's inventory.

The Hurricane had of course earned undying fame for itself in the Battle of Britain, but by the time it reached the Fleet Air Arm it was becoming seriously outclassed by contemporary enemy fighters. Nevertheless, with a wing loading of 26.3 lbs/sq ft and good controls, it was a great dogfighter, and it had sufficient performance and firepower to deal effectively with contemporary bombers.

Perhaps it is sufficient to say that, contrary to logic, it took to the naval environment remarkably well. A thoroughly competent Fleet fighter it was not and could never have been, but it was a great dogfighter with, in its cannon-armed versions, plenty of punch and, most importantly, it reached the Fleet Air Arm at a time when that service desperately needed a relatively fast and reasonably modern single-seat fighter embarked in its carriers.

Approximately 800 Sea Hurricanes would eventually serve with the Fleet Air Arm, and the oldest airworthy example in the world today is the subject aircraft featured in this chapter. As described in further detail in Chapter Sixteen: Hurricane Survivors, Canadian-built Sea Hurricane IB Z7015 was originally delivered to the RAF as a Mk X in March 1941. It was subsequently one of 400 Mk Is and Xs converted into Sea Hurricane configuration by General Aircraft Ltd through the fitment of slinging points, catapult spools and an arrester hook – the airframe was also generally strengthened in order to better withstand the rigours of carrier operations. Taken on charge by the Fleet Air Arm at RNAS Yeovilton, in Somerset, in July 1941, Z7015 was subsequently supplied to 880 Naval Air Squadron (NAS) – the Royal Navy's first Sea Hurricane unit.

880 NAS was one of many such units established in 1941 as the Fleet Air Arm rapidly expanded in order to provide squadrons for the Royal Navy's growing carrier force. The squadron was based at St Merryn, in north Cornwall, where Z7015 was one of more than a dozen Sea Hurricane IBs supplied to it as replacements for three Sea Gladiators and nine standard Hurricane Is that the unit had been flying since January 1941. Its naval aviators were a mix of experienced men, such as squadron CO Lieutenant-Commander F.E.C. 'Butch' Judd and Battle of Britain ace Lieutenant Dickie Cork, and newly winged pilots like Sub-Lieutenant Hugh Popham. All three individuals would fly Z7015 during its time with 880 NAS.

Popham wrote about his impressions of the aeroplane in his autobiography *Sea Flight – A Fleet Air Arm Pilot's Story*:

The Sea Hurricane was splendid, very strong and steady, with a clean, purposeful line to it and no vices, except a tendency to drop a wing on the stall. Its reputation stood high, and it was the best fighter the fleet possessed. Needless to say, the fleet did not

Z7015 has been marked up in the colours and markings it wore when assigned to 880 NAS at St Merryn, in north Cornwall, the fighter being one of more than a dozen Sea Hurricane IBs supplied to the unit as replacements for three Sea Gladiators and nine standard Hurricane Is that it had been flying since January 1941. 880 NAS's naval aviators were a mix of experienced men such as squadron CO, Lieutenant Commander F.E.C. 'Butch' Judd, and Lieutenant Dickie Cork, as well as newly winged pilots like Sub-Lieutenant Hugh Popham. All three individuals would fly Z7015 during its time with 880 NAS.

One of the Royal Navy's most successful fighter pilots, and the only one to claim five aircraft destroyed in a day, Lieutenant Dickie Cork of 880 NAS is seen here seated in the cockpit of his Sea Hurricane soon after Operation *Pedestal*. Cork was credited with nine and two shared destroyed, one probable, four damaged and seven destroyed on the ground, flying both Hurricanes (with No 242 Sqn) and Sea Hurricanes (with 880 NAS). He was killed in a flying accident on 14 April 1944 when his Corsair collided with another Vought fighter at China Bay airfield in Ceylon. (Andy Thomas)

possess very many of them (as the wings didn't fold, none of the *Illustrious* class of carrier could accommodate them), and in any case, by the summer of 1941 the Mk I was already obsolescent.

Popham's CO, South African Francis 'Butch' Judd, was a veteran aviator who had transferred to the Royal Navy from the RAF in the mid-1930s. Having flown numerous types over the years, and previously commanded 764 and 771 NASs, he had garnered something of a reputation by the time he took charge of 880 NAS upon its formation. Hugh Popham recalled:

'The Butcher', known familiarly as 'Butch', was certainly unsettling in appearance. He was tall, perhaps 6 ft 2 in, and wore a reddish beard and moustache. They require separate mention, for

ABOVE Never designed as a naval fighter, the Hurricane nevertheless provided the Fleet Air Arm (FAA) with a relatively modern monoplane fighter that was available in adequate numbers when it was needed most.

while his beard was trimmed somewhat after the fashion of King George V's, his moustaches were allowed to run wild. They sprang out horizontally from his upper lip, stiff, plentiful and coarse, like a couple of tarred rope's ends in need of whipping. He was forever handling them; thrusting them away from his mouth in a pensive way when he was in good humour; grabbing and tugging at them when, as was more usual, he was angry. His temper was volcanic, and his ferocity a matter of legend.

Judd and Sub-Lieutenant R.B. Haworth would share the Sea Hurricane's first aerial victory on 31 July 1941 when they downed a Do 18 flying boat while embarked in HMS *Furious* as fighter cover for a Fleet Air Arm carrier strike on merchant shipping in the Finnish port of Petsamo. Only four Sea Hurricanes (not Z7015) from 'A' Flight were embarked for this operation. 880 NAS moved in its entirety to RNAS Tern, in the Orkneys, in mid-August, and then on to nearby Sumburgh. Z7015 was flown from the latter site on several occasions during this period by Sub-Lieutenant Popham, the unit carrying out convoy patrols and other general duties. Although 880 NAS left Sumburgh in early October to embark in the newly commissioned carrier HMS *Indomitable*, which was about to join the Eastern Fleet in Ceylon via work-ups in Bermuda and the West Indies, Z7015 went unserviceable between the Shetlands and Machrihanish and failed to join the vessel prior to its departure from Greenock on 18 October. The aeroplane was destined to spend the rest of its brief career in the Fleet Air Arm with second-line training units.

880 NAS, however, would experience considerable combat, particularly in the Mediterranean during the summer of 1942 at the height of the Malta campaign. Indeed, many of the naval aviators that had flown Z7015 the previous year were engaged in a bitterly fought series of actions during Operation *Pedestal* in support of vital convoys trying the reach the embattled islands. With conditions on Malta becoming increasingly desperate, *Pedestal* was planned in an effort to fight a convoy of 13 fast, modern freighters and a tanker through the gauntlet of enemy attacks to the beleaguered islands. Additional Spitfires were also to be flown off to Malta as part of this operation. A large escort was assembled which, with the intensity of anticipated opposition, included no fewer than four aircraft carriers, although *Furious* was to exclusively ferry the Spitfires.

HMS *Eagle* embarked the Sea Hurricanes of 801 NAS and 813 NAS's Fighter Flight, whilst on board HMS *Victorious* were the Fulmars of 809 and 884 NASs and the six Sea Hurricanes of 885 NAS, under the command of Lieutenant-Commander 'Buster' Hallett – all three units were relatively inexperienced. In contrast, *Indomitable*'s units contained a wealth of experience. Sea Hurricanes equipped Lieutenant-Commander Bill Bruen's 800 NAS, whilst 880 NAS was led by the fiery 'Butch' Judd and had Lieutenant Dickie Cork as its senior pilot. Completing the carrier's fighter force was Lieutenant Robert 'Sloppy' Johnston's 806 NAS, equipped with recently acquired Martlets. The armada transited the Straits of Gibraltar in the early hours of 10 August 1942 and headed into the Mediterranean to participate in possibly the greatest convoy battle of the war.

During the late afternoon of the 10th, a Vichy-French civilian flying boat en route to Algeria flew over the fleet, and although allowed to pass unhindered, it radioed a sighting, which was of course picked up by the Germans. Following the French sighting, at dawn the next day the first enemy reconnaissance aircraft was detected and it duly sent off its report before escaping. The location reports had allowed submarine patrols to position themselves, and shortly after midday, as *Furious* prepared to fly off its Spitfires, *U-73* hit HMS *Eagle* with four torpedoes and it went down in six minutes. Four of the vessel's precious Sea Hurricanes, from 801 NAS, were airborne at the time, and three landed on *Victorious* and the other on *Indomitable* – the remaining 16 were lost, however. With the enemy fully alerted as to the convoy's position, further attacks were expected, although with its task achieved, *Furious* and its escorts returned to Gibraltar.

The following morning – 12 August – one of 1(F)./*Aufklärungsgruppe* 122's Ju 88Ds regained contact at around 0600 hrs. It was the start of a very long day for the convoy defences. The first

'Short in range, with the ditching propensities of a submarine, harsh stalling characteristics, a very mediocre view for deck landing and an undercarriage that was as likely as not to bounce it over the arrester wires', recalled 'Winkle' Brown from first-hand experience. 'Yet, ... the Hurricane was to take to the nautical environment extraordinarily well'. This example is being waved aboard an unidentified carrier during 1942–43. (Phil Jarrett)

LEFT Approximately 800 Sea Hurricanes would eventually serve with the FAA, and the oldest airworthy example in the world today is this aircraft, Z7015. Destined never to see combat, the fighter was unserviceable when 880 NAS joined *Indomitable* in October 1941 and departed Greenock for the Eastern Fleet in Ceylon. It would spend the rest of its brief career in the FAA with second line training units.

ABOVE RIGHT Ploughing its way through a Mediterranean swell with draft screens up and Sea Hurricanes parked, the modified Illustrious-class carrier *Indomitable* was soon to play a key role in the *Pedestal* convoy drama. Indeed, the vessel was involved in many of the critical actions in this theatre in 1942. Capable of embarking up to 48 aircraft, the 23,000-ton carrier had received five Battle honours by VJ Day. (Andy Thomas)

More Sea Hurricanes under the leadership of the charismatic Lieutenant-Commander Bill Bruen of 800 NAS then entered the fray, and he destroyed a Ju 88 and hit another. As this attack ended, fighters from 880 NAS, led by Cork, arrived. Afterwards, in an interview given in 1943, he described the scene:

The sky at first sight seemed filled with aircraft. The enemy kept in tight formation and our fighters snapped at their heels, forcing them to break in all directions, though most continued to press on in the direction of the convoy. We were in the narrowest of corridors between Sicily and Tunis, and couldn't afford the luxury of biding our time. So we hit them as hard as we could. One Junkers turned away from the main group and I led my section down towards it. I was well ahead and fired when it filled my sights. Smoke poured from its wings and it disappeared below me into the sea. A few minutes later I saw another Ju 88 out of the corner of my eye heading along the coast of North Africa, so I set off in pursuit by myself. At 1,000 ft I came within range and fired. It seemed to stagger in the air, then dropped into the sea with a big splash.

Later in the morning torpedo-bombers from the *Regia Aeronautica* and German Ju 88s from Sicily approached. Hurricanes of 801 NAS, led by Lieutenant-Commander Rupert Brabner, were up, and with Lieutenant 'Sloppy' Johnston of 806 NAS heading four Martlets, they countered the raid. Also in the air were Fulmars from *Victorious*, led by 884 NAS CO 'Buster' Hallett. As the raid built further, Sea Hurricanes led by Lieutenant-

engagements were made soon after 0700 hrs when Fulmars of 884 NAS, led by Lieutenant Churchill, sent a Z.1007bis into the sea in flames. Two hours later, Sea Hurricanes of 800 and 880 NASs from *Indomitable,* backed up by three more Sea Hurricanes and four Fulmars from *Victorious*, were directed to the north-east to intercept an incoming raid by 24 Ju 88s. Canadian Lieutenant W.H. 'Moose' Martyn of 800 NAS led his section in an attack on two of the Ju 88s, with Martyn himself hitting the starboard engine of one that was in turn attacked by Sub-Lieutenant Hastings, whose fire caused it to spiral into the sea. This shared victory saw Martyn become the first of several Royal Navy pilots to 'make ace' that day.

LEFT Lacking an arrester hook, Mk I V7438 was one of a number of surplus RAF Hurricane Is and IIs that were transferred to the FAA in 1941–42 for use as fighter trainers whilst the Royal Navy awaited the delivery of Sea Hurricanes and, eventually, Seafires. Having previously served with Nos 151 and 46 Sqns, this Hawker-built fighter was handed over to the Admiralty in April 1942, and it was photographed shortly thereafter serving with 759 NAS at Yeovilton. (John Dibbs)

Commander Bill Bruen were scrambled from *Indomitable*. It was the Fulmars that attacked first, as the Ju 88s, having dropped their special 'motor bombs', turned for home. Three were reportedly seen falling in flames, with the crews bailing out, and a fourth left the area trailing smoke. Brabner's Sea Hurricanes then intercepted the approaching S.84 torpedo-bombers. Brabner hit two that were credited to him as destroyed, thus making him an ace as well – as the MP for Hythe, he was the first sitting Member of Parliament to claim five aerial victories! Then Bruen's section from 800 NAS arrived and he claimed another S.84 destroyed in concert with Sub-Lieutenant Andy Thomson, who also attacked an S.79 that then crashed into the sea – he made two further claims later in the day.

Elsewhere, others too were fighting desperately, and despite these successes, some of the enemy bombers had got through. As they left, Lieutenant Johnston attacked a Ju 88 that he reported over the radio had crashed, before he then headed back to *Indomitable* and was killed when his Martlet crashed off the side of the carrier's flightdeck on landing. 'Sloppy' Johnston was not the only CO lost, as 880 NAS's Lieutenant-Commander 'Butch' Judd also perished whilst attacking a formation of He 111s. His loss hit 880 NAS hard. 'We had thought him indestructible', was the response from one of his pilots upon hearing of his CO's demise. Dickie Cork duly assumed command of the unit, which now had only six serviceable Sea Hurricanes following the morning's fierce fighting – it had started the day with 12.

After several further engagements, there followed something of a hiatus before attacks resumed in the late afternoon. Italian-flown Ju 87Rs, with a large escort of C.202 fighters, made an appearance, as did various Luftwaffe bombers from the island of Pantelleria, protected by Bf 109s. The standing patrols of Fleet Air Arm fighters were initially vectored to intercept the approaching aircraft, and other aeroplanes were hastily launched. They were then ordered to clear the area due to their proximity to the fleet barrage, and eventually they were vectored onto new threats. During his interview, Cork recalled, 'I counted ten bombers following their

usual tactic of flying close to the sea in a tight group, but one lagged behind and I picked him off and he crashed beside a group of destroyers, which then opened fire on me!' Cork scored further victories during the evening, and his final success – an S.79 – made him the only Royal Navy pilot of the war to claim five destroyed in a day. His account of this action was reported as follows:

Circling over the fleet I saw a flight of Fulmars being harried by waves of enemy fighters and went to their rescue. There were German and Italian aircraft everywhere, diving in from all directions. In the confusion it was almost impossible to catch anything, and my section soon split up, twisting and turning to avoid being shot down. After several minutes I found myself on the edge of the combat area and saw a lone S.79 preparing to attack one of our ships. Diving on it unawares, my gunfire hit wings and engines and it went down towards the sea, one member of the crew jumping out when it was still more than 50 ft up. As I turned away I saw the Savoia's crew take to their rubber dinghy and push off, before the aircraft sank.

From above and behind four Reggiane 2002s came down and started to knock lumps off my Hurricane. I had run out of ammunition so there was little I could do, except skim over the sea, making myself a difficult target and head back towards the fleet. More by luck than judgement I escaped, but my engine had been hit and began to lose power, so I had to get down very smartly.

Unfortunately for Cork, just as *Indomitable* launched its last section of Sea Hurricanes, 12 German-flown Ju 87s began their dives and struck the carrier with two direct hits and three near misses. One of the last aircraft launched before the attack was the Sea Hurricane flown by young Scot Sub-Lieutenant Blythe Ritchie of 800 NAS, and he fired on one of the Stukas as it pulled out of its dive. He saw the canopy fly off just prior to the aircraft hitting the sea. Ritchie subsequently downed two more Ju 87s during this sortie, setting him well on the way to becoming an ace.

With *Indomitable* unable to recover its aircraft, Cork was told to 'pancake' (land) on *Victorious* instead:

Out of necessity I had to get down on her deck as quickly as possible, and virtually barged into other aircraft waiting to land. My motor was just about stopped, and as I got my nose over the round-down it actually conked out. Luckily my hook took a wire and pulled me up. The handlers pushed me backwards to release the hook, then forward, beyond the barrier, where, after a brief examination, they unceremoniously pushed the Hurricane over the side, it being a total write off.

Cork duly received the DSO for his exploits on 12 August 1942, having already been awarded the Distinguished Service Cross (DSC) after the Battle of Britain.

When the heavy Royal Navy escort was forced to turn west soon afterwards, not a single merchant ship had been lost. However, with its carrier-based air cover gone, the *Pedestal* convoy was to suffer grievous losses before coming under the protection of land-based air cover. Nevertheless, sufficient materiel reached Malta to ensure its survival. It had been an epic struggle, and possibly the finest hour for the Fleet Air Arm's fighters and, in particular, the makeshift Sea Hurricane.

Part of the Shuttleworth Collection since 1961, Sea Hurricane Z7015 took almost ten years to restore to airworthiness between June 1986 and September 1995. The fighter made its first post-rebuild flight at Duxford on 17 September 1995. For the first few years after restoration it was based at Duxford, making (literally) flying visits to Old Warden, but it is now permanently located at the latter site with the Shuttleworth Collection, where it often flies in company with the Collection's Westland Lysander and, more recently, Hurricane I R4118.

# CHAPTER TWELVE

# 'HURRIBOMBER'

Few surviving Hurricanes have been restored as 'Hurribombers' over the years, and presently Canadian-built Mk XIIA 1374 seen in this chapter is the only airworthy example in the world. It has been painted in the colours of No 174 Sqn Hurricane IIB BE505, which was one of five aircraft lost by the unit whilst supporting the ill-fated Operation *Jubilee* – the Dieppe raid – on 19 August 1942.

Although the Hurricane is best remembered for its exploits as a fighter, defending Britain from Luftwaffe hordes during the summer of 1940 or attacking formations of Italian aircraft attempting to neutralize Malta the following year, for much of its frontline service the aeroplane was employed in the ground-attack role. The first examples of the 'Hurribomber', as the aircraft was unofficially christened in the frontline, reached Fighter Command units in May 1941. Essentially a Hurricane II modified to carry external ordnance, the aeroplane's primary structural difference from the Mk I of Battle of Britain fame was its employment of a universal wing. The latter had been slightly redesigned by Hawker so that it could carry a single pylon beneath each wing, to which could be attached fuel tanks to extend the aircraft's range, unguided rocket projectiles, gun pods or two 250-lb (and eventually 500-lb) bombs.

The Mk IIA was the first of the 'Hurribombers', and this was followed by the Mk IIB that boasted 12 0.303-in machine guns, the Mk IIC with four Hispano 20 mm cannon in place of the Browning machine guns, and, finally, the Mk IID. The latter had two Vickers Type S 40 mm cannon in pods beneath the wings and a solitary machine gun armed with tracer ammunition for sighting purposes only. The ultimate ground-attack Hurricane was the Mk IV, which was also fitted with the universal wing that allowed it to be configured with all the weaponry options of the Mk II, combined with the increased power of the Merlin 27 engine, dust filters for desert operations and 350 lbs of additional armour plating to protect the pilot, radiators, fuel tanks and engine.

Few surviving Hurricanes have been restored as 'Hurribombers' over the years, and presently Canadian-built

Mk XIIA 1374 seen in this chapter is the only airworthy example in the world. It has been painted in the colours of No 174 Sqn Hurricane IIB BE505, which was one of five aircraft lost by the unit whilst supporting the ill-fated Operation *Jubilee* – the Dieppe raid – on 19 August 1942. One of 600 Hurricane IIBs and IICs built between July and November 1941 by Hawker in its Langley and Weybridge factories, BE505 had initially been supplied to No 607 'County of Durham' Sqn at Martlesham Heath in the early autumn of that year as the unit replaced its Mk IIAs with Mk IIBs.

Like the majority of other units equipped with Hurricanes in Fighter Command at this time (there were ten such squadrons on 1 January 1942), No 607 Sqn was principally employed in the ground-attack role against coastal shipping and targets of opportunity during low-level 'Roadsteads' and 'Ramrods' and larger scale 'Circus' operations across the Channel. Indeed, it had been officially designated as the first Hurricane bomber squadron in Fighter Command in August 1941.

Posted to Manston in October 1941 in order to be closer to the enemy, No 607 Sqn was informed early in the new year that it was being shipped off to India as the RAF hastily attempted to bolster its forces in the region in the wake of the fall of Singapore to the rampant Japanese. When the unit departed in March, eight of its pilots and all 17 of its Hurricane IIBs remained at Manston to form the nucleus of newly established No 174 'Mauritius' Sqn. Amongst the aviators to stay in Kent was 24-year-old Australian Flight Sergeant Charles Watson. He had enlisted in his home state of Victoria in June 1940, and by the following August he had completed his flying training in Australia, bidden farewell to his wife Peggy and their newborn daughter and travelled to Sydney to embark on a troopship bound for the UK. Following conversion to the Hurricane at No 59 OTU at Crosby-on-Eden, in Cumbria, Watson joined No 607 Sqn in December 1941. Once BE505 was assigned to No 174 Sqn, the aeroplane became Watson's regular mount to the extent that he marked his Antipodean heritage onto the fighter. The cowling sported a small boxing kangaroo with

a machine gun-firing joey in its pouch. Aft of the artwork was the name *Pegs*, after Watson's wife.

On 14 August, No 174 Sqn was sent to join five other units at Ford, on the West Sussex coast, in preparation for *Jubilee*. Four days later brought the briefing that confirmed the pilots' suspicions of an impending big operation. The target was the French harbour of Dieppe, which Allied forces would try to capture and briefly hold in a mass practice invasion as the prelude for a bigger assault on 'Fortress Europe' at a much later date. Vice Admiral Lord Louis Mountbatten had more than 6,000 troops, mostly Canadian, under his control for this operation, which would hopefully end in a tactical withdrawal back to England. They would be transported across the Channel in a flotilla of Royal Navy vessels, and the whole operation was to be supported by more than 70 RAF squadrons. This made *Jubilee* one of the RAF's largest one-day aerial battles of the war. In fact, the force available to Air Vice-Marshal Trafford Leigh-Mallory, Air Officer Commanding No 11 Group, was larger than that fielded by Fighter Command at any point during the Battle of Britain. As well as 48 Spitfire squadrons, Leigh-Mallory had eight Hurricane units – six armed with cannon-equipped fighters and two with 'Hurribombers'.

Following in No 607 Sqn's footsteps, No 174 Sqn had shown its effectiveness in combat in the previous five months. Frequently teaming up with cannon-armed Spitfires or Hurricanes, the unit would dive-bomb German shipping or fixed targets with 250-lb bombs shortly after they had been attacked by the cannon-armed fighters. It was the job of the latter aircraft to try and keep the flak batteries at bay, which were becoming increasingly more effective against the RAF fighter-bombers –

The Hurricane's mixed construction is highlighted in this close-up shot of 1374 at its North Weald home. With the Hurricane's primary structure being rectangular in shape, a secondary structure was required to round the fuselage out – hence the adoption of wooden formers that were attached to the longerons by metal clips, and the fabric-carrying stringers. All the various coverings for the aircraft's structure – Irish linen, duralumin and plywood – can be seen here.

The muzzles for the outer four 0.303-in machine guns are visible on 1374, fitted at different heights within the wing. The majority of the 'Hurribombers' in frontline service with Fighter Command were ten-gun aircraft, with the third 0.303-in weapon in each block of four having been deleted as the space for the gun was occupied by the bolts that secured the underwing bomb racks.

No 174 Sqn had lost ten Hurricanes in combat in the five months prior to *Jubilee*, most of them to flak.

Flight Sergeant John Brooks was a squadron mate of Charles Watson in 1942, both pilots having served together in No 607 Sqn and remained behind at Manston after the unit was sent to India. He candidly recalled No 174 Sqn's early operations in the Hurricane:

> We flew the 'new' 'Hurribombers' – 'new' in the sense that the Hurricane was by then considered as outclassed by the new German fighters, so it was fitted with a single 250-lb bomb under each wing. By the time we participated in *Jubilee* the squadron was fully operational and experienced in low-level work, and although the chop rate was high, there was no lack of enthusiasm.

At 0440 hrs the first flight of No 174 Sqn aircraft took off from Ford and headed for Dieppe, led by newly appointed CO, and Battle of Britain veteran, Squadron Leader Emil Fayolle of the Free French Air Force. He had replaced fellow Battle of Britain pilot Squadron Leader Cyril Page on 1 August. The darkness prevented their usual forming up as a squadron, and forced the unit to instead venture out in three sections of four. Codenamed 'Hitler', the target for their 500-lb bombs was a heavy naval gun emplacement to the rear of Dieppe that was in range of the sea and beaches where the troops would soon be coming ashore. To preserve the element of surprise, no previous bombardment from ship or air to 'soften up' the targets had been sanctioned. The first wave of pilots from No 174 Sqn faced a double challenge – not only would they be carrying twice their usual payload, with the 500-lb bombs instead of the usual 250-lb, but they would be formation dive-bombing in the dark.

Flight Sergeant Brooks remembered his dismay upon hearing that they would be 'the first lot in, before first light'. He recalled that it took them about 40 minutes to cross the Channel, skimming the waves at low level to preserve the element of surprise. Looming through the darkness were the flames of a burning German ship that had wandered into the invasion fleet. Fayolle decided that stealth was no longer required – it was time to lead his aircraft up to a few thousand feet to give them sufficient height to dive-bomb their targets.

Although the 'Hitler' guns were not firing, the German flak batteries were manned and ready for action, as Brooks recalled:

> The light flak was coming up thick and fast and we were flying at a very vulnerable height. I could see the 40 mm stuff curving up towards us, for all the world like a strike of bright glowing beads on a string. It would flash past us and explode just above our heads – or so it appeared. Flak always looked worse at night.

As previously noted in this volume, the Hurricane cockpit lacks a floor, being fitted with just an adjustable seat and trays for the pilot's feet to sit on when operating the rudder pedals.

LEFT Every aspect of the colour scheme that adorned BE505 in 1942 has been replicated on 1374, even down to the personal markings that its regular pilot, 24-year-old Victorian Flight Sergeant Charles Watson, had applied to the cowling. To the right of the small boxing kangaroo with a machine gun-firing joey in its pouch is the name *Pegs*, which Watson had added to the 'Hurribomber' in honour of his wife, Peggy.

FAR LEFT Flight Sergeant Charles Bryce Watson poses perched on a wheel chock in front of his 'Hurribomber', BE505, at Manston. Watson had travelled to Britain from Australia in 1941 and converted to the Hurricane at No 59 OTU at Crosby-on-Eden, in Cumbria. He joined No 607 Sqn in December 1941, three months before the unit was posted abroad. (John Dibbs)

After spotting the target, Brooks' section started its dive, releasing bombs at the last possible moment. 'Some light flak came up from the gun site but it wasn't really enough to put us off. My main concern was that we would all pull out and miss the surrounding trees'. After feeling the crump of the exploding bombs shudder through his Hurricane, Brooks looked for the other members of his section, while firing his guns at anything that moved below, weaving frantically to avoid incoming rounds.

The dawn light revealed the landing craft and troops arriving on the beaches. Turning back out to sea, and giving the trigger-happy Royal Navy a wide berth, Brooks formed up with other members of the squadron to make their way back to Ford. Three never made it, including Squadron Leader Fayolle, who had collided with an intercepting Fw 190. Squadron mate and fellow Free French pilot Pilot Officer R.L.N. van Wymeersch had also hit a Focke-Wulf fighter, but survived and was captured (he was later executed after participating in the 'Great Escape' in March 1944). The third pilot, Sergeant C.F. James, was killed when his Hurricane was hit by flak.

Such losses were not uncommon in 'Hurribomber' squadrons in Fighter Command, which had a high turnover of pilots. 'Sometimes you hardly got to know a chap before he was killed or went missing,' Brooks recalled. 'It was said that if you managed to survive your first three "ops" then you had a good chance of completing your airframe tour.' While the Hurricane's could take severe punishment, just a single bullet in the radiator could quickly cause the loss of an aircraft due to engine overheating. Frequently flying at low level, the pilots of No 174 Sqn had little opportunity to bale out, and pulling up to altitude made them easy targets for flak.

Brookes was friendly with Flight Sergeant Charles Watson, the Australian having visited him at his home in London. By the time of the *Jubilee* operation, Watson had flown close to 100 hours on Hurricanes, and by Brookes' estimation had gained the necessary operational experience required to ensure his survival. Watson went up in BE505 on No 174 Sqn's second sortie of the day, with three sections taking off at 1025 hrs. The 12 aircraft joined their escorts of two Spitfire squadrons and one unit equipped with cannon-armed Hurricanes and headed out to sea.

As the morning wore on, it became apparent that the raid was turning into a disaster. The harbour's terrain was awkward to cross in tracked vehicles and German defences had been grossly underestimated by planners of the operation. The majority of the troops were pinned down on the beaches amid heavy fire and scenes of carnage. After a slow start, the Luftwaffe was making its presence felt above. The scheduled withdrawal was hastily brought forward by several hours to 1100 hrs. To distract the enemy's attention from the incoming naval vessels, the RAF was tasked with targeting defensive positions inland. No 174 Sqn approached Dieppe and received instructions from the Royal Navy command ship to bomb the

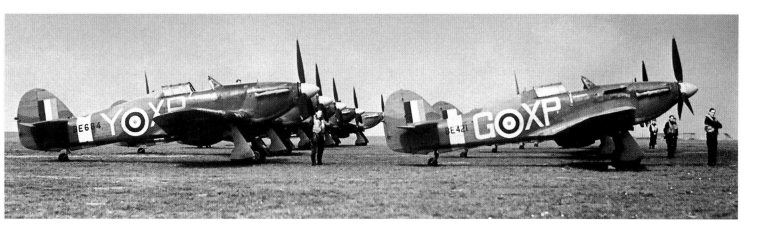

An impressive line-up of No 174 Sqn 'Hurribombers' and their pilots, at Manston. This photograph was taken in May 1942, just two months after the unit had formed at the Kent fighter station. Both the aircraft closest to the camera were lost on operations before the Dieppe raid. (John Dibbs)

eastern heights of the town. Low-hanging smoke and a 2,000-ft cloud base hindered their ability to locate their targets and prevented them from setting up a steep dive.

As they commenced a turn bringing them over the target area, the Hurricane flown by Pilot Officer M.H. 'Doofy' du Fretay had its wing hit by flak. Streaming flames, the fighter-bomber was flown into a column of enemy armoured vehicles by its Free French Air Force pilot, who, according to Brookes, 'loathed Germans'. Frustrated by the poor visibility, the remaining Hurricane pilots set up a shallow dive and dropped their bombs in a wooded area to the east of the town where enemy troops had been reported.

High above Dieppe a massive aerial battle was now taking place, but the low-flying Hurricanes, ducking through the smoke and cloud, avoided any enemy aircraft – but only just. Brookes recalled:

We formed up to go home (there were now just five of us) at about 200 ft, when I saw to my horror a big formation of Messerschmitt 109s and Focke-Wulf 190s flying parallel to the coast. They passed directly over the top of us at not more than about 200 ft. It was possible to make out the individual markings, and one I noticed had a big black oil streak underneath. I held my breath, as I'm sure the others did, since we had used most of our ammunition in the ground attacks. Besides this, we would have been slaughtered, being outclassed, outnumbered and short of fuel.

Shortly after forming up, Brookes and his surviving squadron mates realized that Flight Sergeant Watson was missing. The Australian had the following to say about his demise:

While flying over our own shipping convoy at approximately 2,000 ft I received a direct flak hit.

No 174 Sqn's pilots and Intelligence Officer pose for a group photograph at Manston during the late spring of 1942. The four pilots seated on the wings with crosses just above their heads were killed in action serving with the unit. Standing in front of the bombed-up 'Hurribomber' is Battle of Britain veteran Squadron Leader Cyril Page, who led No 174 Sqn from May through to August 1942. (John Dibbs)

The 'Hurribomber', as the aircraft was unofficially christened in the frontline, was essentially a Hurricane II modified to carry external ordnance. The aeroplane's primary structural difference from the Mk I of Battle of Britain frame was its employment of a universal wing, slightly redesigned by Hawker so that it could mount a single pylon beneath each wing. The pylons could carry external fuel tanks to extend the aircraft's range, unguided rocket projectiles, gun pods or two 250-lb (and eventually 500-lb) bombs.

A combat-weary 'Hurribomber' of No 607 Sqn has a single 250-lb bomb secured to its two underwing pylons. Note the blanked-off port for the missing 0.303-in machine gun in the starboard wing – the corresponding weapon in the port wing was also deleted. To the right of the inboard guns is the gun ciné camera, installed within the leading edge of the starboard wing. (John Dibbs)

Damage was done to the port mainplane and the aircraft developed a slight glycol leak in the port side. Dropped out of formation, nursing engine, and received another hit which caused engine to splutter and eventually die. Fair amount of smoke and glycol came from port side of engine. Decided to bail out. Height approximately 700 ft. Aircraft crashed in sea approximately two miles off Dieppe Harbour.

Watson, his aircraft having probably been hit by friendly fire, survived his low-altitude egress with only an injury to his knee. Having clambered into his dinghy, he spent seven long hours battling an onshore wind in a desperate attempt to get back to the English coast. He eventually came across another dinghy containing severely injured Canadian Spitfire pilot Pilot Officer D. Linton of No 411 Sqn, who had been shot down by an enemy fighter. At this point Watson stopped fighting the tide and took both dinghies directly towards the French coast. They were captured by the Germans as soon as they reached the beach. Despite Watson's attempts to save Linton, the young Canadian pilot succumbed to his injuries.

No 174 Sqn sent its third, and final, flight of the day up at 1330 hrs, the unit managing to despatch ten aircraft. This time they carried 250-lb bombs, enabling the pilots to make a more successful low-

level attack on the heavy gun emplacement codenamed 'Rommel'. They scored at least one direct hit on the guns, and all ten aircraft made it back to Ford. The 19 August 1942 entry in No 174 Sqn's Operations Record Book (ORB) shows that in the space of ten hours, the unit had generated 34 sorties and dropped a total of 25,500 lbs of bombs. Its acting (and subsequently permanent) CO, Battle of Britain veteran Flight Lieutenant W.W. McConnell, noted that the 500-lb bombs were ineffective when conditions forced shallow-dive low-level attacks – just one of the many costly lessons learned by the Allies that day.

Despite the incredible bravery of the forces involved, Operation *Jubilee* had been a spectacular failure, barely achieving any of its objectives. The planned withdrawal left more than half of the infantry behind, with 3,623 men either dead or wounded. It was also the most costly single day in the history of the RAF, with more than 100 aircraft destroyed. As previously mentioned, five of these machines were No 174 Sqn 'Hurribombers', and only van Wymeersch and Watson survived being shot down. Losses in men and materiel were soon made good, however, with the unit retaining its Hurricane IIBs until they were replaced by Typhoon IBs in April 1943 – by which time No 174 Sqn was the very last frontline unit in No 11 Group to be equipped with the Hurricane.

Peter Teichman enjoys himself in 1374 during a photoshoot from North Weald. 'This aeroplane can out-turn any other fighter I have flown', Teichman states. 'No doubt it is slower than a Bf 109 and less well-armed, but no way the "Hun" pilot would be able to get guns onto a Hurricane if she was flown by a competent pilot.'

# CHAPTER THIRTEEN

# Mk XII

No fewer than 1,451 Hurricanes were constructed by The Canadian Car and Foundry Company Ltd between January 1940 and June 1943, as well as myriad spare parts (including more than 1,200 wings and almost as many oleo legs). Although more than 20 Canadian-built Hurricanes have survived, and at present nine of these aircraft are classified as airworthy, only one flyer, Mk XIIA BW881 seen in this chapter, is in RCAF colours.

Some 1,451 Hurricanes were constructed by the Canadian Car and Foundry Company Ltd – CCF – between January 1940 and June 1943, as well as myriad spare parts (including more than 1,200 wings and almost as many oleo legs). More than 20 Canadian-built Hurricanes have survived, and at present nine of these aircraft are classified as airworthy. However, only one of these flyers, Mk XIIA BW881 seen in this chapter, is in RCAF colours.

Canada's premier manufacturer of railway rolling stock, CCF (today part of Bombardier Transportation Canada) branched out into the aviation industry in 1936 when it obtained a licence to assemble Grumman FF-1 two-seat biplane fighters – designated G-23s in Canada – for foreign sale. In November 1938 CCF secured a contract to build 40 Hurricane I airframes (to be delivered without engines) for the RAF at its Fort William, Ontario, plant. The completion of these aircraft initially relied almost entirely on British-supplied materials including steel tubing, aluminium sheeting and metal castings that were then formed, pressed and machined at Fort William. Imported British materials were key to the manufacturing process, as the fledgling Canadian aircraft industry lacked the capability to produce such items. Hawker also supplied CCF with a pattern Hurricane I (L2144) and two sets of production drawings on microfilm in March 1939.

The outbreak of war drastically affected production of Canadian Hurricanes, as a steady flow of imported British materials for the Fort William plant could no longer be guaranteed. Although shortages hindered production well into 1941, the first CCF Hurricane (P5170) completed its maiden flight on 10 January 1940. The lack of essential imported

No 135 (F) Sqn Hurricane XII 5405 flies in close formation with a second aircraft from the unit at 15,000 ft over Patricia Bay, in British Columbia, in the autumn of 1942. This aeroplane was delivered to the RCAF on 20 July 1942 and it suffered a Category C accident on 4 February 1943 and survived a mid-air collision with Mk XII 5408 on 8 May 1943. Repaired on both occasions, it was replaced in frontline service by a Kittyhawk IV in August 1944 and eventually struck off charge and sold for scrap in June 1947. (Mark Peapell)

LEFT Although No 135 (F) Sqn had initially been led by Squadron Leader Ed Reyno, who had seen combat with No 1 Sqn RCAF during the Battle of Britain, he was soon replaced by fellow Battle of Britain pilot Squadron Leader William Connell (who served with both No 1 Sqn RCAF and No 32 Sqn). A seasoned combat veteran, Connell had also participated in the defence of Malta. (Mark Peapell)

materials notwithstanding, all Canadian Hurricanes had aluminium-covered wings, unlike the early Mk Is built in England. However, problems with obtaining a sufficient number of Merlin engines for aircraft that were subsequently retained in Canada for the RCAF were not rectified until the introduction of the Packard-built Merlin 28 and 29 in the autumn of 1941.

The first 40 Hurricane Is were followed by an order for a further 160 examples, built in five different batches. The bulk of these were shipped to Britain, where they were assigned as attrition replacements to various units, rather than en masse to any one squadron. The widespread distribution of CCF airframes was made possible by the interchangeability of the components between British- and Canadian-built Hurricane Is. Just 20 had reached Fighter Command prior to the Battle of Britain, however, and a number of them were lost during the bitter fighting that summer. The first of these is believed to have been P5185 of No 253 Sqn on 1 September 1940, which was shot down whilst engaging Do 17s and Bf 110s over Dungeness – its pilot, Pilot Officer John Clifton, was killed when the fighter crashed in Staplehurst. Later CCF Mk Is saw action in the defence of Malta and in ground-attack sorties and convoy patrols in the Middle East in 1941. By then all Canadian Hurricane Is had been redesignated Mk Xs so as to differentiate them from British-built examples.

ABOVE The vast majority of Canadian-built Hurricanes were fitted with Hamilton-Standard three-bladed metal propellers manufactured locally under license rather than the Rotol or de Havilland propellers favoured in Britain. The hub change mechanism for the American-designed propeller proved to be too large for the Rotol or de Havilland spinners so it was simply left uncovered. This unidentified Hurricane XII of No 135 (F) Sqn was photographed at Patricia Bay on 10 November 1942. (Mark Peapell)

RIGHT Mk XIIA BW881 wears a scheme that is representative of No 135 (F) Sqn aircraft 5429 of Western Command, complete with a Disney-inspired bulldog emblem on the left side of its nose. The latter was the official squadron emblem, the bulldog motif being a modified version of one created by Disney Studios for the USAAF's 62nd Fighter Squadron of the 56th Fighter Group.

Mk XIIA BW881 was the fifth
Hurricane returned to airworthy
status by HRL, the fighter being
acquired by the Flying Heritage
Collection from Sir Tim Wallis
of the Alpine Fighter Collection
as part of a package including a
Bf 109E, I-16 and Spitfire FVB. Still
being worked on when it was
bought, BW881 made its first flight,
from Wattisham, in the hands of
Stu Goldspink on 15 March 2006.

'King', one of No 135 (F) Sqn's two British bulldog mascots, walks along the wing root of a Hurricane at Mossbank. According to the squadron diary, on 5 August 1942 'The Squadron Mascot, a British bull pup, as purchased today in Regina, Saskatchewan, to be known as Cpl Piccadilly Regina, Regimental No 166762, nicknamed "King". "King" reported by air from Regina, Saskatchewan, at 1200 hrs today, and he is entitled to Rations and Quarters, effective the same date.' (Mark Peapell)

The broadness of the Hurricane's wing is readily apparent from this near head-on view of BW881. Sydney Camm chose to adapt tried and tested wing spars of bulbous steel polygonal section. He strengthened the Hurricane's flying surfaces through building the wing spars into a frame, which was then braced and stiffened by diagonal drag members that ran in zigzag fashion between the top and bottom spars. They were bolted to the spars via strong forgings, which were in turn fastened to the spar booms by horizontal bolts.

Just as with the parent company in England, CCF shifted production to the improved Hurricane II from early 1941. Both this later variant, known as the Mk XII, and the earlier Mk X could be fitted with Packard Merlins from Detroit – the Merlin 28 for the Mk X and the Merlin 29 for the Mk XII. The Hurricane XII also had 12 Browning 0.303-in machine guns, four more than the Mk X – this 'up-gunning' was unique to CCF aircraft. A number of Mk Xs were modified once in Britain, becoming Sea Hurricane IAs with catapult spools but no arrester hook for use from catapult ships, and Sea Hurricane IBs with spools and an arrester hook for carrier deck operations. Some were re-engined as Mk IIA/B/Cs, also being equipped with universal wings, a variety of armament and the ability to carry underwing stores.

The vast majority of the Hurricane XIIs remained in Canada, although some airframes devoid of engines, instruments and armament were shipped to Britain and fitted with Merlin XXs and either 12-machine gun or four-cannon wings. Those Hurricanes completed by CCF and issued to the RCAF were sent to either coast to serve with Eastern and Western Commands. BW881 was one such aircraft, being delivered to No 118 (F) Sqn of Eastern Command at Dartmouth, Nova Scotia, in January 1942. Its subsequent operational history is detailed in Chapter Sixteen: Hurricane Survivors. The aeroplane wears a scheme that is representative

BW881 was built as a Sea Hurricane I with eight-gun wings, a Merlin III engine and de Havilland propeller – hence the spinner. Originally intended for use by the FAA, it was fitted with catapult spools and an arrester hook, together with general strengthening. The first aircraft from this 50-strong production went to the RAF's Merchant Ship Fighter Unit in November 1941. However, following the Japanese strike on Pearl Harbor on 7 December 1941, all but two were transferred to RCAF charge to be issued to East Coast units to help plug gaps in the Canadian fighter defence caused by aircraft being transferred to the West Coast to face what was believed to be an impending Japanese attack.

ABOVE No 135 (F) Sqn's newly arrived Hurricane XIIs bask in the warm sunshine at Mossbank, Saskatchewan, in July 1942. Parked behind 5405 is 5418, which was involved in a fatal mid-air collision with 5419 on 30 May 1943 during a formation low flying exercise in British Columbia. The propeller of 5418 cut off the tailplane of 5419, causing the latter machine to dive into the water near Sydney Island. Despite its near destruction, 5418 survived the war and now is beautifully restored at the Reynolds-Alberta Museum at Wetaskiwin, Alberta – home of Canada's Aviation Hall of Fame. (Mark Peapell)

LEFT As with all HRL restorations, the cockpit of BW881 has been rebuilt using as many genuine 'fixtures and fittings' as possible. Current Virgin Galactic Chief Test Pilot and former Shuttleworth Collection pilot David Mackay felt that the cockpit of the Hurricane was 'disorganised – wherever you looked you saw controls. At first it looked as if it had been thrown together. You'd have to be careful not to drop anything, because you wouldn't get it back. Once you became more familiar with the cockpit, everything fell pretty much into place.'

of No 135 (F) Sqn aircraft 5429 of Western Command, complete with a Disney-inspired bulldog emblem on the left side of its nose. The latter was the official squadron emblem, the bulldog motif being a modified version of one created by Disney Studios for the USAAF's 62nd Fighter Squadron of the 56th Fighter Group – the unit, and emblem, still exist today within the modern USAF, the squadron training future F-35 Lightning II pilots at Luke AFB, Arizona.

No 135 (F) Sqn was one of a number of Home War Effort (HWE) defensive fighter units hastily established once Canada entered World War 2, these squadrons being stationed on either coast. Typically, they would be manned by a mix of newly trained pilots and combat veterans who had been sent home on a rest posting after completing a tour overseas. Frequently, pilots new to HWE squadrons had no flying time in Hurricanes at all, and the units would therefore double as OTUs that quickly got them up to speed. The experienced pilots on rest tours would instruct their novice squadron mates on operational tactics, general flying and the fighting skills they had learned following time in the frontline on the Channel front, on Malta or in North Africa. Later in the war, when the RCAF's Hurricane OTU at Bagotville, Quebec, was up and running, pilots sent to HWE fighter squadrons had already spent several weeks at 'finishing school', known as the Advanced Tactical Training Detachment. Of the pilots graduating from the Hurricane OTU, roughly half would be posted immediately overseas and the remainder went to HWE units on either coast.

No 135 (F) Sqn was formed at Mossbank, Saskatchewan, as part of No 4 Training Command on 15 June 1942 – just six months after the Japanese attack on Pearl Harbor. A total of nine HWE units would fly CCF Hurricanes, those in Western Command being charged with providing air defence against possible attacks by Japanese carrier-based aircraft. Sister-squadron No 133 (F) Sqn was formed at Lethbridge, Alberta, at the same time. Most of No 135 (F) Sqn's initial cadre of aircraft came directly from CCF's Fort William factory between 8 July and

10 August 1942, the unit having 24 Hurricanes on strength (along with four Harvards) by the latter date. No 135 (F) Sqn moved to Patricia Bay, near Victoria in British Columbia, in September 1942. Squadron Leader Ed Reyno, who had experienced combat with No 1 RCAF Sqn during the Battle of Britain, had overseen the stand-up, recruitment and assembly of the unit's pilots, although he was soon replaced by fellow Battle of Britain pilot Squadron Leader William Connell. A seasoned combat veteran, Connell, had also participated in the defence of Malta.

No 135 (F) Sqn would remain at Patricia Bay until August 1943, when the unit moved its Hurricanes and personnel to Annette Island, Alaska. Three months later the squadron was transferred to Terrace, British Columbia, before returning to Patricia Bay in March 1944. In May of that year No 135 (F) Sqn transitioned to Kittyhawk IVs, having by then become the last unit in Western Command to still be equipped with Hurricanes. The CCF aircraft were eventually sent by rail to eastern Canada for overhaul or placed directly in storage.

CCF Hurricane Mk XII 5584 was selected for preservation by the RCAF at the end of the war, with the remainder being disposed of from various military depots across Canada. Most of these aircraft were unceremoniously scrapped, but others were acquired by farmers, who found varied agricultural uses for their parts. During the early 1960s, Canadian and American aviation enthusiasts started collecting Hurricane parts from farms, scrapyards and crash sites across the country, and most of today's surviving CCF airframes can be traced back to these 'barn finds'.

The colour scheme chosen for BW881 upon the completion of its restoration is representative of RCAF Hurricane XII 5429, which served with No 135 (F) 'Bulldog' Sqn, a Canadian Home Defence unit formed at Mossbank, Saskatchewan, in June 1942 as part of Western Air Command, and which was disbanded at Patricia Bay, British Columbia, in September 1945. BW881 was shipped to Arlington, Washington, in August 2006, from where it moved to the Flying Heritage Collection's new home at Paine Field, in Everett, Washington. The fighter is routinely flown from here during the summer months.

# CHAPTER FOURTEEN

# FINNISH STORM

One of the lesser known users of the Hurricane was Finland, which received just 11 examples – ten Mk Is and a solitary Mk II – between March 1940 and May 1944. All the Hurricane Is were supplied by the British government, whilst the Mk II was a Soviet Air Force example that ran out of fuel and crash-landed on the ice of Lake Topozero on the Finnish side of the frontline in February 1942 following aerial combat.

One of the lesser-known users of the Hurricane was Finland, which flew a total of just 11 examples – ten Mk Is and a solitary Mk II – between March 1940 and May 1944. All the Hurricane Is were supplied by the British government, whilst the Mk II was a Soviet Air Forces example that ran out of fuel and crash-landed on the ice of Lake Topozero on the Finnish side of the frontline in February 1942 following aerial combat. Although the latter aircraft – coded HC-465 in Finnish service – was scrapped post-war, in 2014 newly restored Sea Hurricane IB BW874 was temporarily painted in its markings by then owner Phil Lawton, who is married to a Finn and lives in Helsinki. He then had the aeroplane flown from England to northern Finland in August 2014 so that the fighter could participate in the Tour de Sky international airshow held in the city of Oulu.

The Hurricane's history in Finnish skies goes back to late 1939 when, on 30 November, the Winter War broke out between Finland and its neighbour, the USSR. The conflict centred on Finland's refusal to agree to Soviet demands for military bases on Finnish territory and a 'readjustment' of the border on the Karelian Isthmus – the latter would have effectively seen the Mannerheim Line (Finland's main line of defence against the USSR) surrendered to Soviet forces. At that time the USSR was allied to Germany, so the British and French governments agreed to supply Finland with weapons to help in its fight against the communist aggressors.

An order for 12 Hurricane Is was duly agreed on 2 February 1940, with the aircraft being drawn from stocks held by Nos 5 and 20 Maintenance Units (MUs). The fighters, which were all built by Hawker as part of its second Hurricane contract for the

Personnel from the Hurricane flight Detachment 'Kalaja' of LLv 32 pose in front of HC-456 at Lappeenranta in early August 1941. They are, from left to right, Private Rosengren, Corporals Kuusisto and Kärki, Private Porkka, Corporals Karvonen, Sopanen and Nykänen, Second Lieutenant Ruotsila, Staff Sergeant Aikala, First Lieutenant Koponen, Mechanic Naukkarinen, Captain Kalaja, Sergeant Jutila, First Lieutenant Taskinen, Sergeant Suominen, Corporal Tuominen and Warrant Officers Pajas and Soininen. (Kari Stenman)

Air Ministry, had cost the Finns £9,875 each. According to Hurricane historian Frank Mason, these aeroplanes had originally been sold to Poland in the summer of 1939, and they were in transit when Germany invaded on 1 September. The crated fighters were returned to Britain and placed in storage with Nos 5 and 20 MUs, from where they were selected by the Finns. Twelve Finnish Air Force pilots, led by Lieutenant Antti Jussi Räty of *Lentolaivue* (LLv) 26, travelled to Britain to collect the fighters, the aviators receiving training on Hurricanes at No 11 Group Air Fighting School at St Athan, in Wales. Lieutenant Räty sent a progress report back to his superiors in Finland on 10 February after five days in Wales:

Flights at first in the American two-seat Harvard I trainer – 95 per cent of the power it generates transforms to sound; terrible noise – Brewster [Buffalo] is a mosquito compared to it – then on to the Hurricane except for two pilots, who didn't get the opportunity to fly HC [Hurricane] by 10 February. Flights gone well. The aeroplane is more comfortable than the FR [Fokker D.XXI, which the Finns hoped the Hurricane would replace in frontline service], and can manoeuvre without fear of 'fault'. Sensitive controls, especially flaps. Good stability. Firing programme in the second week. Ten–fifteen flight hours in all. If good weather, the course is finished in two weeks. A third week is reserved for departure, so there is time to receive our own aeroplanes. Flights in RAF aeroplanes only so far. Reception at Gloster factories. Planned departure is therefore 25 February.

On 21 February the Finnish pilots started collecting the 12 Hurricanes from Gloster's Brockworth factory, flying them in threes back to St Athan. The deal for these aircraft had in fact been done directly between Gloster and the Finnish government because the British government was anxious to avoid any confrontation with the USSR over the supply of aircraft to its enemy.

Once at the Welsh airfield, the Hurricane's machine guns were calibrated and loaded, radios tested and the aeroplanes taken aloft for an air test

RIGHT BW874 is actually painted in the colours of all-silver Canadian-built Hurricane AG244, which was operated by the Central Flying School of the Royal Rhodesian Air Force from Norton air base, Rhodesia, in 1945. The restored Hurricane took to the air at Thruxton for the first time on 16 July 2014, and just a few days later its colour scheme was put to the test when Peter and Faye Medley of Flying Colours Contracts Ltd applied this temporary Finnish Air Force camouflage scheme to represent Hurricane II HC-465.

BOTTOM RIGHT The scheme applied to BW874 was an accurate rendition of a late-war Finnish Hurricane; Flying Colours Contracts used the remarkably preserved HC-452 – originally built at Brooklands for the RAF as N2394 – in the Aviation Museum of Central Finland at Luonetjarvi air base as a guide. A veritable time capsule, the latter fighter retains most of its original paintwork.

BELOW All versions of the Hurricane had landing lamps fitted in the centre section of the leading edge of each wing. Each lamp has a completely independent electrical circuit which is controlled by two-way and OFF tumbler switches mounted at the extreme left corner of the instrument panel.

and gunnery firing over the Bristol Channel. Finally, the protective mesh over the carburettor air intake was removed to prevent it from freezing up in the cold conditions expected in Finland. On 25 February the first group of six aircraft departed St Athan for Finland, with overnight stops at Wick, in Scotland, Sola, in Norway, and Västerås Hässlö, in Sweden. The fighters would be escorted to Wick by an RAF Blenheim I, after which two Hudsons and a Sunderland flying boat would accompany them over the North Sea to Norway. One of the aeroplanes (HU-455) hit soft ground whilst taxiing at Västerås Hässlö, tipping it up on its nose and bending the propeller blades. All six aircraft would remain here for a week while the aeroplane was repaired by mechanics flown in from Britain.

On 28 February the second group of Hurricanes left St Athan, following the same route as the first. One of the aircraft (HU-461) ground-looped on landing at Wick and was never delivered to Finland. A second Hurricane (HU-462) was written off in a forced landing near Sola airfield on 2 March after its pilot became lost in thick fog – the remaining four got down safely, however. All ten surviving Hurricane Is eventually came together at Västerås Hässlö, where they waited for repairs to be completed on HU-455's damaged propeller, before pressing on to Finland. The aircraft that had crash-landed was taken to Stavanger, in Norway, where it was stripped

of useable parts (including four Browning 0.303-in machine guns). All ten aeroplanes reached Finland between 7 and 10 March.

The Hurricanes were initially assigned to Detachment Räty of LLv 22, flying from Säkylä, in south-west Finland. Soviet bombers attacked nearby Turku just prior to the Hurricanes' arrival there, so the fighters were kept on standby through to 13 March in case another attack was attempted. However, an armistice signed between the Finnish and Soviet governments that day meant the Hurricanes had arrived too late to see combat in the Winter War.

With their tailwheels replaced by snowskids to make the aircraft easier to operate from snow-covered airfields, the ten Hurricanes were subsequently transferred to LLv 28, which was primarily equipped with Morane-Saulnier MS.406s, on 27 May 1940. On 3 June one of the Hurricanes (HC-457 – the aircraft codes had been changed from HU- to HC- upon the fighters' arrival in Finland) was lost in a flying accident that killed Second Lieutenant Viljo Pinomaa. The remaining nine aircraft were transferred to LLv 30 on 29 August that same year, where they were flown alongside the unit's 25 D.XXIs. Despite an absence of spare parts, the Finns succeeded in keeping their small Hurricane force operational through to the start of the Continuation War with the USSR on

OPPOSITE HC-452, which is the aeroplane preserved in the Aviation Museum of Central Finland, was photographed at Tiiksjarvi airfield in the summer of 1942 covered in pine tree branches as camouflage to hide it from Soviet reconnaissance aircraft. Second Lieutenant Esko Ruotsila claimed two-and-a-half victories in this machine in 1941–42 whilst serving with LLv 32. (John Dibbs)

Also seen in Chapter One being refuelled whilst serving with No 1 Sqn in France as N2358, HC-454 of 2/LeLv 26 was photographed at Kilpasilta, on the Karelian Isthmus, having its reserve tank topped off in May 1943. The fighter, which bore the tactical number '4' on its rudder, survived more than three years of frontline service with the Finnish Air Force before being placed in storage just weeks after this shot was taken. (Kari Stenman)

RIGHT The last airworthy Hurricane in Finnish service was the solitary Mk II that had run out of fuel and crash-landed on the ice of Lake Topozero, near the White Sea, on 4 February 1942 following aerial combat. Mk IIB Z2585 was assigned to 152nd IAP, 103rd SAD of the Karelian Front Air Force, flying from Boyarskaya. Its pilot, Lieutenant F. G. Zadorozhniy, managed to escape and return to his unit, while the Hurricane was eventually repaired using parts from two other downed Soviet Mk IIs and impressed into service from 16 March 1944. (Kari Stenman)

25 June 1941, this time as a reluctant ally of Germany. Five Hurricanes were serving with the 1st Flight of LLv 30 at Hollola when the fighting erupted, and one of these aircraft (HC-453) was written off when it crashed on take-off on the opening day of the war – its pilot, Veikko Teuri, was killed.

On 1 July the flight was transferred to Utti and assigned to D.XXI-equipped LLv 32, five Hurricanes flying with Detachment Kalaja. The flight was given the task of intercepting enemy aircraft attempting to attack targets in south-eastern Finland. Twenty-four hours after the aircraft had arrived in Utti, one of the Hurricanes (HC-459) was shot at in error by a Finnish flak battery. The aeroplane caught fire as it was coming in to land at Utti and its pilot, Sergeant Lauri Suominen, was injured during the subsequent crash-landing that destroyed the Hurricane. On 3 July Second Lieutenant Esko Ruotsila, in HC-452, was leading a second Hurricane on a patrol over the Karelian Isthmus when he intercepted three I-153 Chaikas from 7th *Istrebitel'nyj Aviacionnyj Polk* (IAP – Fighter Air Regiment) near the border town of Enso. Two of the biplane fighters were shot down, thus giving the Hurricane its first aerial success with the Finns. The following day Captain Heikki Kalaja intercepted three DB-3 twin-engined bombers and shot one of them down too.

On 15 July Second Lieutenant Ruotsila was again in combat with I-153s from 7th IAP over the Karelian Isthmus in HC-452, as his combat report from this engagement recalled:

Air surveillance reported five fighters over Simola. We met a three-aeroplane patrol approaching from the east at an altitude of 1,000 m south of Simola. We attacked them with the sun at our backs. After the first pass Sgt [Päavo] Aikala and I separated from each other and engaged enemy aeroplanes individually. I saw one evading in the direction of Merijoki and chased it to Nurmi, at which point my engine started to run roughly. I turned back for home. A short while later I saw Sgt Aikala chasing an enemy aircraft towards Vilajoki. I turned towards them and the enemy aeroplane took evasive action. Sgt Aikala reported that he too was having problems

with his engine. When both aircraft were checked after we had landed, it was found that their superchargers had come loose, allowing oil to drain from the engines to the point where they were both almost dry. Simola observation post confirmed that two enemy aircraft had crashed after our first attacking pass.

On 19 August Detachment Kalaja sent three Hurricanes to Tiiksjarvi to form the 1st Flight of LLv 10 – a ground-attack and reconnaissance squadron equipped with Fokker C.VE and Blackburn Ripon biplanes and D.XXIs that worked closely with the Finnish Army's 14th Division. The Hurricane pilots exclusively flew reconnaissance missions with this unit since there were no Soviet aircraft to be found. On 16 September the flight suffered a serious blow when Captain Kalaja was shot down and killed in HC-458 whilst strafing Soviet troops – his was the only Finnish Hurricane that was ever lost to enemy action. The remaining two aeroplanes from Detachment Kalaja were flown to Suulajärvi a week later and returned to LLv 32. They were rarely flown from then on due to a lack of spares.

Nevertheless, on 8 January 1942, six Curtiss Hawk 75As (which had been issued to LLv 32 in May of the previous year) and a solitary Hurricane, flown by First Lieutenant Nurminen, engaged three I-15bis from 7th IAP over the Karelian Isthmus and shot all of them down near Leipäsuo. This proved to be the last aerial victory credited to the Hurricane, as the surviving airframes were subsequently grounded for long periods due to unserviceability. On 23 June 1942, two airworthy Hurricanes were passed on to the 2nd Flight of LLv 26, which was otherwise equipped with Fiat G.50s, at Malmi. A further three Hurricanes joined the unit shortly thereafter, and Staff Sergeant Päavo Aikala was killed when one of these aircraft (HC-455) crashed on 30 July. On 18 March 1943, the 2nd Flight was transferred to Kilpasilta, and two months later, two Hurricanes were placed in storage there when they could no longer be kept airworthy. Two more suffered this fate in July.

The last airworthy Hurricane in Finnish service was the solitary Mk II that had run out of fuel and

Stu Goldspink holds BW874 in position off the starboard wing of the cameraship as both aeroplanes perform a gentle banking turn to port during a late afternoon flight from Thruxton in the autumn of 2014.

crash-landed on the ice of Lake Topozero on 4 February 1942 following aerial combat. Mk IIB Z2585 was assigned to 152nd IAP, 103rd *Smešannaja Aviacionnaja Divizija* (SAD – Composite Aviation Division) of the Karelian Front Air Force, flying from Boyarskaya. Its pilot, Lieutenant F.G. Zadorozhniy, managed to escape and return to his unit, while the Hurricane was eventually repaired using parts from two other downed Soviet Mk IIs and impressed into service from 16 March 1944.

Originally delivered to the RAF in early 1941, Z2585 had flown with Nos 56 and 316 Sqns prior to becoming one of 3,360 Hurricanes supplied to the Soviet Union as part of the Lend-Lease agreement with Britain. The aircraft had been shipped to the USSR in December 1941.

Allocated the Finnish serial HC-465, Z2585 had fulfilled the fighter evaluation and target aircraft training roles for just ten weeks when it was grounded on 31 May 1944. All bar one (HC-452) of the surviving Hurricanes, including HC-465, were retired in the early autumn of 1944 and scrapped. HC-452 – originally built at Brooklands for the RAF as N2394 – is now preserved in the Aviation Museum of Central Finland at Luonetjarvi airbase, where a superb conservation effort has retained most of its original paintwork.

# CHAPTER FIFTEEN

# HURRICANE SPECTACULAR

LEFT Spitfire F IA X4650 and Hurricane Mk I R4118

BELOW Spitfire F VB AB910 and Hurricane Mk IIC LF363

Hurricane Mk IIC LF363

Hurricane Mk IIC PZ865

Hurricane Mk IIC PZ865

Hurricane Mk IV KZ321

Workers at Hawker's Langley factory crowd around the last Hurricane to leave the production line in September 1944. A Hurricane survivor, PZ865 still flies today as part of the Battle of Britain Memorial Flight. (Kent Ramsey)

# CHAPTER EIGHTEEN

# HURRICANE SURVIVORS

There are currently around 70 Hurricanes surviving worldwide, ranging from the superbly restored flying examples featured in this volume to conserved wreckage displayed in museums. This chapter gives detailed histories of the airworthy Hurricanes featured herein.

## HURRICANE I/IIA P3351/DR393

Jan Friso Roozen, Cannes–Mandelieu Airport, France

Unique as the only Hurricane to have seen action during the Battle of France and still be flying today, P3351 was the first of the HRL fighters to return to the sky when it was test-flown at Christchurch, in New Zealand, on 12 January 2000. Built as a Mk I at Brooklands by Hawker Aircraft Ltd as part of a batch of 500 Hurricanes ordered against Contract No 962371/38, the aircraft bore serials between P3265 and P3984, with P3351 falling into the second serial block (P3345–P3364). Powered by a 1,280 hp Merlin III (No 148156), it was allocated to No 5 MU at Kemble, in Wiltshire, on 28 March 1940 and taken on charge nine days later, having been designated as a Reserve Aircraft.

According to RAF records, P3351 was allocated to RAF Tangmere, in West Sussex, on 13 June 1940 and issued to No 73 Sqn five days later. It had actually been issued directly to No 73 Sqn as a replacement aircraft at the end of May, and this was probably an example of paperwork trying to keep up with events on the ground. At the outbreak of World War 2, Nos 1 and 73 Sqns had been the only two Hurricane units attached to the

AASF, which was despatched to France, with No 73's first base being Le Havre/Octeville. Following the German attack in May 1940, No 73 Sqn helped to cover Allied airfields and bases, retreating as its airfields were overrun by enemy troops. By the start of June the squadron was based at a temporary aerodrome on farmland at Gaye, south of Reims in the Champagne region, and P3351 flew a defensive patrol to Hautmont in the hands of Pilot Officer Peter Carter (Red Section of 'A' Flight) between 1010 hrs and 1120 hrs on 1 June 1940. At this time the squadron did not carry unit codes ('TP') on most of its aircraft, instead using individual aircraft letters – P3351 was coded 'K'.

On 1 June, No 73 Sqn was awaiting orders to move to a new base at Raudin, east of Le Mans, and the signal confirming that this would take place on the 3rd was received the following day. Doubts were expressed that the ground component of the AASF would be able to cover the 300 km distance without enemy interference, so the Hurricanes would provide air support from a temporary base at Échimenes. The first aircraft left for the latter site at 0430 hrs on 3 June, with two spare Hurricanes being flown directly to Le Mans. The day proved to be remarkably sunny and hot, and the ground convoy made excellent progress, arriving at the village of Raudin at 1800 hrs with the loss of just one vehicle due to a fire caused by a dropped match!

P3351 was one of the aircraft that operated from Échimenes, being ferried there by Pilot Officer Carter – he landed at 1815 hrs on 3 June. He also seems to have flown it from Gaye on a 2 hr 20 min defensive patrol over Reims four days later. The squadron ORB indicates that the aircraft moved between bases as operational requirements dictated, and were to be found flying from Gaye, Échimenes, Le Mans (Raudin), Saumur, Bagneux and Nantes throughout the remainder of the month. It has been suggested that P3351 was used by Squadron Leader J.W.C. More to fly from Le Mans to attend the funeral of Flight Lieutenant E.J. 'Cobber' Kain at Troyes on 8 June following his death in a flying accident at Échimenes the previous day, but this has not been substantiated.

No 73 Sqn's final base in France was Nantes, which it reached on 15 June in order to cover the retreating members of the AASF as part of Operation *Ariel*. P3351 was flown by Sergeant A.E. Scott a defensive patrol over the port of St Nazaire on the morning of 17 June. The squadron's final patrols were undertaken the following day, with Peter Carter flying P3351 three times: the first patrol was between 0440 hrs and 0550 hrs, the next between 1105 hrs and 1155 hrs and the last time was the dash home. Carter and P3351 left Nantes at 1415 hrs in a group led by Flight Lieutenant C.W.K. Nicholls, landing to refuel at Boscombe Down, in Wiltshire, before proceeding to Tangmere, where they received orders to move to Church Fenton, in North Yorkshire, finally arriving there that evening.

Most of the ground personnel had already left for St Nazaire to embark on the troop ship RMS *Lancastria*, together with the headquarters of British Air Forces in France and hundreds of other RAF personnel. No fewer than 38 members of the squadron were killed when the *Lancastria* was sunk by three bombs from a Ju 88 during the afternoon of 17 June. The remaining groundcrew, under the command of Flight Lieutenant Brown of No 67 Wing, set fire to the unserviceable Hurricanes left behind and escaped in a Bristol Bombay and Avro Anson – making No 73 Sqn the last RAF unit to leave France. This scene was famously recreated in the opening sequences of the film *The Battle of Britain*.

Following their arrival at Church Fenton, the squadron enjoyed a brief respite, with its personnel being given home leave and its surviving aircraft thoroughly overhauled – P3351 was repainted with its full squadron codes of 'TP-K' at this time. By 7 July, No 73 had resumed operations, however. Twelve days later, 'A' Flight flew to Prestwick, in Scotland, for night-flying experience. All went well until, in the early hours of Sunday 21 July, Sergeant Alf Scott undershot the runway in P3351, causing the undercarriage to collapse and tipping the aircraft onto its nose. That night saw three Hurricanes damaged (including another by Scott), and all were set aside for repair.

As the Battle of Britain developed in the south, P3351 underwent repairs at No 4 MU from 27 July, although the note 'Rolls-Royce' is made on its Movements Card so it is quite possible that the work was carried out at Hucknall, in Nottinghamshire, rather than Hanworth, in Middlesex, Rolls-Royce being part of the Hurricane Repair Organisation (HRO). By 27 August, P3351 was ready for despatch to No 22 MU at Silloth, in Cumbria, and on 6 September, complete with a replacement Merlin, it was allocated to No 32 Sqn at Acklington, in Northumberland. This unit had been transferred to No 13 Group on 27 August and tasked with convoy patrols and fighter cover, having had a torrid time 'down south' at Biggin Hill, in Kent.

For three months, P3351 was flown mainly by Pilot Officer Jack Rose over north-eastern England until 16 December, when No 32 Sqn moved south to Middle Wallop, in Hampshire, as part of No 10 Group. Within five days, P3351 was reassigned to the American volunteers of No 71 'Eagle' Sqn based at Kirton-in-Lindsey, in north Lincolnshire, under the command of Squadron Leader Walter M. Churchill, probably flying directly from its old base at Acklington the few miles south to join the unit. It would have been coded 'XR-' but records are incomplete for this period. Although P3351 arrived on 21 December 1940, its first recorded flight with No 71 Sqn was not until 16 February 1941. On 10 March, P3351 was one of two Hurricanes that undertook a patrol over the Humber Estuary, but on returning in the early evening, Pilot Officer Kenneth Samson-Taylor crashed on landing and damaged P3351.

After a month undergoing repairs, the Hurricane rejoined its unit on 18 April 1941, which by then was based at Martlesham Heath, near Ipswich, in Suffolk, ready for further operational flying. However, by the beginning of May, new Hurricane IIAs had begun to arrive as replacement aircraft, and P3351 was transferred to No 55 OTU at Usworth, near Sunderland, where it would have taken up a unit code commencing 'PA-'. No sooner had it arrived than on 13 May 1941, Polish flying instructor Sergeant Stanislaw Karubin flew it into some high-tension power lines. Fortunately, he managed to land safely at Ouston, in Northumberland, where the damaged wing leading edge was repaired on-site. P3351 also received a new engine – presumably the propeller or reduction gear had been affected by impact with the power cables. It is interesting to note that when the wreck was recovered from Russia, it was found to carry Polish red and white chequerboard markings on both the port and starboard cowlings – probably added when being flown by Karubin or other Polish pilots at Usworth.

Upon P3351's return to Usworth, two remarkable coincidences occurred. Student Pilot Officer William Miller, from Invercargill, New Zealand, flew the aircraft twice. 'Dusty' Miller was to retire to Wanaka, New Zealand, where decades later he would be reunited with P3351, acting until his death as a guide at the New Zealand Fighter Pilots Museum, where he was especially proud to show visitors 'his' Hurricane. Meanwhile, on 9 September 1941, another Invercargill pilot, Sergeant Ness Polson was flying P3351 on an evening training mission when – officially – the Merlin engine overheated and seized. Polson carried out a wheels-up landing in a field near Headingley, Leeds. Unofficially, it seems that Polson was competing with his wingman to see how low each could fly – Polson won, flying low enough to hit a hedge, which precipitated the forced-landing!

This ended P3351's RAF flying career, the fighter being allocated to Rolls-Royce at Hucknall on 16 September 1941 for a Repair in Works (RIW). It was upgraded to Mk IIA Series 2 specification with a Merlin XX engine as part of a batch of 40 aircraft being prepared for shipping to Russia under the Lend-Lease programme. As part of the upgrade it was given a new serial, DR393. Whether all of the work took place at Rolls-Royce is not clear, as it seems to have passed from one facility to another with notes on its Form 78 as Repaired and Awaiting Allocation (RAAA) on 8 November, allocated to No 51 MU (at Lichfield, in Staffordshire), a storage/packing unit, on 20 November, then further modifications at works (location not specified) on 23 January 1942, another RAAA comment on 14 February, allocated to No 29 MU (at High Ercall, in Shropshire) on 20 February and then on to the Packing Unit at No 52 MU, in Cardiff, on 9/10 March, before finally being taken by road to the Port of Glasgow.

On 3 May 1942, accompanied by 23 other Hurricanes, it was loaded onboard the SS *Ocean Voice* and the vessel sailed with Convoy PQ 16 for Murmansk, in northern Russia. Routed via Iceland, PQ 16 was subjected to incessant aerial attack as the convoy approached its destination. The *Ocean Voice* suffered serious bomb damage that opened a 20-ft hole barely 2 ft above its waterline and set the ship on fire. Miraculously, it managed to berth safely at Murmansk, Convoy PQ 16 having lost 'only' 770 vehicles, 147 tanks and 77 aircraft during the voyage – a success by Arctic Convoy standards at that time.

Once in Russian hands, DR393 was quickly unloaded and re-assembled. It then flew in Soviet service – cannon-armed – for the following year. No operational details have been located but it would undoubtedly have been used in combat against the Luftwaffe in the northern sector of the Eastern Front. It is believed that the aeroplane ultimately crashed in the winter of 1943. During the restoration a 7.9 mm copper-jacketed projectile was found lodged in the oil-cooler, having passed through the radiator from the lower face. Possibly ground fire, it is certain that this was the bullet which brought the aeroplane down.

The Hurricane's very substantial remains were recovered in 1991. Following temporary display at Archangel in September 1992 as part of the 'Dervish 91' celebrations to mark the 50th anniversary of the arrival of PQ 16, they were brought to the UK by Sussex-based Jim Pierce before being purchased by New Zealand-based aviation enthusiast Sir Tim Wallis. Sir Tim's joint HRL venture undertook the rebuilding of the fuselage, while the wings were sub-contracted to Airframe Assemblies at Sandown, on the Isle of Wight. Air New Zealand Engineering Services (ANZES) reached agreement with Sir Tim Wallis to participate in the restoration project from its base in Christchurch, and the rebuild programme progressed under the company's stringent ANZES

Quality Management System. The original Hurricane Type Data had been located and agreement was made not to deviate from these design specifications, with full engineering design support provided by ANZES's Technical Services.

The Hurricane's tube-framed fuselage construction is – though essentially simple – quite sophisticated and demands special tooling. Tony Ditheridge gained access to the original equipment needed to form the 12-sided steel tube stock used in the construction of the fuselage, wing centre section, fin and tailplane spars. ANZES salvaged many parts from the original airframe, which were then shipped to HRL for restoration and inclusion in the rebuilt structure. Having thoroughly researched the history of this particular airframe, it was decided to restore the fighter as P3351 – making it the only airworthy Hurricane that had fought in the Battle of France, although the airframe still retains its Mk IIA configuration and is powered by a post-war Merlin 35 (as fitted to the Boulton Paul Balliol). This engine has the advantage of having a pre-oiler and other features that extend its Time Between Overhaul life considerably when compared with the Merlin XX.

In late 1995, the restored fuselage and empennage, centre section and wings were returned to New Zealand for completion by ANZES. Many enthusiastic individuals and organizations contributed to P3351's completion. The radiator core was made by Replicore in Whangarei, New Zealand, and the casing and assembly by Auto Restorations in Christchurch. The propeller hub was secured by the Alpine Fighter Collection, the complex wooden propeller blades were made by Hoffman of Germany and Dowty Rotol approved Skycraft Ltd in Britain to make the remainder of the parts and to overhaul and test the completed propeller. The Croydon Aircraft Company in Mandeville, New Zealand, applied the fabric fuselage covering at ANZES. The outer wings were re-attached in early 1998 and by December 1998, P3351 was ready for painting.

In late 1999, the Merlin 35 was started up at Christchurch Airport and in early January 2000, P3351 was ready to fly. The civil registration

ZK-TPL bore testimony to its codes when serving with No 73 Sqn – although the paint scheme chosen only replicated the single 'K' individual aircraft letter and large red/white/flue rudder markings that were applied in France to counter attacks by French forces. The undersurfaces were finished with one wing black and the other silver, as worn by RAF fighters during the first six months of 1940.

The first post-restoration flight took place on 12 January 2000, with P3351 taking pride of place in Sir Tim Wallis's collection at Wanaka. Flying on numerous occasions at the prestigious Warbirds Over Wanaka airshow, the aeroplane was finally advertised for sale following Sir Tim's decision to

close his collection. Fittingly, it eventually found a new home in France, leaving New Zealand by ship on 10 February 2013. The fighter was assembled at Dijon-Darois by Bruno Ducreux's Aero Restauration Service for owner Jan Friso Roozen, who bases it, now registered as F-AZXR, at Cannes–Mandelieu Airport, in south-east France. The aeroplane made its British airshow debut at the Flying Legends airshow at Duxford in July 2013, and returned for this event the following year. In May 2015, the Hurricane suffered a landing accident at its base, but the fighter returned to the air during 2016 following extensive repairs, which were carried out by Aero Restauration Service.

# HURRICANE I R4118

Hurricane Heritage, Old Warden, Bedfordshire, England

Restored in its original markings as worn while in service with No 605 Sqn, R4118 is presently the world's only airworthy Hurricane to have seen service in the Battle of Britain – let alone scored victories in it. Furthermore, the aircraft is probably the most authentic Hurricane of them all, as it is still powered by its original Merlin III engine and is armed with its original (deactivated) Browning 0.303-in machine guns, in addition to a host of internal fittings such as a TR 9 radio and Identification Friend or Foe (IFF) equipment.

Peter Vacher first set eyes on R4118 in March 1982 when he and a friend, John Fasal, were searching for historic Rolls-Royce motor cars in India. During a visit to Banaras Hindu University, the pair stumbled across two derelict aircraft, one of which Peter assumed to be a Spitfire. Eleven years later Peter showed a photograph of the aircraft to his wife's flying instructor – Pete Thorn, once a pilot with the BBMF – who immediately pointed out that the 'Spitfire' was in fact a Hurricane! Having personally restored ten vintage cars, including four Rolls-Royces, Peter decided to attempt to acquire the mystery Hurricane and have it restored to fly, and to that end he arrived in Banaras – now known as Varanasi – on 5 January

1996. The story of how Peter managed to buy the Hurricane and return it to England is the subject of a book in itself, *Hurricane R4118*, written by Peter and published in 2005.

R4118 was built as a Mk I at Brockworth by the Gloster Aircraft Company (a subsidiary of Hawker Aircraft Ltd) as part of a batch of 100 Hurricanes ordered against Contract No 19773/39. The aircraft were allocated serials between R4074 and R4232, with R4118 forming part of the first block (R4074–R4123). Powered by a 1,280 hp Merlin III (No 24927 – incredibly, this engine was still installed in the airframe when found), it was flown from Brockworth to No 22 MU at Silloth between 18 and 23 July 1940. Following preparation for service use, it joined its first unit, No 605 'County of Warwick' Sqn at Drem, in Scotland, on 17 August, where the unit was 'resting' following a period of intense activity. This had included the loss of its CO, Squadron Leader G.V. Perry, whilst covering the BEF withdrawal from France from a temporary base at Hawkinge, in Kent, during May. The squadron flew south to Croydon, rejoining No 11 Group, on 7 September, with R4118 being flown by Pilot Officer (later Wing Commander, DSO, DFC and Bar) C.F. 'Bunny' Currant – who

R4118 'JU-J' at rear serving with No 111 Sqn based at Montrose, in Ayrshire. This photograph was taken on 9 March 1941, with Sergeant John Stein at the controls of R4118. (Peter Vacher)

dropped in to Abingdon to refuel en route. 'Bunny' was to provide many details and stories about R4118 to Peter Vacher during the restoration of 'his' old Hurricane prior his death in March 2006 at the age of 95, some 15 months after it had returned to the skies following restoration.

Once the squadron arrived at Croydon it was thrown into the thick of the Battle of Britain, R4118 being flown by the CO, Squadron Leader Walter M. Churchill, on 9 September when Flight Lieutenant Archie McKellar, leading 'B' Flight, picked off three He 111s in a single attack. Churchill had earlier led his section in to draw off the fighter escort and had his knee grazed by a bullet – sending him spinning out of formation. Churchill was injured by a bullet in his arm two days later on 11 September, and R4118 was then turned over to Pilot Officer 'Jock' Muirhead. On 24 September, Muirhead shared a 'Do 215' with Pilot Officer Witold Glowacki – who did not return and was posted as missing. Muirhead himself was killed in action on 15 October, on which date R4118 was air-tested by Pilot Officer Alec Scott and, starting on 26 September, it became the regular

mount of Pilot Officer J.A. 'Archie' Milne, a Scots Canadian who had volunteered for the RAF in May 1939 and joined No 605 Sqn in August 1940. The next day, 27 September, 'Archie' downed a Bf 110 in R4118. Other pilots who flew R4118 at the time included Pilot Officer (later Wing Commander, DFC) Bob Foster, who damaged a Ju 88 on 28 September and shared another on 1 October. Bob was another of the pilots to be reunited with his old Hurricane during the restoration process, and he wrote the foreword to Peter Vacher's book. Bob died on 30 July 2014, aged 94.

Pilot Officer (later Wing Commander, DFC) Alec Ingle flew R4118 just once, but it was his logbook entry for that flight which confirmed the individual squadron code letter worn by the fighter. Alec had written 'W' alongside R4118, confirming the full code as UP-W – letters which now grace the restored Hurricane once again. Another ace to fly R4118 was none other than Pilot Officer (later Group Captain, DFC) Peter Thompson who, when serving as Commanding Officer of Biggin Hill in 1957, managed to secure the RAF's last airworthy

Hurricane, LF363, as the very first aircraft of what developed into the BBMF.

R4118's luck ran out on 22 October when 12 Hurricanes took off from Croydon at 1411 hrs to patrol Kenley and Biggin Hill at 20,000 ft ('angels 20'). A dogfight with a group of Bf 109s broke out to the east of Tonbridge at 22,000 ft, and R4118, flown by Flying Officer Derek Forde as 'Yellow 1', sustained Cat 2 damage (beyond repair at site). In less than two months, it had flown 49 sorties with 11 different pilots and had been directly or partially responsible for the destruction of five enemy aircraft.

The Hurricane was despatched to the Service Aircraft Section of the Austin Motor Company at Longbridge, in Birmingham, on 23 October, Austin being part of the HRO – R4118 was one of 13 Hurricanes it repaired that year. Austin also built 300 Hurricane IIBs, virtually all of which were shipped to Russia, one of which (AP740) survives as a static museum exhibit in Moscow. R4118 was ready for collection by 17 December, when it was allocated to No 18 MU at Dumfries, in Scotland. The aeroplane remained here in storage until issued to No 111 Sqn on 18 January 1941. The unit was 'resting' at Aberdeen (Dyce) at the time, R4118 being assigned to 'A' Flight and ferried to the detached base at Montrose on 3 February by the squadron commander, Squadron Leader A.J. Biggar.

No 111 Sqn was acting as a training unit at the time, and no fewer than 11 pilots flew it over the next eight weeks, with the aircraft itself making up to seven sorties in a single day. In service with No 111 Sqn, R4118 was coded 'JU-J' and Peter Vacher tracked down the family of one of its pilots – another Canadian, 'Skid' Hanes – who were able to provide an air-to-air photograph of him flying R4118 from Montrose on 9 March 1941. Alongside its training role, the squadron took part in sorties against raids mounted from German bases in Norway, R4118 participating in one on 24 March whilst being flown by Sergeant W. Seaman.

On 26 April, R4118 was posted to join No 59 OTU at Crosby-on-Eden, in Cumbria. This unit, by coincidence, was commanded by Alec Ingle, who had flown the aircraft once during the Battle of Britain with No 605 Sqn. It survived the hazardous

life of an advanced training aircraft unscathed until 7 October, when New Zealander Sergeant (later Flight Lieutenant) F.J.M. Palmer hit a lorry at the end of his landing run at Longtown, in Cumbria, which was a satellite airfield for No 59 OTU. Peter Vacher contacted Palmer in Auckland and he recounted how the wind had changed direction, causing the runway to be switched, but that a contractor's vehicle somehow strayed onto the active runway. The damage was sufficient for R4118 to be despatched to Taylorcraft at Rearsby, in Leicestershire – a major contractor within the HRO, which repaired 64 Hurricanes during 1941 alone. When the airframe was being surveyed prior to restoration, a Taylorcraft inspection stamp was found on the rudder.

It was repaired and awaiting collection by 12 December, and ten days later it had been allocated to No 44 MU at Edzell, in Angus, Scotland, where it was initially stored. During a test flight on 23 February 1942, R4118 swung on landing and was damaged when it hit a snow bank. The accident was put down to insufficient brake pressure having built up in the pneumatic system and the damage was repaired on site by a civilian contractor starting on 1 March, with the Hurricane back on charge by 1 April.

Its next unit was No 56 OTU at Tealing, north of Dundee, to which it was allocated on 24 May and where it probably served mainly on air gunnery training – possibly even acting as a target tug, as well as firing live ammunition at towed drogue targets. R4118 survived unscathed for a further 11 months until it was allocated to David Rosenfield Ltd, part of the HRO, which received it at Barton, in Manchester, on 5 April 1943. During the overhaul/repair, the company placed a stamped aluminium plate over the top of the original Hawker Aircraft Ltd brass constructors' plate, and both were still in place in the cockpit when the aircraft was recovered from India, confirming the identity beyond question as R4118. Oddly enough, the plates on both wings indicate that they were manufactured by CCF at Fort William (now Thunder Bay), in Ontario, and rebuilt or repaired in Derby in the workshops of the London, Midland & Scottish Railway Company. Whether they were fitted during repairs carried out by Austin Motors, David Rosenfield or Taylorcraft cannot be established. Other components came from a variety of subcontractors.

The repaired and rebuilt R4118 was awaiting collection from Barton on 28 May 1943 and it was despatched to No 5 MU at Kemble, in Wiltshire, on 16 June as one of a batch of 203 Hurricanes received that month that were to be overhauled and sent to Air Command, South East Asia (ACSEA) as training aircraft for Indian pilots. The Japanese army had invaded Burma and was advancing towards India, so the plan was to boost pilot numbers in the region by sending war-weary Hurricanes to ACSEA for use as trainers. On 11 November, R4118 was sent to the Packing Unit of No 52 MU at Cardiff, where it was crated; by 12 December, the aeroplane was on board the cargo ship SS *Singkep*, a 6,607-ton Dutch merchantman built in 1924. Following a perilous journey at just 12 knots, R4118 reached the Aircraft Erection Unit at Santa Cruz, in Bombay (Mumbai), India, between 6 and 12 February 1944. Being a relatively ancient Mk I, it remained in its packing crate and, following an order issued in July 1944, was Converted to Ground Instructional on 4 October, being finally Struck Off Charge on 1 January 1947.

How and when it was moved from Santa Cruz to Banaras Hindu University – a distance of approximately 1,500 km – to be utilized as an instructional aid is not recorded, but move it certainly did. In the event, the aircraft was simply removed from its crate and left in the open until Peter Vacher was lucky enough to stumble upon it some 40-odd years later.

After tortuous negotiations, the aircraft finally returned to the UK in July 2001. Having been removed from its shipping container, it was reunited with several of its former pilots at the Oxfordshire home of Peter and Polly Vacher. The gathering also included the families of many pilots, as well as Test Pilot Duncan Simpson, who had flown PZ865 when owned by Hawker Siddeley and the Strathallan Collection's example, G-AWLW, which was subsequently destroyed in a hangar fire at Hamilton, Ontario, in February 1993.

R4118 was placed on the UK civil aircraft register in August 2001 as G-HUPW (a reference to its code letters with No 605 Sqn). The initial work of stripping the airframe was carried out in Peter's own workshop, with new and repaired parts being provided by HRL. Much preparation and bead-blasting was carried out in Oxfordshire and as many original components and fittings as possible were renovated, but – as with all airworthy Hurricane restorations – the steel tubing was remanufactured using modern equivalents. The wings were rebuilt in Bob Cunningham's specialist workshop in Bournemouth, the stripped fuselage was shipped to HRL in Suffolk in January 2002 and the Merlin III was despatched to Maurice Hammond's Eye Tech Engineering at Eye, in Suffolk. Many detailed components and sub-assemblies were provided by Guy Black, and a Griffon engine – purchased from the university at the same time as the Hurricane – was exchanged for a Rotol propeller hub with Stephen Grey of The Fighter Collection. New blades were made by Hoffman in Germany and the whole propeller was assembled by Mike Barnett of Skycraft Services Ltd, Andrew Wood of P & A Wood having come up with a constant speed unit.

The aircraft was assembled in the Suffolk workshops of HRL, the paint scheme being applied by Clive Denny of Vintage Fabrics. The aircraft was finally taken by road to Cambridge Airport, where Terry Holloway of Marshalls had offered hangarage and flight test facilities. The great day finally came on 23 December 2004 when, despite a wind gusting to 25 knots, Pete Kynsey lifted the Hurricane off the ground on its first flight since 1943. Three weeks later on 13 January 2005, R4118 made its official launch flight in front of an invited audience including families of World War 2 pilots Peter Thompson, Denis Winton, Walter Churchill and Alec Ingle. Also in attendance for this historical flight was Bob Foster, who had flown nine operational sorties on R4118.

The fighter made its home at Kidlington Airport, near to Peter and Polly Vacher's Oxfordshire home, until 29 September 2015 when it was sold to software entrepreneur James Brown who has set up a new organization called Hurricane Heritage operating from Old Warden aerodrome, home of the Shuttleworth Collection. Here it shares a hangar with the collection's own Hurricane, Z7015, and several other Hawker aircraft.

# SEA HURRICANE IB Z7015

The Shuttleworth Collection, Old Warden, Bedfordshire, England

During 1938, the British and Canadian governments reached an agreement to begin licensed production of the Hurricane in Canada. Production was undertaken by CCF at Fort William and was helped by the delivery of a pattern aircraft (L2144) together with two sets of production drawings on microfilm (a total of 82,000 individual items). The first Canadian Hurricane, P5170, completed its maiden flight on 10 January 1940 and a further 1,450 examples were built, although only 1,449 unique serials have been confirmed.

The first 40 Canadian Hurricanes were built to Contract No 964753/38 as Hurricane Is, with serials P5170–P5209, and were delivered to Britain by sea between March and July 1940. P5170 was tested at Brooklands, in Farnborough, and at Boscombe Down between March and August 1940, Group Captain 'Sammy' Wroath flying it several times between 17 July and 3 August 1940 at Boscombe Down. The aircraft were assembled at No 13 MU at

Henlow, in Bedfordshire, and issued to RAF squadrons starting in September 1940. Two further batches of Mk Is were delivered, 20 aircraft with serials between T9519 and T9538 and 100 aircraft with serials between Z6983 and Z7162, which were broken down into three blocks – Z6983–Z7017 (35), Z7049–Z7093 (45) and Z7143–Z7162 (20).

The vast majority of these 160 aircraft were delivered to the UK without engines. Those that did have them would have been fitted with UK-manufactured Rolls-Royce Merlin IIIs, as Canada had opted not to put the engine into production. It is estimated that about one in ten Canadian Mk Is were flight-tested before despatch to the UK – oddly enough, Z7015 was one of them. Many of these aircraft were later converted to Sea Hurricane IB configuration – including Z7015.

Z7015 was ordered against Contract No BSB 166 and carries the construction number CCF/41H/4013, making it the oldest surviving

Z7105 was only used for static scenes during the making of *The Battle of Britain* in the summer of 1968 (it is seen here at Duxford on 28 July that year), the Hurricane's serviceable Rotol propeller having been fitted to Spitfire LF XVI TB382. (Gary R. Brown collection)

Canadian-built Hurricane. Although allocated to No 13 MU at Henlow on 30 July 1940, this was simply a paperwork exercise as it did not make its first test flight until 18 January 1941, at the CCF plant at Fort William in the hands of V.J. Hatton, who took it up for 35 minutes at 0920 hrs. Due to the ground temperature that day being -20°C, part of the oil-cooler had to be blanked off. The same pilot made a further 20-minute flight at 1400 hrs that afternoon.

Originally built as a Merlin III-powered Hurricane I, Z7015 was delivered to Henlow (just a short hop from Old Warden) on 18 March 1941 and assembled by No 13 MU. It was then despatched to No 5 MU at Kemble, where it was placed in store on 20 April. At this time, many Hurricane Is were being converted to Sea Hurricane configuration, and Z7015 was one of those selected, being allocated to General Aircraft Ltd at Hanworth on 27 June. Here, it was modified with slinging points, catapult spools and an arrester hook – in addition to general strengthening – prior to delivery to RNAS Yeovilton (HMS *Heron*) on 29 July. There it was taken on charge by the Fleet Air Arm and allocated to 880 NAS, which was replacing its three Sea Gladiators and nine Sea Hurricane IAs with newer equipment.

The squadron was due to embark in HMS *Indomitable* but, as the ship was still working up, 'A' Flight went aboard HMS *Furious* for the strike on the Finnish port of Petsamo, during which the CO, Lieutenant-Commander F.E.C. Judd, shot down a Do 18. The rest of the squadron, including Z7015, remained at St Merryn, in Cornwall, before moving to Twatt and then Sumburgh, both in the Orkneys, where Sub-Lieutenant Hugh Popham flew it several times during September on convoy patrols and other duties. The unit left Sumburgh in early October, rejoining 'A' Flight at Machrihanish, in Scotland, to embark in *Indomitable* and sail to join the Eastern Fleet. For some reason Z7015 did not join the ship, being retained in Britain in a training capacity instead. The fighter was next noted on 10 February 1942 when it was flown from Hatston (HMS *Sparrowhawk*) near Kirkwall, in the Orkneys, to RNAS Donibristle (HMS *Merlin*), near Rosyth, in Scotland, by Peter Hutton of 801 NAS.

Z7015 was allocated to David Rosenfield Ltd (part of the HRO) at Barton, in Manchester, on 5 April 1942, where it underwent repairs to the centre section and undercarriage – this suggests a landing accident of some sort. It is interesting to note that when the aircraft was stripped for restoration in 1995, the centre section was found to have been built at Kingston in 1939, but as Hawker supplied CCF with spar webs until the latter started local manufacture, it is not conclusive that the centre section was replaced during this repair. The repairs took some time to complete and Z7015 was not ready for collection from Barton until 26 November 1942, being taken on charge at Yeovilton (HMS *Heron*) on 8 December, where it was allocated to 759 NAS of the Advanced Fighter School and coded 'Y1-L'. Z7015 seems to have served at Yeovilton for about another 12 months before it was retired and transferred to Loughborough College of Technology, which had an aircraft engineering department training ground engineers for the Royal Navy. Here it joined another Hurricane (KX829), a Spitfire (AR501) and a Grumman Martlet (AL246), all of which survive today.

At Loughborough the aircraft was initially kept in the camouflage and markings from its time with 759 NAS, but it was soon re-doped overall silver. On arrival at the college, it was fitted with a DH variable pitch propeller – normal for the majority of Sea Hurricanes, as it was found that the heavier metal blades of the DH prop helped counterbalance the additional weight of the arrester hook and improved the aircraft's longitudinal stability in the air. On 21 February 1961, Loughborough College exchanged Z7015 and Spitfire AR501 with the Shuttleworth Collection, receiving the Hunting Jet Provost prototype G-AOBU in return – a far better airframe for training a new generation of engineers.

On arrival at Old Warden, the Hurricane was reassembled by a team from Hawkers at Dunsfold and was seen to have acquired the Rotol propeller from AR501 and lost its arrester hook. It is interesting to note that following Z7015's restoration to flight, its Pilot's Notes mention the aeroplane's longitudinal instability. Furthermore, the Airworthiness Approval Note (AAN) lodged with the Civil Aviation Authority (CAA) mentions that in order to solve Centre of Gravity problems, the original 20-lb arrester hook had been replaced by a 6-lb aluminium reproduction. Perhaps the DH prop should have been reinstalled instead – by then, however, it had been acquired by Personal Plane Services Ltd of Booker, in Buckinghamshire, and is now fitted to Spitfire F IA AR213.

Although initially displayed at Old Warden in all-silver, Z7015 was soon repainted in green/brown camouflage with a red spinner and acted as a Gate Guard alongside Spitfire PR XI PL983 until the summer of 1967, when it was moved into the blister hangar and the fabric stripped in order to survey it for a possible restoration to flying condition for the forthcoming film *The Battle of Britain*. The Merlin III was ground-run, but an unserviceable radiator prevented any chance of a return to flight – a lucky break, as the restoration team had no idea that the tailplane spar was so badly corroded that it would probably have broken up if flight loads had been applied to it. In the event, Z7015 was used as airfield dressing at Duxford as 'H3428/L', and it is seen in the early part of the film being doused with 'petrol' as the squadron abandons its French landing ground (the aeroplane is lacking a propeller, as its serviceable Rotol prop had been fitted to Spitfire LF XVI TB382 at Henlow in May 1968).

With the filming over, Z7015 returned to Old Warden for a further stint as a Gate Guard, the damp grass wreaking even more havoc on the steel tube structure and tailplane spar. Here it remained until Dowty at Cheltenham, in Gloucestershire, undertook to carry out a restoration to flying condition. On arrival at Staverton, in Gloucestershire, the true extent of the corrosion was discovered and the attempt abandoned, the fuselage and wing centre section being returned to Old Warden for storage whilst the outer wings were sent to British Airways at Heathrow, where they were refurbished in 1980. The fuselage was moved to Duxford in 1982 and placed in what is now known as Hangar 5, where volunteers from the Duxford Aviation Society started yet another restoration attempt before lack of resources brought the project to a halt. It was not until June 1986 that the project was put onto a

formal footing, with the Imperial War Museum agreeing to provide the funding to get the aircraft restored to flying condition. David Lee reformed the team that had previously restored Shuttleworth's ex-Loughborough Spitfire LF VC AR501, with Keith Taylor as Crew Chief (and Merlin engine specialist), Steve McManus as Deputy Crew Chief and Norman Gardiner as overall Project Manager.

The task was enormous, hampered by the previous attempts, and the first job was to catalogue how much of the airframe they had and what condition it was in. Norman Chapman was the Licensed Engineer on the aircraft and he oversaw all of the work. No stranger to Hurricanes, he had first worked on them in 1940.

Reconstruction work began in earnest in 1987, and one of the first requirements was the building of a tube-squaring machine to roll the square ends onto the circular section steel tubing used in the Hurricane's construction. Although much of the stainless steel and other fittings could be cleaned and reused, the four main longerons and many of the other fuselage tubes were badly corroded and had to be replaced. The centre section was rebuilt first, followed by the fuselage and engine bearer. The undercarriage, radiator and dog-house were sent off to specialist sub-contractors whilst the tailplane was despatched to Cranfield, where the College of Aeronautics had developed an approved modification for the tailplane spar which had already been utilized by the BBMF on its Hurricanes. This 'mod' has now been superseded as HRL have developed the capability of remanufacturing the spars used in the Hurricane's wings and tailplane.

Over the next few years, the various parts started to return: the dog-house from Maurice Bayliss, the radiator from Cambridge Radiators and the propeller – complete with new Hoffman blades – from Skycraft. The wings were inspected and found to be serviceable following the restoration work carried out by British Airways in 1980, and in 1990 Keith Taylor started work on getting the Merlin III back to airworthy condition following an inspection by one of the engine's original design team, A. Harvey-Bailey. The fuselage fabric was applied and doped by Chris Morris from Old Warden in early 1993, the

Shuttleworth Collection being responsible for all the fabric work. On 13 March 1994, the fuselage – resplendent in the markings of 880 NAS – was moved into the Restoration hangar, with the wings being fitted the following June. The long-missing arrester hook had been located and re-installed, but it was modified for display purposes. Originally, once the hook was lowered, it could not be raised again until after the aircraft had landed. The modification allows retraction via a pneumatic spring brake actuator system, and a slide ensures that actuator loads cannot be transferred into the airframe if the hook remains latched when the actuator is operated. The CAA have not assessed the hook in use and the aircraft is therefore not approved for arrested landings! Following flight tests, it was decided that in order to solve Centre of Gravity problems the original 20-lb hook should be replaced by a 6-lb aluminium reproduction, as mentioned earlier.

The Merlin III was first run on 23 July 1994, but it took a full year of further work – including rebuilding the propeller – before the aircraft was at long last ready for its first taxi tests with John Lewis at the helm on 23 July 1995. The CAA signed off the paperwork on 5 September 1995 and the first flight, in the hands of Andy Sephton, took place at Duxford on 17 September – nine years, nine months and nine days after restoration work had commenced. For certification purposes the Hurricane had been registered G-BKTH with the CAA on 24 May 1983, but this is not carried externally.

For the first few years after restoration, Z7015 was based at Duxford, making flying visits to Old Warden, but it is now permanently based at the latter site with the Shuttleworth Collection, where it often flies in company with the Collection's Westland Lysander and, more recently, Hurricane I R4118.

## HURRICANE IA AE977

Peter Monk, Biggin Hill, Kent, England

AE977 was the first of HRL's rebuilt Hurricanes to fly in Britain, having been preceded by P3351, which had flown in New Zealand six months earlier in January 2000. This Hurricane is a Canadian-built Mk IA that had been ordered for the RAF from CCF against Contract No BSB 166, which called for 340 Hurricane Is with serials originally intended to be allocated in the range BH732–BJ257. However, new guidelines were set by the British Purchasing Commission in North America and the serials were amended, before production commenced, and the aircraft were built with serials ranging between AE958 and AG684. Bearing the construction number CCF/41H/8020, it would have become BH751, but emerged instead as the 20th, and final, aircraft of the serial block AE958–AE977. Some of these aircraft were redesignated as Hurricane Xs so as to differentiate them from their UK-built cousins, but according to its Form 78 Aircraft Movements Card, AE977 seems to have kept its original designation as a Hurricane IA.

The contract allocated AE977 to the Hurricane specialists of No 13 MU at Henlow on 1 September 1940, but it was not built until much later and was actually delivered on 21 April 1941. On arrival, the aeroplane was assembled at Henlow before despatch to No 10 MU at Hullavington, in Wiltshire, on 27 May, where it was placed in storage, probably at the dispersed site at Down Farm near Westonbirt, in Gloucestershire, on 3 June 1941. By this time the Hurricane I was outdated, and many were being sent to General Aircraft Ltd at Hanworth to be converted to Sea Hurricane configuration through the addition of slinging points, catapult spools and an arrester hook – in addition to general strengthening – prior to delivery to the Fleet Air Arm. When the wreckage of AE977 was delivered to HRL in 1994, there was no sign of any Sea Hurricane features, however, which suggests that it was never converted and was simply one of many Hurricane IAs operated from shore bases by the Fleet Air Arm.

AE977, coded 'S', flies in formation with other Hurricanes from 759/760 NAS during a training flight from Yeovilton on 9 December 1941. (John Dibbs)

AE977 was transferred from No 10 MU to No 22 MU at Aston Down, in Gloucestershire, on 11 July 1941, where it was prepared for service and issued to the RNAS Deposit Account eight days later – this simply meant that it was a Royal Navy aircraft being stored at an RAF facility. AE977 was delivered to RNAS Yeovilton (HMS *Heron*), where it was issued to 759/760 NASs in August 1941 and coded 'S'. This combined unit was a shore-based operational training squadron, part of the Fleet Fighter School, which prepared fighter pilots who were going to become carrier-based in due course. AE977 served without any serious mishaps until 11 July 1942, when it suffered Category X damage due to a burst tyre on landing, which caused the pilot, Squadron Leader A.D.R. Webber of the Royal New Zealand Navy, to taxi off the runway due to a jammed wheel. It was soon back in action again, but on 5 December 1942 it was involved in a mid-air collision with Hurricane Z4702 and crashed near Godney, in the Somerset Levels near Glastonbury. The pilot escaped unharmed but the Hurricane was beyond repair, classified as Category Z, and was written off.

It appears that large portions of the airframe remained in situ at the crash site and were recovered in the 1960s, eventually coming into the possession of Malcolm Clube, well known in motor racing circles. Speaking in February 2015, Clube explained that he had acquired it from a motorcycling associate, Julian Ide, whose father had overheard two farm workers discussing the crash in a Somerset pub many years previously! Intrigued by the conversation, Julian's father had asked them to show him the crash site and then arranged for the wreckage to be removed and taken to his home in Milford, Surrey, where it was stored for several decades. Clube himself stored it for several years before it came to the notice of Tony Ditheridge, who was in the process of forming HRL in association with Sir Tim Wallis. A deal was struck and a very large chunk of battered Hurricane was delivered to Milden, in Suffolk, in 1994. The aircraft was registered to HRL as G-TWTD on 6 May that year, the registration incorporating the initials of the founders of the company Tim Wallis and Tony Ditheridge.

Over the next six years, the recovered components were stripped and assessed to see if they could be re-utilized in the restored aircraft. It was possible to use all of the fuselage stainless steel plates and attachment brackets, but the T50 tubular steel structure was corroded and had to be replaced with modern material of the same gauge. The same applied to the centre section and tailplane. A new radiator, new header tank and new oil-cooler were manufactured by Anglia Radiators, the main undercarriage legs were stripped and salvaged where possible, with the outer casings and axles being replaced, whilst the Dowty tailwheel unit was stripped and repaired. Other parts such as the outer wing panels were subcontracted to specialist suppliers, the wings being built and assembled by Airframe Assemblies Ltd in its workshops at Sandown. No armament is fitted to the rebuilt wings, the space being taken up by additional fuel tanks

AE977 was originally fitted with a Merlin III and a DH 'bracket' prop when it was assembled by No 13 MU in May 1941, but during the restoration it was decided to fit a Packard Merlin 224 with a Hamilton Standard three-bladed constant speed propeller. This engine is the Packard equivalent of the Rolls-Royce Merlin 24 and effectively brings AE977 up to Mk II standard – as evidenced by the deeper radiator and oil cooler so characteristic of the later Hurricanes. The colour scheme chosen was representative of Squadron Leader Douglas Bader's 'LE-D' of No 242 Sqn during 1940, although AE977 retained its own serial. First engine tests were carried out at Milden, before the aircraft was transported by road to the nearby military airfield of RAF Wattisham, in Suffolk, where Stuart Goldspink took it up for its first test flight on 7 June 2000. It made its first public

appearance at the Flying Legends airshow held at Duxford the following month.

Sold to American collector Tom Friedkin, AE977 left Duxford on 27 April 2001 and was transported to Southampton Docks, from where it was shipped to Galveston, Texas, together with Tom's Spitfire LF IXE ML417. It was then taken by truck to Houston, where it was reassembled – the registration G-TWTD was cancelled on 25 September 2001. Registered in the USA to Tom's company, Chino Warbirds Inc, as N33TF, the Hurricane was flown to Chino, California, where it was based and displayed with the Planes of Fame Museum until 19 April 2012, when it was re-registered to Tom's new company, Comanche Warbirds Inc, and flown to his private airfield near Houston. It was soon sold, however, and on 12 March 2013, it was re-registered in the UK as G-CHTK, joining Peter Monk's Biggin Hill Heritage Hangar Collection at the Kent Battle of Britain fighter base.

Once it arrived at Biggin Hill, AE977 was repainted in the markings of Hurricane I P3886 'UF-K' of No 601 Sqn, which had been flown by American volunteers Pilot Officer Billy Fiske and double ace Flying Officer Carl R. Davis. It flew in this scheme as part of the 'Eagle Squadron' demonstration team, commemorating US airmen who flew from Britain during World War 2, between March 2013 and October 2014, when the markings were changed to represent P2921 'GZ-L' of No 32 Sqn, which was flown from Biggin Hill by Flight Lieutenant Pete Brothers during July and August 1940.

In September 2016, AE977 undertook an epic flight to Kjeller, in Norway, in order to participate in the weekend air display organized by the Norwegian Spitfire Foundation.

## HURRICANE XIIA BW874

Karl-Friedemann Grimminger, Munich, Germany

As with many of the Canadian Hurricanes, there has been some confusion over the identity of this example, but its true serial number was finally confirmed in 2014. Despite some sources, including

the CAA, quoting 'RCAF 5487', the CCF plate is clearly stamped CCF R30040, which makes it BW874 beyond all doubt. This confirmation was only made possible thanks to many years of dedicated research by Jerry Vernon, Norman Malayney and Jon Leake, who managed to decode the connection between CCF construction numbers and individual aircraft serial numbers. This research was not available when the wreckage was first recovered, and it is assumed that one of its previous owners came up with 'RCAF 5487' as a possible identity, which has followed it around ever since.

BW874 was built by CCF as a Sea Hurricane IB and taken on strength by No 118 (F) Sqn RCAF at Dartmouth, in Nova Scotia, on 8 January 1942. As such it would have featured the longer engine bearer of the Hurricane II but would have been fitted with a Merlin III and DH propeller (removed from a Fairey Battle) together with eight-gun wings, an arrester hook and catapult spools. Originally intended for Fleet Air Arm use, it was diverted to RCAF East Coast defence use following the Japanese attack on Pearl Harbor in December 1941. Following 18 months as a home-defence fighter, it was eventually returned to CCF at Fort William on 23 June 1943 for conversion to Mk XIIA standard, with a Packard Merlin 28 or 29 and Hamilton Standard propeller.

Following the upgrade, it was issued to No 1 (F) OTU at Bagotville, in Quebec, on 20 September, but the fighter went missing on a training flight on 15 November 1943 whilst being flown by Sergeant Raymond W. Bailey, RAF Volunteer Reserve. Five aircraft had been up from their base at Bagotville on a local formation flying exercise when a very sudden, heavy snowstorm covered the entire area with zero-zero conditions. An extensive search was made for Bailey and his aircraft, and it was thought at the time that he had crashed through the ice of a lake 30 miles east-south-east of Bagotville. The real crash site was not found for another 40 years, when a logging crew discovered the wreck, and the body of its pilot, in dense woodland in 1973. Bailey was buried with full military honours at Chicoutimi (St Francois Xavier), in Quebec.

The precise details surrounding the recovery of the wreck remain unclear, but it appears in lists supplied by both Tex Lavallee and Jack Arnold, both noted Hurricane collectors in the 1970s. Lavallee said it was recovered in poor condition following a crash, whilst Arnold said it was recovered from northern Quebec on the side of a hill near Bagotville. It is known that Jack Arnold acquired some of Lavallee's collection of Hurricane parts, and that the crash site of BW874 was visited several times following its initial discovery, which has led to salvaged parts being offered for sale on internet auction sites and elsewhere.

BW874's damaged centre section as received by Classic Aero Engineering Ltd at Thruxton in 2002. (Phil Lawton)

What is certain is that a damaged Hurricane centre-section was sold by Jack Arnold to Matt Sattler of Carp, Ontario, and he in turn sold it to Tony Ditheridge, then trading as AJD Engineering Ltd. This, together with other parts including the construction number plate from CCF R30040, was sold by HRL to Classic Aero Engineering Ltd at Thruxton aerodrome, Hampshire, and was registered G-CBOE on 24 May 2002, quoting 'RCAF 5487' as its previous identity – Classic Aero was owned by Peter Tuplin and the late Paul Portelli. Chief Engineer Bruce Ellis was concentrating on rebuilding Paul's Spitfire Tr 9, SM520/G-ILDA, so work on the Hurricane was subcontracted back to HRL, which rebuilt the fuselage. The registration was transferred into Peter and Paul's ownership on 24 February 2005, but following Paul's death in May 2007, all efforts were focused on completing and selling the Spitfire, and the Hurricane project remained unfinished.

At this point Phil Lawton enters the story. Phil had acquired another Hurricane project, Z5207/G-BYDL, which he had placed with Classic Aero for restoration, but as that company started to wind down its operation following Paul Portelli's death, Phil was faced with a dilemma – how to get Z5207 completed? The solution came in 2011 when Phil purchased the Classic Aero Hurricane project, G-CBOE, and some workshop machinery, setting up Phoenix Aero Services Ltd in the same Thruxton hangar in order to complete both Hurricanes. With G-CBOE being much more advanced, it was decided to concentrate all efforts into getting it completed, and work on Z5207 ceased in March 2011.

In addition to these two Hurricanes, Phil had a third Hurricane project, G-RLEF, which he had purchased from Maurice Bayliss, and two containers full of recovered Hurricane components on site at Thruxton. G-RLEF was abandoned but some of the restored parts from the tail group were used on G-CBOE. A Merlin 500-29, which had previously been installed in a Spanish Air Force CASA 2.111, was overhauled by Retro Track and Air Ltd for fitment to G-CBOE, while the aeroplane's propeller was a Hamilton Standard 23EX, as originally fitted to Canadian-built Hurricanes. Its spinner used an original backplate but a newly manufactured cone. The wings were assembled at Thruxton in a wing jig loaned by Retro Track and Air Ltd, using a kit manufactured by Bob Cunningham at Bournemouth.

The civil registration was transferred to Phoenix Aero Services Ltd on 30 January 2013, but on 30 April that same year, it was changed to Phil Lawton's name. It had always been Phil's intention to sell this Hurricane to fund the completion of Z5207, and to that end he chose a colour scheme which could be easily painted over if need be. The all-silver colours represent CCF-built Hurricane AG244, which was operated by the Central Flying School of the Royal Rhodesian Air Force from Norton airbase, Rhodesia, in 1945. The restored Hurricane took to the air at Thruxton on 16 July 2014, and just a few days later the all-silver colour scheme was put to the test when Peter and Faye Medley of Flying Colours Contracts Ltd applied a temporary Finnish Air Force camouflage scheme to represent HC-465, formerly Z2585, which was operated by the Finns after it was captured from the Soviet Air Forces in February 1942. Phil is married to a Finn and lives in Helsinki, and the colours were specially applied for the Hurricane's appearance in the Oulu International airshow, which was held on 9–10 August 2014. On its return to Thruxton, the washable paint was removed and the silver finish restored.

Although Phil had been planning to sell just BW874/G-CBOE, he received an offer from Munich-based collector Karl-Friedemann Grimminger in December 2014 which resulted in the sale of both BW874 and Z5207, together with the assets of Phoenix Aero Services Ltd, including his North American AT-6D Harvard III G-TXAN. BW874 returned to the UK when it visited Goodwood for the 75th anniversary of the Battle of Britain in September 2015, and it continues to grace the skies of mainland Europe in its striking and unique silver colour scheme.

# SEA HURRICANE I/HURRICANE XIIA BW881

Flying Heritage Collection, Paine Field, Everett, Washington, USA

BW881 was one of a pair of Hurricane hulks that were at one time owned by Tex Lavallee as part of his 'Cultural and Aeronautical Collection', located in St Chrysostome, Quebec. When Lavalle disposed of his collection, the pair were acquired by Matt Sattler of Carp, Ontario, who in turn sold them to Tony Ditheridge in the summer of 1987. Tony's company, AJD Engineering Ltd, had a track record of having restored or rebuilt many different aircraft types over the years, but once he looked at the Hurricanes in depth, he realized the work was well beyond AJD's budget, and so the company sold its two Hurricanes.

BW881, construction number CCF R32007, had been built in 1941 as part of CCF's fourth production batch, comprising 50 aircraft with serials between BW835 and BW884. They were built as Sea Hurricane Is with eight-gun wings, Merlin III engines and DH propellers, apart from BW841 and BW880, which were standard Hurricane Xs. Originally intended for use by the Fleet Air Arm, they featured catapult spools and arrester hooks, together with general strengthening, and the first few were ferried from the factory to the Halifax-based pool of the RAF's Merchant Ship Fighter Unit by RAF pilots in November 1941. Following the Japanese attack on Pearl Harbor on 7 December 1941, all but two were transferred to RCAF charge to be issued to East Coast units to help plug gaps in the Canadian fighter defence caused by aircraft being transferred to the West Coast to face what was believed to be an impending Japanese attack.

RAF records show BW881 being taken on charge by the RCAF in Nova Scotia on 17 January 1942, RCAF records indicating that Eastern Air Command (EAC) took it on charge on 22 January 1942 when it was assigned to No 118 (F) Sqn at Dartmouth. It seems to have remained with the unit until 23 June, when it was returned to the manufacturers at Fort William and converted to Hurricane XIIA standard through the removal of the arrester hook and catapult spools and the replacement of its Merlin III with a Packard Merlin 29 driving a Hamilton Standard propeller.

Returned to EAC on 20 September 1943, BW881 was issued to No 1 (F) OTU at RCAF Bagotville. Just after take-off on 10 December that same year, Flight Sergeant E.E. Whitehead was climbing through 4,000 ft about 3 miles north-west of St Anne, Quebec, when his aircraft suffered an engine failure. Whitehead was uninjured in the subsequent wheels-up landing and an investigation determined that the engine had thrown oil through the breather, possibly as a result of a failure of the scavenge pump. BW881 suffered Category D damage and was despatched for repair, eventually returning to the unit. On 7 September 1944, with only a month to go before the OTU's final course was due to finish, Flying Officer E.L. Banks was testing a new Merlin in BW881 when a con-rod failed and Banks brought it down for another wheels-up landing, this time behind the hospital at Chicoutimi, in Quebec. Banks was not harmed but the aircraft suffered Category B damage and was allocated to No 9 Repair Depot at RCAF Station St John/Jean, in Quebec, where on 28 September 1944, it was written off as 'spares and produce'.

Quite how it survived to become the property of Tex Lavalle is not clear, but its battered remains – together with those of BW853 – eventually made it to the UK and passed into the hands of William Tassell and Henry Pearman. Moved to Tassell's farm at Ulcombe, in Kent, some restoration work was performed on Tassell's aircraft, BW853, but Pearman's project remained untouched and, after several years in storage, BW881 was sold to Maurice Hammond of Eye Tech Engineering Ltd, who registered it as G-KAMM on 23 February 1995. Hammond did no work on it either, and BW881 found its way back to Tony Ditheridge at Milden where, on 10 December 1998, it was re-registered to Sir Tim Wallis's Alpine Deer Group Ltd in Wanaka.

Tony had formed a new company, HRL, in partnership with Sir Tim Wallis, specifically to remanufacture Hurricanes, and Wallis's own Hurricane I, P3351/DR393, had been the first to fly, followed by AE977, 'KZ321' and R4118 – so by the time that BW881 came along they were well-versed in the technique.

The Flying Heritage Collection acquired BW881 from Sir Tim Wallis as part of a package including a Messerschmitt Bf 109E, Polikarpov I-16 and Supermarine Spitfire F VB. Restoration continued at Milden until 2006, when the completed aircraft, now fitted with a Packard Merlin 224 driving a Hamilton Standard Hydromatic propeller, was taken by road to Wattisham, where it made its first flight in the hands of Stu Goldspink on 15 March.

The colour scheme chosen for the aeroplane is representative of RCAF Hurricane XII 5429, which served with No 135 (F) 'Bulldog' Sqn, a Canadian Home Defence unit formed at Mossbank, Saskatchewan, in June 1942 as part of Western Air Command and which was disbanded at Patricia Bay, British Columbia, in September 1945. Following further test flights, BW881 was shipped to Arlington, Washington, in August 2006, where it was reassembled by John Norman of JNE Aircraft Restoration Services – who had restored ex-Soviet Hurricane AM274 – before its final move to the Flying Heritage Collection's new home at Paine Field, in Everett, Washington, where it is regularly flown. The UK civil registration G-KAMM was cancelled on 23 August 2007 and the fighter is now registered in the USA as N54FH.

## HURRICANE I/XIIA RCAF 1374

Hangar 11 Collection, North Weald, Essex, England

Originally believed to be RCAF 5403, research has shown that this aircraft is actually RCAF 1374, construction number R20023. The fighter was originally laid down for the RAF as Hurricane I AG287, but it was part of a batch of aircraft transferred to the RCAF for assignment to East Coast defensive units and given new serials in the block RCAF 1351–1380.

Despite being ordered as a Mk I, it is almost certainly the first Hurricane built by CCF to RAF Mk II standard, with eight-gun wings and the longer nose of the Hurricane II airframe. It was transferred to RCAF charge as RCAF 1374 without its intended Packard Merlin engine. Like other Hurricanes of the RCAF 1351–1380 batch (from the AG287–AG332 range), it was subsequently fitted with a Merlin III and DH propeller, which had been removed from an RCAF Fairey Battle trainer, and in this form it was designated a Hurricane I in RCAF service.

As RCAF 1374, it entered service with No 125 (F) Sqn, EAC, on 30 April 1942 at Sydney, transferring to No 128 (F) Sqn when the latter unit formed at Sydney on 7 June 1942 for East Coast air defence. It suffered a Category C accident on the runway at RCAF Station Sydney at 1335 hrs on 1 July 1942 whilst being flown by Sergeant W.S. Fowler and was issued to No 4 Repair Depot at Scoudouc, New Brunswick, on 24 July for repair, after which it was allocated to the war reserve at Sydney on 5 September. Following nine months in store, the fighter returned to active service with EAC on 7 June 1943, possibly serving again with No 125 (F) Sqn at Sydney, before it was sent to CCF at Fort William on 2 September 1943 for conversion to Mk XIIA standard with the installation of a Packard Merlin 29 and fitting of 12-gun wings.

Following conversion, it was issued to No 1 (F) OTU at Bagotville on 18 November, but the conversion to Mk XIIA standard was not noted on the RCAF record card until 22 April 1944, when it was allocated to No 9 Repair Depot at RCAF Station St John/Jean (Cap de la Madeleine) for salvage and disposal after a crash at Bagotville which resulted in its eventual write-off. The aeroplane was finally written off on 6 September 1944, just weeks before No 1 (F) OTU ran its final course.

This was one of many Hurricane wrecks salvaged and collected by Jack Arnold of Brantford, Ontario, who personally started the restoration of RCAF 5481 and traded parts for Hurricanes worldwide. Arnold sold several of his Hurricanes to the late David Tallichet and Bob Schneider in the late 1980s, and 1374 is known to have been one of them. Schneider, trading as RRS Aviation, had a business relationship with Tallichet's Military Aircraft Restoration Corporation (MARC) and restored several aircraft at his workshop in Hawkins, Texas, including the P-40 and Bristol Beaufort in the RAF Museum at Hendon. All of his work involved static museum aircraft, none of them being restored to fly. Schneider built two static Hurricanes, using welded steel tubing as the main fuselage structure; one of these is now displayed in the Pima Air & Space Museum in Tucson, Arizona, and the other is at the National Museum of the US Air Force at Wright-Patterson AFB in Dayton, Ohio. The latter aircraft was subsequently rebuilt by HRL using non-airworthy fuselage tubing to bring it up to a proper standard for museum display.

When RRS Aviation closed down, the remaining Hurricane parts, drawings and other material, comprising parts from at least three aircraft, were sold to HRL and transported to Milden. Here, the best components were selected to rebuild this aircraft, utilizing the centre section of RCAF 1374, which still carried the manufacturer's data-plate stamped CCF/R20023. As with all of the Hurricanes restored by the company, as much of the original material that could be salvaged was retained and refurbished, although most if not all of the fuselage tubing had to be replaced. The wings were built by Bob Cunningham and his team in Bournemouth in the correct 12-gun configuration, uniquely incorporating full gun mounting fittings, ammunition boxes and feed chutes. As a Hurricane XIIA it would have been fitted with a Packard Merlin 29, and an example was sourced and rebuilt by Maurice Hammond of Eye Tech Engineering Ltd to be paired with a Hamilton Standard propeller that was overhauled by California Propellers in the USA.

The aircraft was placed on the UK civil aircraft register by HRL as G-HRLO on 26 September 2005, but following the sale of the partially completed project to Peter Teichman's Hangar 11 Collection, the registration was amended and on 5 April 2007 the aircraft became G-HHII. The decision was made to complete the restoration as a fighter-bomber in order to represent an important aspect of the Hurricanes extensive operational career. As such the wings feature the distinctive faired bomb-racks, together with a full set of ten Browning 0.303-in machine guns and ammunition belts (the third gun in each block is deleted as the space is occupied by the bolts which secure the bomb racks).

The comprehensive restoration was completed in January 2009 and saw the aeroplane rolled out resplendent in the markings of 'BE505', a Manston-based Mk IIB fighter-bomber operated by No 174 'Mauritius' Sqn in the spring of 1942. The aircraft's first post-restoration flight took place from North Weald on 27 January 2009 and it rapidly became a firm favourite on the British and European airshow circuits. In December 2015 Peter Teichman decided to rationalize his collection and G-HHII was advertised for sale, but as of November 2016 it remained unsold.

## HURRICANE XII RCAF 5481

Galway Scone Pty Ltd, Scone, New South Wales, Australia

The original restoration of this aircraft was started by noted Canadian collector Jack Arnold, who attempted to restore it to flying condition at Brantford. As with many of his recoveries, there is some degree of confusion regarding its precise identity – the construction number quoted as '60372' is probably a part number, as the real construction number of 5481 would have been CCF 46036, but this would not have been known to Arnold at the time. Arnold claimed that this

Hurricane was found in or near 'bush near a lake' in northern Quebec in 1980.

RCAF 5481 was one of a batch of aircraft built by CCF at Fort William for the RCAF with serials between 5376 and 5675. They were constructed in 1942 and all were built as Hurricane XIIs with 12-gun wings and Merlin 29 engines. RCAF records relate that 5481 was taken on strength by No 3 Training Command on 7 October 1942 and flown to No 1 Wireless School (WS) at Derbert, Nova Scotia, that same day to be used in the Third Victory Loan Campaign. This may be a reference to No 1 WS, although the latter was situated at Montreal, in Quebec. Debert was the home of No 31 OTU, later redesignated as No 7 OTU.

5481 was then transferred to EAC and taken on charge by No 1 (F) OTU at RCAF Station Bagotville on 4 November 1942. After 11 months of hard flying, it was assigned to No 9 Repair Depot at St John/Jean between 22 October 1943 and 24 June 1944 for overhaul, before being issued to No 3 Training Command. Allocated to No 9 Bombing & Gunnery School at Mont Joli, in Quebec, on 6 July 1944, the aircraft remained in service until 3 November, when it was returned to No 9 Repair Depot at St John/Jean and writen off – it was allegedly 'Stored in field' after being struck off on 29 November that year. How this ties in with Arnold's claim that it was found in 'bush near a lake' in northern Quebec is impossible to fathom after so many years.

Whatever its origins, this Hurricane underwent a long period of 'restoration', first in Arnold's workshop and later in his hangar at Brantford, using parts taken from several of the other Hurricanes that he had recovered and utilizing a lot of new steel tubing. Following an accident in which a Harvard fell onto him, Arnold started to dispose of his aircraft collection, and in 1984 the project was acquired by Terry Dieno of Davidson, Saskatchewan, who continued the rebuild using new 4130 aircraft grade steel tubing. Terry had acquired his pilot's licence in 1973 when he began a lengthy career in commercial crop spraying, pipeline patrol and aerobatics, the latter with a Yak and a Pitts Special. He and his sons are currently restoring P-51D Mustang 44-63350 *Lou IV*, which they acquired in 2007 following a landing accident at Camarillo, in California.

The Hurricane project was sold to Charles Church of Micheldever, in Hampshire, in 1986 and shipped to England, where the restoration was started once again, this time by Paul Mercer at Sandown. As the 4130 grade steel tubing previously used was not acceptable to the British CAA, the fuselage was completely taken apart and rebuilt with new T50 tubing that was squared to fit between the salvaged assembly plates, load bearing gussets and engine support mounts. The centre section was restored by RGC Aeronautical Engineering using modern materials to the original drawings and jigs. Completely new woodwork was made up whilst the construction of a new set of outer wings was subcontracted to Airframe Assemblies Ltd, the leading and trailing edges being completed by Dick Melton Aviation at Roundwood Farm, also at Micheldever. The tailplane was overhauled by RGC using the original spars and webs from BBMF Hurricane LF363, with the cross-brace members and inter-spar ribs fabricated by RGC. The Merlin 29 originally installed was replaced with a Merlin 500/224, serial no 306773, which was overhauled and test run by Mike Nixon of Tehachapi, in California, whilst the cowlings were completely refabricated in thicker 18-gauge material.

Following Charles Church's death in the crash of his Spitfire V EE606 on 1 July 1989, the Hurricane project was registered as G-ORGI on 20 November 1989 in the name of Charles Church Displays Ltd and transferred to Dick Melton's workshop on the Church estate at Roundwood Farm, Micheldever. Here it was completed and test flown for the first time, with a four-bladed Spitfire propeller and in a silver dope and yellow chromate finish, on 8 September 1991. The correct RX5 three-bladed propeller was installed when it was returned from overhaul by Dowty.

The aircraft had already been sold to David Price of Santa Monica, California, and the UK registration was cancelled on 31 January 1992. The Hurricane was shipped by sea to California, where

RCAF 5481 being rebuilt by Paul Mercer at RGC Aeronautical Engineering's premises at Sandown, on the Isle of Wight in the late 1980s. (Chris Michell)

it arrived in March 1992. Following assembly at Chino by Craig Charleston, it was issued with a US Certificate of Airworthiness on 10 April, prior to its first flight from US soil on 17 April. The markings chosen were representative of those worn during the Battle of Britain by Pilot Officer Geoffrey Page's No 56 Sqn Hurricane P2970 'US-X', and it was unusual in that it was rebuilt and flown with no aerial mast. Registered NX678DP, the Hurricane was initially based at Santa Monica with the Museum of Flying, but was later loaned to the Camarillo-based Southern California Wing of the Commemorative Air Force, to which it was delivered by air on 1 April 2003.

David Price parted with the Hurricane the following year, the US registration being cancelled on 27 April 2004 following sale to Ed Russell of Niagara Falls, Ontario, although it was not registered in Canada until 30 May 2005, the civil registration C-FDNL being applied beneath the tailplane. The Hurricane became a firm favourite at Canadian and US air shows for the next few years, but in 2013 Ed Russell decided to part with his

collection and on 16 December the Hurricane was cancelled from the Canadian civil register following sale to a group of private owners in Australia.

5481 was shipped to Scone, in New South Wales, becoming the only Hurricane in Australia when it was unpacked at Pay's Air Service on 7 April 2014. Since then the fabric has been removed and the aircraft has undergone a thorough overhaul, culminating in the application of No 46 Sqn 'PO' Battle of Britain colours. The aeroplane has been marked up as Mk I V6748 in which Queenslander Pilot Officer John Crossman was shot down and killed on 30 September 1940 – he was buried at Chalfont St Giles churchyard, Buckinghamshire. The Hurricane was re-registered as VH-JFW on 3 September 2015, with the owner named as Galway Scone Pty Ltd, an industrial machinery manufacturing business located in Scone. Its first flight from Australian soil took place at 1030 hrs on 2 October 2016 when Ross Pay took it up for a 20-minute test flight – the first time a Hurricane had flown in Australia since 1944!

# HURRICANE XII RCAF 5711

Historic Aircraft Collection Ltd, Duxford, Cambridgeshire, England

The precise identity of this Hurricane has been the subject of much discussion and conjecture over the years since it arrived in Britain from Canada in 1982, but the truth is simply that it is a complex 'hybrid' of parts donated by at least seven Canadian Hurricanes – one of which was RCAF 5711 (construction number CCF 72036). This identity was chosen as representative of the airframe by one of its previous owners, Stephen Grey, who found the constructor's plate attached to the centre section in its normal location on the port side of the cockpit above the fuel cock. At that time the correlation between construction number and serial number was not properly understood, but extensive research by Jerry Vernon, Norman Malayney and Jon Leake over the past 35 years has now established it without doubt.

It must be taken into account that during the period 1970–85, most restorers were not at all interested in the identities of the aircraft they obtained. They were just seen as sources of spares. With companies like HRL decades away from being formed, the only way to get a flyable Hurricane was to cannibalize the good parts from many hulks. In doing so the identities got mixed and matched, not only between airframes but also between owners. When and if they got a flyable aircraft was when they worried about an identity, and that was purely for paperwork purposes. It is for this reason that the identities of most of the Hurricanes rebuilt at the time – including this one – have been called into question by modern-day historians anxious to pin down a specific serial number. Unfortunately, this is not a simple matter.

G-HURI was brought to England in 1982 by Stephen Grey as an unfinished project that he had bought from a four-man group based in Regina, Saskatchewan. Rem Walker, Bob Hamilton, Gary Rice and Laurie Wright, prompted by Bob Hamilton's discovery of a Rolls-Royce Merlin III on a farm east of Regina, harboured aspirations of finding and rebuilding a Spitfire. The latter type has always been a rarity in Canada, but Hurricanes were not, and the group soon started to locate and acquire large quantities of Hurricane components.

In January 1970, the four visited Shaunavon, Saskatchewan, as a result of a tip-off given to them by Dave Klaiman, a member of the Experimental Airplane Association, who told them he had a tailplane, elevators, fin and rudder from a Hurricane which he had originally intended using on a homebuilt project that he was working on. Having collected the parts, the group made further enquiries, which led them to a farm to the south of Shaunavon. Here they found a pair of Hurricane wings buried under two feet of snow; the only problem – besides the snow – was that they were two *port* wings. The wings were in very good condition and showed little damage, so they agreed to return the following May when the snow should have melted. The farm was owned by the Songh brothers, who explained that the fuselage had been sold on to another farmer, Ed Kronberg, who had towed it on its undercarriage, complete with engine and prop, to his own farm further to the south and west. The hunt was on.

On arriving at Kronberg's farm, the group discovered that Ed had put the fuselage into his workshop and systematically taken it apart, very carefully, down to the last nut and bolt. Nothing remained that resembled a Hurricane fuselage, although it was mainly still there – just in a different form. Examples of his ingenuity included a main undercarriage leg that had been converted into a working drill press, and the centre section spars that had been cut and welded to build a small trailer! All of the valves, brackets, special fittings, bolts, etc were stored in two large boxes. The Merlin had been disassembled and the block cut up to be melted down for aluminium, whilst the rest of the airframe – apart from the tail, which had started the whole search in the first place – was in a snow-covered scrap pile. When Ed learned what the group planned, he apologized for dismantling the Hurricane, but he was consoled

Two port Hurricane XII wings that were discovered on the Songh brothers' farm at Shaunavon, Saskatchewan, buried under two feet of snow behind a chicken coop in 1970. One of these was later used on RCAF 5711. (Rem Walker)

by the fact that many of the parts were usable due to the care that he had taken. In the end his farm provided numerous fuselage parts and other fittings, including three good propeller blades, hub parts, radiator, one main undercarriage leg, canopy, windscreen, hydraulics, switches and many other components.

The group returned to Shaunavon on 23 May 1970 to start the process of loading up the parts, and on 8 June they left the Songh brothers' farm with the two port wings on a trailer. It took several trips to transport all the parts back to Regina. The identity of the Shaunavon Hurricane has never been established, but it is assumed to have been one sold as surplus from RCAF Station Swift Current, Saskatchewan.

The problem of the two port wings was solved when they learned that Neil Rose of Vancouver, Washington, USA, had two starboard wings with his Hurricane project. A trade was arranged, and in August 1970 Neil and Harry Whereatt delivered

a starboard wing on a trailer and the exchange was made. The group continued to make many trips throughout Saskatchewan, Manitoba and Alberta in an effort to locate a fuselage and other parts but these were not successful.

The breakthrough came in early September 1970 when they received a call from the Air Museum in Calgary, which wanted to exchange the ex-Neil Rose starboard wing for a forward fuselage and centre section (no undercarriage or tail) plus two de-skinned but rebuildable wings and other miscellaneous parts. The exchange took place over the weekend of 19–20 September 1970 and the group brought back to Regina the partial fuselage from RCAF 5424, which had been part of Lynn Garrison's collection dating back to 1962. Following Garrison's move to Ireland, where he set up Blue Max Aviation, the Air Museum that he had established was closed and eventually disbanded in 1971. The aircraft and assets were subsequently turned over to the City of Calgary to be housed at the city's Planetarium for safekeeping and display. In 1975 the Aero Space Museum Association of Calgary was registered as a non-profit, charitable organization and assumed the care and upkeep of these artifacts. At the time of the sale to Stephen Grey, the Association had made a legal attempt to claim title to the Hurricane on the basis that it had only been leased to the Regina group, but this was not successful.

Whilst work on the fuselage and wings continued in Regina, the group was still looking for more parts to complete the puzzle, and in 1972 they visited Cameron Logan's farm in Scotland, Ontario, in order to obtain more hard-to-find components. Logan had purchased more than 200 surplus aircraft in the immediate post-war period, including two Halifaxes and an Me 262, all of which were scrapped on his property. Amongst the aircraft were no fewer than 72 Hurricanes, but by 1972 the few remaining hulks were badly corroded due to having been left in open fields of alfalfa. Luckily Logan had stored some components in a building on the property, and the group found a good pair of main undercarriage legs, a set of wheel spindles, brakes, pitot tube, wobble pump, a set of wheels and a flap jack. All were in very good condition and when cleaned up they were as good as new.

In September 1972, another Hurricane centre section, comprising the wing centre section and partial cockpit, turned up right under their noses in Schragg Steel's scrapyard in Regina. Needless to say, this was acquired to join the growing collection of essential parts required to create a flyable Hurricane. This was followed by another trip to Calgary when, on 11 November 1972, the group collected a Merlin 29, still inhibited and in its original crate, which had been located in Kelowna, British Columbia, the existence of which was passed on to the group by the Calgary Centennial Planetarium.

The group spent 12 years working on rebuilding an airworthy Hurricane from the best components that they had to hand, until they eventually realized that the task was beyond their means. In 1982, they made it known that the project was available for sale. Stephen Grey telephoned Rem Walker on a Tuesday, arrived in Regina the following Friday,

and a 40-ft container was subsequently loaded at Gary Rice's premises with the main Hurricane project, plus parts from at least six other aircraft. On arrival in England the container was initially stored in Coventry, where Stephen Grey was the Managing Director of the Coventry Climax company, before moving on to Coningsby, in Lincolnshire, where Paul Mercer had been contracted to carry out the restoration to flying condition. Mercer, assisted by Peter Rushen, had just completed rebuilding Spitfire F VIII MT719/I-SPIT for Franco Actis in Italy and was later responsible for the airworthy rebuild of Hurricane RCAF 5481/G-ORGI on behalf of Charles Church Displays Ltd.

Part of the confusion surrounding the identity of this Hurricane is that it was first registered to Stephen Grey as G-HURI on 9 June 1983, quoting the RCAF serial '5547' as its previous identity. That aircraft had been shipped to the UK during 1943 and had never returned to Canada, but Grey had contacted Harry Whereatt requesting information, and it is known that Harry had misidentified his own Hurricane variously as '5445', '5455' and '5545' (it is actually 5447), so it is likely that this was a simple transcription error. When the civil registration was amended on 10 January 1989, with the owner now being listed as Patina Ltd – the operating company behind The Fighter Collection – the identity '5547' that had originally been quoted to the CAA was amended to CCF construction number 72036. The latter equates to RCAF 5711, which was one of the last 100 Hurricanes built at the Fort William plant. 5711 was one of the 72 Hurricanes that were sold as scrap to Cameron Logan, and was presumably one of the derelict wrecks that were still present when Rem Walker and others visited the farm in the 1970s. In a letter dated 13 October 1988, Stephen Grey clearly stated that 'this centre section and fuselage structure very definitely and permanently carried 72036, so that is the correct historical identity of my aircraft'.

Whilst lacking the active wartime history of many of the newly rebuilt Hurricanes produced in the past 20 years, G-HURI is, without doubt, one of the most original Hurricanes flying today, having been rebuilt using the best remaining parts of the original structure from several Canadian examples. Without any specific history or identity, it assumed the identity of CCF construction number 72036. The plate is no longer carried within the aircraft, but this is not unusual. Indeed, neither LF363 nor PZ865 carry their identity plates on the fuselage structure any longer, having both been rebuilt in recent years.

With the development of The Fighter Collection, the Hurricane was delivered to Duxford in January 1988; much work was seen to have been done since its arrival in the UK some five years earlier. Paul Mercer continued to oversee the restoration process, assisted by Peter Rushen and other engineers from The Fighter Collection. During the next few months the final systems were installed, and when the aeroplane made its first flight, on 1 September 1989, it was finished in RAF markings representing Z3781 'XR-T' of No 71 'Eagle' Sqn. This unit had been equipped with the Hurricane IIA from May to August 1941 when based at Martlesham Heath and North Weald. The original Z3781 had been destroyed in a fatal accident as a result of bad weather on 8 October 1941 near Maughold, Ramsey, Isle of Man, whilst on a transit flight from Fowlmere, near Duxford, to Eglinton, Northern Ireland, which took the life of its pilot, Connecticut-born Pilot Officer Andrew Mamedoff. His is buried in Brookwood Military Cemetery.

G-HURI flew in these markings until 2004 when it emerged from an 18-month-long overhaul at Duxford in new colours representing Z5140, a Gloster-built Hurricane IIB flown by No 126 Sqn during the siege of Malta from June 1941 to March 1942. The identity was chosen as it could carry the squadron code letters 'HA-C', the initials of the Historic Aircraft Collection Ltd, which had acquired the aircraft in August 2002 in exchange for Hawker Nimrod I S1581 (G-BWWK). The original Z5140 arrived on Malta on 6 June 1941 during Operation *Rocket*, having flown off HMS *Ark Royal*. The Malta squadrons were happy to receive any aircraft regardless of colour, and the first Hurricanes were delivered in the north-west European temperate camouflage scheme. In September 2005, the 'new' Z5140 became the first

Hurricane to return to Malta since World War 2. It flew there together with HAC's Spitfire, BM597, as part of the 'Merlins Over Malta' project.

In August 2012, G-HURI undertook an epic long-distance flight to Russia and back to participate in the centenary celebrations of the Russian Air Force, at Ramenskoye airfield, south-east of Moscow. In successfully fulfilling this mission, 'HA-C' became the first Hurricane to fly in Russian skies since approximately 3,000 of them were supplied via hazardous Arctic convoys to the Soviet Air Forces from 1941 onwards. G-HURI was flown at Ramenskoye before President Vladimir Putin by serving RAF instructor and display specialist Flight Lieutenant Dave Harvey. He then ferried the fighter home via Lithuania, Poland, Germany and Belgium, displaying the aircraft at the Belgian Air Force's Zoersel airbase en route. During this ambitious flight, the old warrior flew 18 sorties and completed some 21 operational hours before returning to its long-time home at Duxford.

During the winter of 2014/15, G-HURI underwent some refurbishment, part of which was a change of colour scheme. Bearing in mind that 2015 was the 75th anniversary of the Battle of Britain, the markings chosen were those of P3700 'RF-E', which was flown by No 303 'Warsaw-Kosciuszko' Sqn and abandoned by Sergeant Kazimierz Wünsche over Poynings, Kent, on 9 September 1940, having sustained damage from a Bf 109 during combat over Beachy Head. The crash site of the original P3700 had been excavated by the Wealden Aviation Archaeology Group in September 1979, when various components were recovered, but a further, more detailed, excavation took place starting on 9 September 2015 to mark the 75th anniversary of the crash. The second excavation was carried out as part of Operation *Nightingale* by a team of archaeologists and historians supported by Polish and British veterans of foreign missions in Iraq and Afghanistan. Sergeant Wünsche was badly burned but survived the war, passing away in Warsaw on 10 July 1980 aged 61. His daughter Grazyna and granddaughter Joanna were both present at the dig site during *Nightingale*, which saw a number of artefacts being recovered from his Hurricane.

# HURRICANE IV 'KZ321'

Vintage Wings of Canada, Gatineau, Quebec, Canada

The true identity of this aircraft is not known, as all manufacturer's plates, together with its original Merlin engine, disappeared in the years between its discovery by Robs Lamplough in a Jaffa scrapyard in 1983 and its acquisition by Stephen Grey of The Fighter Collection some eight years later. As it was found in Israel alongside the hulk of another Hurricane IV (KZ191), which is known to have served post-World War 2 with No 6 Sqn, RAF, it is reasonable to assume that the aeroplane was part of the eighth or ninth production blocks (Contract No 62305/39) and was built at Langley, in Berkshire, but that is all. The aircraft in these blocks were a mixture of Mks IIB, IIC, IID and IV, with serials in the range KW696–LD999, although 60 aircraft were delivered as Sea Hurricanes and given new serials between NF668 and NF703 (36), and NF716 and NF739 (24).

Although Robs was primarily looking for P-51D Mustangs, he brought the fuselage and centre section of KZ191 back to the UK and alerted the late Doug Arnold about the other one. Arnold repatriated the anonymous Hurricane a few months later, and it was soon to be found in one of his hangars at Blackbushe, in Hampshire, where some preliminary work was carried out on it. Arnold had purchased a pair of Hurricane wings from The Doon School, in Dehra Dun, India, during a visit in February 1976. The same school also possessed the reduction gear, propeller and spinner from a Hurricane that Arnold had acquired at the same time, so these parts were combined with the ex-Jaffa fuselage to create a reasonable Hurricane project, which was registered as G-HURY on 31 March 1989.

The aircraft was moved from Blackbushe to Arnold's new base at Biggin Hill, and it was from here that it was obtained by Stephen Grey of The Fighter Collection during 1991. He in turn had it moved to his base at Duxford and re-registered to Patina Ltd on 25 April 1991. Some work was carried out here, but in the end the decision was made to transfer the project to HRL, where a full restoration to flying condition was carried out between 2001 and 2003. During the work all of the steel tubing was replaced, although the stainless steel plates and attachments brackets, and items such as forgings that could be non-destructive tested, were restored for use in the rebuilt aircraft. The Indian wings were rebuilt and fitted with four dummy Hispano cannon barrels, the gun bays being used for overload fuel tanks, and a civilian Merlin 500 driving a Rotol RS5/13 propeller was installed.

The final configuration chosen for the restored aircraft is representative of a cannon-armed Hurricane IID in the colours of No 6 Sqn when it was based in the Western Desert and Tunisia between December 1942 and September 1943. As such, some 'artistic licence' has been used for it should be armed with a pair of Vickers 'S' guns and be fitted with a tropical Vokes filter. The squadron was re-equipped with rocket-armed Mk IVs in September 1943 and moved to Italy, being based at Grottaglie between February and July 1944. The serial number represents one of these Mk IVs, KZ321, which served with No 6 Sqn at Grottaglie as 'JV-N' until it was lost on 24 May 1944 whilst being flown by Pilot Officer Grey. It may have been hit by ground fire or possibly crashed as a result of damage caused by its own exploding rocket projectiles. Grey bailed out at about 1,000 ft and was seen floating in the sea, apparently lifeless. His body was never recovered and he has no known grave. The real KZ321 would have carried the European 'Temperate' camouflage scheme of Dark Green and Ocean Grey.

As this Hurricane was found alongside KZ191, it is obvious that it must have served with No 6 Sqn in Palestine, and may well have seen previous service at Prkos, in Yugoslavia, either with No 6 itself or with the Yugoslavian Hurricane unit, No 351 Sqn. On 13 September 1946, the squadron received orders to pack up and leave Palestine for Nicosia, in Cyprus. The ground equipment was to be crated by the 16th and shipped from Haifa on the 18th, whilst it was planned that the aircraft would fly out on the 21st. Any unserviceable Hurricanes were stripped of parts and disabled (by smashing the reduction gear on the Merlin XX with a sledgehammer) so that they would be of little military value in the forthcoming 1948 Palestine War. With no physical evidence to show on the airframe, it unlikely that we will ever be able to determine which Hurricane this really is. Analysis of squadron records suggests that KZ726, KZ916, LE292 or LE659 may be considered as possible candidates, but that is no more than conjecture.

The restored aircraft made its first flight from Earls Colne, in Essex, on 8 July 2003 and was flown to Duxford the following day, where it appeared in the Flying Legends airshow. The Hurricane remained based at Duxford for three more years until it was sold to Michael Potter's Vintage Wings of Canada and the UK civil registration cancelled on 20 February 2006. It arrived at its new home at Gatineau Executive Airport, Quebec, on 18 May and made its first flight from Canadian soil on 15 June 2006. 'KZ321' is now registered in Canada as C-FTPM and retains the markings of No 6 Sqn.

## HURRICANE MK IIC LF363

RAF Battle of Britain Memorial Flight, Coningsby, Lincolnshire, England

There is much misinformation surrounding the history of this particular Hurricane. Depending on which source you read, it has been claimed that it was 'the last Hurricane to enter service with the RAF' or that it was 'found abandoned and awaiting scrapping at the Hawker airfield at Langley, where Sir Sydney Camm personally arranged for it to be restored'. Neither of these tales is correct and the following is the true history of this remarkable old warrior.

LF363 was ordered from Hawker Aircraft Ltd as part of the tenth production block (Contract No 62305/39) and built at Langley in the winter of 1943/44 as a cannon-armed Mk IIC. The aircraft in this block of 1,961 were a mixture of Mks IIB, IIC and IV with serials in the range LB542–LF956, LF363 falling into the serial batch LF313–LF346 (34 aircraft). Powered by a Rolls-Royce Merlin XX, engine number 142613/418645, it made its first flight on 1 January 1944 and, following 50 minutes of air testing, it was delivered to No 5 MU at Kemble on 28 January. The flight from Langley to Kemble took just 30 minutes, and it remained here until 30 March when an Air Transport Auxiliary ferry pilot from No 16 Ferry Pool at Kirkbride picked it up for delivery to its first unit, No 63 Sqn at Turnhouse, near Edinburgh, the flight lasting 1 hr 40 min.

The unit, which had reformed in June 1942 from an element of No 239 Sqn, was initially equipped with the Mustang I and had commenced tactical reconnaissance missions along the French coast in early 1943. It re-equipped with Hurricanes in March 1944 and moved to Scotland from Odiham, in Hampshire, in January 1944. The Hurricanes were a temporary measure as the squadron converted to Spitfires in May. Its primary role was cooperating with either the Army – taking part in training exercises – or with the Navy, providing spotter aircraft for the naval bombardment on D-Day and during the Walcheren landings. The squadron continued to perform tactical reconnaissance too, and it was for this reason that on 7 April 1944 LF363 was fitted with camera bearers in the rear fuselage, with two F 24 cameras installed the following day.

The aircraft has continued to carry the blanked off camera ports for the rest of its life, and they were even replaced during the complete restoration undertaken by Historic Flying Limited (HFL) – although nobody realized what they were at that time, their true purpose and origin only coming to light in 2015!

Although based at Turnhouse, the squadron operated detachments at Dundonald and Ballyhalbert, both in Northern Ireland, during April and May 1944 before moving to Lee-on-Solent, in Hampshire, where it re-equipped with Spitfires. As a consequence, LF363 joined No 309 'Polish' Sqn at Drem on 23 May, taking up the code 'WC-F'.

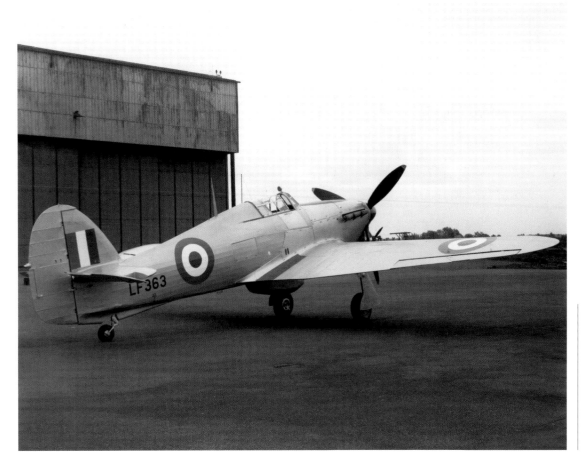

LF363 is seen at Biggin Hill in June 1956, shortly after its arrival at the Kent airfield. Here, it joined the Station Flight, and was regularly flown by Biggin Hill CO, Battle of Britain Hurricane pilot Wing Commander Peter Thompson. (BAE SYSTEMS)

Just like No 63 Sqn, this unit had previously been equipped with the Allison-powered Mustang I – also in the fighter-reconnaissance role – and found the change to the Hurricane somewhat disappointing to say the least. The squadron spent much of its time patrolling the east coast of Scotland and the Firth of Forth after a solitary Ju 88 had dropped some bombs on Edinburgh. In September 1944 the unit converted back to the Mustang I, and on 2 November LF363 rejoined No 63 Sqn, by now based at Manston, before moving to No 26 Sqn at Tangmere on 30 November 1944.

No 26 Sqn was also operating in the fighter-reconnaissance role, but the ageing Hurricanes were not really suited to this and the unit re-equipped with Mustangs in December 1944 – prompting another move for LF363, this time to No 62 OTU at Ouston, near Durham, where it served for the remainder of the war. The aeroplane's four 20 mm cannon were removed on 20 April, although there is no mention of the cameras being taken out – it is

reasonable, however, to assume that this took place before the aircraft was transferred to Ouston.

LF363 was air-tested following repairs at No 22 MU at Silloth on 4 July 1945, at which time it had logged a total of 144 hr 35 min of flying time and had suffered no significant damage or accidents. It was then allocated to No 5 MU at Kemble on 14 August, but was actually taken on charge by the Station Flight at Middle Wallop at the end of the month. Here it remained, possibly as the 'hack' of the station commander or another high-ranking officer, the aeroplane being maintained in flying trim – its Form 700 (servicing logbook) indicates that significant amounts of work had to be done to keep it airworthy, despite the fact that it was only three years old. The Form 78 Aircraft Movements Card has an entry dated 21 June 1947 which notes that LF363 was 'Presumed Struck off Charge'. This further backs up the theory that it was operating in a semi-official capacity at Middle Wallop, for LF363 was certainly being flown regularly as the fuelling figures indicate that the tanks were filled several times a month during the summer of 1947.

There is a suggestion that by August 1947, LF363 had been transferred to the Fighter Command Communications Squadron at Northolt, but the paperwork does not support this. Indeed, the Form 700 confirms that it was still on charge at Middle Wallop, but now with the Station Handling Flight. This state of affairs continued until 6 February 1948, when it was transferred to the Station Flight at Thorney Island, in Hampshire, in accordance with a signal from HQ Fighter Command (Q 123) dated 5 February 1948.

All of this coincides with the period when Air Vice-Marshal Sir Stanley Vincent, DFC, AFC, held the position of Senior Air Staff Officer, RAF Fighter Command. From 1948 he commanded No 11 Group, before requesting retirement in 1950. Vincent was the only RAF pilot to have downed enemy aircraft in both World Wars, firstly when flying with No 60 Sqn RFC during 1916–17 and latterly when serving as Station Commander at Northolt during the Battle of Britain, when he often flew and fought alongside the Polish Hurricane squadrons under his command. Vincent's 'boss' Sir James Robb had Spitfire LF XVIE SL721 as his personal 'hack' at the time, and Vincent 'acquired' LF363 as his. It is interesting to note that SL721 survives in flying condition as part of Michael Potter's Vintage Wings of Canada collection at Gatineau.

Vincent and LF363 led the 1948 Battle of Britain flypast over London on 15 September, but during the flight the accumulator stowage panel (a large panel on the starboard side of the fuselage behind the cockpit) detached itself and Vincent landed at West Malling, in Kent, where a temporary plywood panel was made and fitted in order to get him and 'his' Hurricane home! As a result of this, LF363 was ferried from Thorney Island to Hawker Aircraft Ltd at Langley on 29 October 1948 for significant rectification work to be carried out – by now it had 219 hr 55 min flying time logged.

Following the work at Langley, LF363 was checked on 20 April 1949 and judged to be serviceable for the ferry flight back to Thorney

Island, subject to refuelling at Bovingdon, in Hertfordshire – coincidentally, where Robb's Spitfire, SL721, was based with the Metropolitan Communications Squadron. On the morning of the flight, 22 April, the compressor was found to be not charging the air bottle to sufficient pressure, so the bottle was charged on the ground and the flight plan amended to a direct flight to Thorney Island – where it landed with the undercarriage retracted when the gear failed to come down.

Repair work started immediately, the decision to carry out the work 'in house' being taken on 23 April, and the Merlin XXII (which had only 22.5 hours on it) was removed on 4 May for shock-testing and found to be within limits. The damage to the engine bay was repaired and the engine reinstalled on 13 May, with the team making excellent progress – replacing many components with serviceable units taken from stores. The final inspection took place on 13 June, when the aircraft was signed off for flight testing by Squadron Leader E.J. Andrews. Following the rectification of minor technical snags, a signal was received from Fighter Command HQ that the aircraft was to be resprayed. On 27 June, it was duly repainted in Ice Blue with a red spinner, together with an Air Vice-Marshall's pennant and the crest of No 11 Group, Fighter Command, carried below the cockpit. Further touches were added on 10 September when a locally made personal kit stowage box was fitted in the rear fuselage so that Sir Stanley could pack a few items into 'his' Hurricane when visiting airfields within No 11 Group.

Vincent flew LF363 in the 1949 Battle of Britain flypast over London, without incident, but he was soon to retire and the Hurricane was transferred to Hawker Aircraft at Langley on 28 November. Here, the fighter's engine was inhibited and LF363 was stored until August 1950, when it was reactivated prior to delivery to Waterbeach, in Cambridgeshire, on 1 September (interestingly Vincent now lived in Bury St Edmunds, not far from Waterbeach). The following May saw LF363 flown to No 19 MU at St Athan for servicing, where many problems were discovered and the recommendation was made that 'this aircraft not be flown at speeds exceeding 180 knots as vibration of cockpit section becomes excessive'.

It was then flown to Langley, where Hawker removed the cannon mounting tubes and blanked off the leading edges of the wings, before respraying it in temporary camouflage and markings for a flying role in the film *Angels One Five*, which was filmed at Kenley during July 1951. LF363 was joined by Hawker's own PZ865 plus some Portuguese Air Force Hurricanes, and it flew at Kenley as 'P2617' – making life difficult for historians 60-odd years later trying to work out whether the actual P2617 had flown in the film or not (it hadn't). With the filming over, the cannon tubes were reinstalled on 18 August and LF363 was returned to its Ice Blue colours by the simple expedient of washing off the temporary camouflage. It had been officially recorded as on charge to the Station Flight at Kenley during the filming, but it now moved to Biggin Hill Station Flight and even No 41 Sqn – which was based at Biggin with de Havilland Hornets at the time – before finding its way back to Waterbeach on 6 November 1951.

LF363 remained at Waterbeach for the next four years, in the company of a motley collection of time-expired Hurricanes that had been gathered from other stations as a source of spare parts to keep it – now the last airworthy Hurricane on RAF strength – in the air. These three Hurricanes (Z3687, LF751 and PG953) were progressively cannibalized until their remnants were used to build up a static gate guardian which took on the identity LF751. This aircraft is now displayed as 'BN230' in the Spitfire and Hurricane Memorial Museum at Manston, in Kent.

LF363's film career continued when it was used during the filming of a BBC television series *The War in the Air* and then, in August 1955, it returned to Kenley once more where it was utilized in the film *Reach for the Sky* – the life story of Douglas Bader. Following filming, it was flown to Langley for another major overhaul in September 1955, and on 10 June 1956, resplendent in all-silver and with the cannon tubes finally removed, LF363 was delivered to Biggin Hill, where it joined the Station Flight.

The Station CO was ex-Battle of Britain Hurricane pilot Wing Commander Peter Thompson, DFC, who hatched a plan to set up a Battle of Britain Flight at Biggin Hill, with LF363 as its founding member. Following the acquisition of three Spitfire PR XIXs and then three Spitfire LF XVIEs the following year, Peter's idea became a reality, and developed into what we now know as the BBMF, the newly camouflaged LF363 and Spitfire TE330 performing the Battle of Britain flypast over London on 15 September 1957 as the Flight's first official duty. More filming came the way of LF363 during 1957 when it was used in the film *The One That Got Away* about the German PoW Oberleutnant Franz von Werra, Northolt doubling for the Rolls-Royce airfield at Hucknall, where the real von Werra tried to steal a Hurricane.

Peter Thompson was posted from Biggin Hill in February 1958 and, with the closure of the base, LF363 and the rest of the Flight moved to North Weald the following month, but that closed too, so in May they moved to Martlesham Heath, in Suffolk. Although the Spitfires experienced severe serviceability problems, LF363 soldiered on, moving in November 1961 to a new home at Horsham St Faith, in Norfolk, at which time it and Spitfire PR XIX PM631 were the only airworthy aircraft left on the Flight – a situation which prevailed until 1964, by which time the Flight had moved yet again, this time to Coltishall, in Norfolk, on 1 April 1963, following the closure of Horsham St Faith.

Following the acquisition of Spitfire VB AB910 in 1965, the BBMF started to establish itself more securely, and LF363, in its green and brown camouflage with a red spinner, was a familiar sight at air displays and special events throughout the 1960s until it was 'called up' for duty in the epic motion picture *The Battle of Britain*, which was filmed at North Weald, Debden, Duxford, Hawkinge and other locations throughout the summer of 1968. During the film LF363 carried many different markings as there were only three airworthy Hurricanes available. Once shooting was finished, the aircraft was given a major overhaul and new fuselage fabric – probably by Simpsons Aeroservices

Ltd, who had the contract to prepare and maintain all of the aircraft during the film, and which had done the same to PZ865/G-AMAU at Bovingdon prior to its return to Hawker Siddeley at Dunsfold.

On its return to Coltishall, in all-silver, LF363 was quickly repainted in camouflage and coded 'LE-D' in honour of Squadron Leader Douglas Bader. The Flight had now decided to change the markings on its aircraft whenever they received a major service, and over the following seasons LF363 appeared in a variety of different schemes – some more authentic than others. These were:

> 1969–72: 'LE-D' of No 242 Sqn, Squadron Leader D.R.S. Bader, 1940
> 1973–78: 'LE-D' (thicker grey lettering than the previous version)
> 1979–82: 'GN-F' of No 249 'Gold Coast' Sqn, 1940
> 1983–86: 'VY-X' all-black nightfighter scheme of No 85 Sqn, 1940
> 1987–89: 'NV-L' of No 79 Sqn, 1940
> 1990–91: 'GN-A' of No 249 Sqn, Flight Lieutenant James Nicolson, 1940

The 1991 season saw a catastrophic accident befall LF363, the first in its 47-year life, when on 11 September it was flying from Coningsby to Jersey in a three-ship formation with the Flight's Lancaster and one of the Spitfires. As they approached RAF Wittering, the Hurricane's engine started to run rough and very soon smoke was pouring out of the exhausts. Squadron Leader Allan Martin declared an emergency but, whilst attempting to land at Wittering, the Merlin stopped and LF363 slammed into the ground in a stall, sliding backwards along the runway in a shower of sparks. Martin escaped, despite a broken ankle, and sustained minor burns as the fully fuelled aircraft burst into flames and was reduced to a charred wreck, despite the best efforts of the Wittering fire crew, who were on the scene within seconds. The aircraft was returned to Coningsby on 13 September and the subsequent Board of Inquiry established that the engine had seized due to a broken camshaft.

After three years in storage, the decision was made to sell one of the Flight's three Spitfire PR XIXs in order to raise the funds required to rebuild LF363, PS853 being selected for disposal. LF363 was then transported to Audley End, in Essex, where HFL was contracted to carry out a total rebuild to flying condition. Work started in early 1995, but the damage was so great that virtually everything had to be replaced. Only six of the original fuselage tubes could be re-utilized, the fuselage work being sub-contracted to Retrotec Ltd, whilst the centre section and wings were rebuilt by HFL using parts from LF363 and one of two ex-Russian recoveries as patterns. The 'Cranfield mod' (see Z7015) to the tailplane spar was not repeated as HRL now had the capability to build new spars to the original pattern. A new fin, rudder and elevators were also required, as was totally new woodwork, cowlings and the majority of the aircraft's systems. During the wing rebuild, the cannon mounts were removed and these are now fitted to PZ865 to enable LF363 to represent an eight-gun Hurricane IIA and PZ865 a cannon-armed IIC.

On return to the Flight, the 'US-C' markings chosen were very apt as they represented a Hurricane of No 56 Sqn, a unit then based at Coningsby but equipped with the Tornado F 3, and whose squadron crest represents a Phoenix rising from the ashes. LF363 was collected from Audley End by Squadron Leader Paul Day on 29 September 1998 and flown to Cambridge Airport, where a party from the Flight checked it over before LF363 carried on to Coningsby and landed at 1730 hrs – just over seven years from the date of the accident at Wittering. The aeroplane made its first public display at Duxford on 11 October 1998, flown by Air Marshall Sir John Allison. The No 56 Sqn markings were retained until the winter of 2005/06, when LF363 went to The Aircraft Restoration Company Ltd at Duxford for maintenance and emerged in March 2006 as Flying Officer Harold Bird-Wilson's 'YB-W' of No 17 Sqn during the Battle of Britain. These colours were retained until the winter of 2013, when LF363 underwent a major overhaul at Coningsby from which it emerged in May 2014 in the markings of Flight Lieutenant Arthur Clowes' 'JX-B' of No 1 Sqn, making its first public appearance at the Shuttleworth Collection Pageant at Old Warden on 7 September 2014.

## HURRICANE IIC PZ865

RAF Battle of Britain Memorial Flight, Coningsby, Lincolnshire, England

Ordered from Hawker Aircraft Ltd as the last aircraft in the tenth production block of Hurricanes (Contract No 62305/39), PZ865 was built at Langley in the summer of 1944 as a cannon-armed Mk IIC. The aeroplanes in this block of 1,397 were a mixture of Mks IIB, IIC and IV with serials in the range LE121–PZ865; PZ865 fell into the final batch of 18 aircraft, and was the last Hurricane ever built. It made its maiden flight at Langley in late July 1944 in the hands of Hawker's Chief Test Pilot, P.W.S. 'George' Bulman, who had made the first flight of the prototype at Brooklands some nine years earlier on 6 November 1935. The following month a 'christening' ceremony was held when PZ865 was officially named *The Last of the Many!* by Lady Spencer-Spriggs, wife of Sir Frank Spencer-Spriggs, Managing Director of Hawker Siddeley Aircraft Co Ltd, Bulman flying it again in the company of Bill Humble in Tempest V EJ592 and the company's Hawker Hart G-ABMR.

Being such a significant aircraft, PZ865 was purchased back from the Ministry of Supply by the Directors of Hawker Aircraft Ltd. This meant that it was not actually handed over to the RAF, but was retained at Langley, where the Hurricane was used as a communications aircraft until 9 December 1945. During that time it clocked up approximately 41 hr 55 min of flying time – its original logbooks were returned to RAF Uxbridge upon the aeroplane's sale to Hawker and were subsequently destroyed, so this is an estimate.

PZ865 was inhibited and stored at Langley in 1945, although it was brought out and transported by lorry through Kingston during a victory parade which was held on 8 June 1946. In 1950, Hawker heard that there may be an embargo on flying military aircraft in civilian markings, so the decision was made to bring the Hurricane out of storage and civilianize it for 'Racing, Record and Demonstration purposes'. To this end it received a Special Category Certificate of Airworthiness and was given the civil registration G-AMAU, being test flown at Langley on 12 May 1950 by the Chief Test Pilot, T.S. 'Wimpy' Wade, DFC, AFC, for 25 minutes. 'George' Bulman took it up for 30 minutes the following day, before Wade made a surprise appearance at the Royal Aeronautical Society's garden party at White Waltham on 14 May, where it was seen to be finished in an Oxford Blue and gold civilian colour scheme. These were adopted as Hawker's 'House Colours' and later applied to Hart G-ABMR and Hawker Tomtit G-AFTA. At this stage in its civilian career PZ865 retained the 'sword type' aerial mast, but had the cannon barrels removed and the wing leading edges faired over.

Further test flights were carried out during May, as it had been entered in the King's Cup Air Race as the personal entry of HRH Princess Margaret. The pilot was to be Group Captain Peter Townsend, CVO, DSO, DFC and Bar, who had made his name flying Hurricanes with No 85 Sqn during the Battle of France and later the Battle of Britain. He subsequently became romantically linked to the young princess, until her announcement that she did not intend to marry him was made in 1955. Townsend flew G-AMAU for the first time on 26 May, and a Rotol four-bladed propeller was fitted on 1 June. The race was being staged at Wolverhampton, and Townsend flew G-AMAU there and back on 2 June to test its performance with the new propeller. The speed increase was not considered sufficient to warrant the change, so the original three-bladed prop was reinstalled on 5 June. It is interesting to note that G-AMAU/PZ865 was also flown with a four-bladed Rotol propeller during the 1980s when the BBMF was

The Last of the Many!

The fuselage of PZ865 starts to take shape at Langley in the early summer of 1944. (BAE SYSTEMS)

experiencing issues with spares, the same being true of its stablemate LF363. The aircraft was then fitted with two additional 12.5-gallon fuel tanks in the armament bays outboard of the main wing tanks and was flight-tested with these on 12 June.

The King's Cup Air Race was held on 17 June and G-AMAU was delivered to Wolverhampton the day before by 'Wimpy' Wade, who flew it back to Langley on 18 June. The race consisted of three laps, and Townsend averaged 283 mph in 50 minutes to come home second with an extremely low pass over the finish line. The fact that the race was won by Edward Day in Miles Magister G-AKRV is a testament to the skill of the handicappers, who had set the Hurricane off last in the field of 36 competitors. The race also featured two Spitfires, G-AISU and G-AIDN, but the thrilling finish was marred by a fatal accident to W.H. Moss, who was flying Moss MA 1 G-AEST.

The Hurricane's next appearance was at the Kemsley Challenge Trophy, held on 19 August at Fairwood Common, in Swansea, over three laps of

a 28-mile circuit. This time G-AMAU was flown by another wartime fighter pilot, Squadron Leader Neville Duke, DSO, OBE, DFC and two Bars, AFC, who came third at an average speed of 295 mph. Its original Rolls-Royce Merlin XX (No 75283) had been replaced with a Merlin 24 (No 309303) on 11 August, which may account for the slight performance increase. The final event of the year was the Daily Express International Air Race along the south coast from Hurn to Herne Bay, which was held on 16 September. No fewer than 75 aircraft were chasing the £2,350 prize purse on offer, and G-AMAU was flown by Hawker test pilot Frank Murphy, with Flight Lieutenant Frank Bullen keeping him company in Tomtit G-AFTA.

The Certificate of Airworthiness (C of A) was renewed on 3 May 1951 and the Hurricane appeared at White Waltham three days later, Peter Townsend taking it up for a 30-minute local flight on 21 June and again on the 22nd in preparation for the Jubilee Trophy Air Race. The latter was part of the National Air Races, which were scheduled to be held at Hatfield two days later. Despite Frank Murphy flying G-AMAU to Hatfield on 22 June, bad weather on the 23rd caused the cancellation of the races – in which all three aircraft of the 'Hawker Circus' were entered – and Neville Duke flew the Hurricane back to Langley on 25 June.

Filming of *Angels One Five* took place at Kenley during July 1951, and G-AMAU was painted in temporary RAF camouflage and markings as 'P2619/US-B', joining its latter-day stablemate LF363 and a group of Portuguese Hurricanes at the Surrey airfield on 2 July when it was flown over from Langley by Frank Murphy. The opening sequence of the film shows G-AMAU, with no squadron codes, being flown into the fictitious 'RAF Neethley' by John Gregson's character Pilot Officer 'Septic' Baird – the Hurricane used for the studio shots of the subsequent crash scene has never been identified. Filming took place at Kenley until 27 July, with G-AMAU being flown by Hawker pilots Bullen or Murphy and returning to Langley each night.

The Hurricane 'took leave' during filming to take part in the Fifty Years of Flying exhibition, which was sponsored by the *Daily Express* and held at Hendon, flying in from Langley in full film colours on 18 July and returning six days later, piloted by Frank Murphy. Although A.W. 'Bill' Bedford, OBE, AFC, FRAeS is supposed to have also flown it during filming, this is not borne out by the logbook entries, which show that his first flight in the aircraft was not until 24 September. That day he ferried it back from Shoreham to Langley after Frank Murphy had competed in the *Daily Express* Trophy Race from Shoreham to Brighton, Newhaven, Whitstable, Hythe, Rye Harbour, Hastings, Eastbourne, Beachy Head and back to the finish at Brighton's West Pier on 22 September.

'Bill' Bedford then became one of its regular pilots, and throughout 1952 his name appears frequently alongside his test pilot colleagues Frank Murphy, Frank Bullen and Neville Duke. The latter took the Hurricane on its first flight outside of Britain on 8 June 1952 when he flew it from Dunsfold, in Surrey, to Lympne, in Kent, to clear

customs and then on to the RAF base at Celle, in Lower Saxony, from where he returned by the reverse route the following day. The aircraft had been first flown to Dunsfold on 28 April when Frank Bullen made the 10-minute 'hop' from Langley, and it seems to have been based there for the rest of the year, making visits to a variety of locations including Sywell, Boscombe Down, West Raynham, White Waltham, Brockworth and Baginton.

The pattern continued throughout 1953, although 'Bill' Bedford and Don Lucey were now the main pilots. 9 October was an interesting day as no fewer than nine different Fleet Air Arm pilots all took the controls for ten minutes at a time – probably at the end of a course at Boscombe Down. Don Lucey flew it back to Langley on 16 February 1954, and its next flight was another overseas trip, Neville Duke flying to Schiphol, in Amsterdam, via Lympne on 4 May and returning two days later. For the Battle of Britain Day events that year, G-AMAU was loaned to the RAF, Flight Lieutenant Smith picking it up from Langley on 14 September and flying the aircraft to Waterbeach, from where he participated in the London flypast on 15 September, returning the fighter to Dunsfold on 17 September. This may indicate that the Waterbeach-based LF363 was unavailable for the flypast, and with G-AMAU the only other flyable Hurricane in the UK, it was pressed into service.

Two more test pilots from the Hawker team took their first flights towards the end of 1954, Duncan Simpson on 12 November and Hugh Merewether on 20 December. Meanwhile, 19 August 1955 saw none other than Group Captain 'Sammy' Wroath, Commandant of the Empire Test Pilots' School (ETPS) at Boscombe Down – he had founded the school in 1943 – taking the Hurricane up for 25 minutes. Wroath had returned to the ETPS in 1953 and was Commandant until 1957.

Another familiar name to grace the logbook is none other than Wing Commander Peter Thompson, DFC, who founded the BBMF at Biggin Hill. LF363 was obviously unavailable again, so on 13 September 1956, he picked up G-AMAU from Dunsfold and flew it to his base at North Weald, where he landed at 0935 hrs and handed it over to Group Captain Jamieson, who carried out two 50-minute flypasts, taking off at 1030 hrs and 1500 hrs. Thompson returned the aeroplane to Dunsfold on 14 September and 'Bill' Bedford took off in it the following morning for displays at Wymeswold, Thorney Island and Benson – a somewhat circuitous trip!

June 1957 saw the start of G-AMAU's regular trips to and from the Hawker factory at Blackpool's Squires Gate airfield. The factory had originally been built by the Ministry of Aircraft Production during 1939–40, and it was used by Vickers-Armstrong to manufacture Wellington bombers during World War 2. In order to keep pace with orders for the Hunter, Hawker leased the factory and reopened it in the early 1950s, and it was here that the company also chose to set up a small facility converting ex-Fleet Air Arm Sea Furies for foreign use. To this end Hawker received an order to convert a batch of two-seat Sea Furies into target tugs for the German company Deutsche-Luftfahrt Beratungsdienst; the Hurricane was the aircraft of choice for the Hawker test pilots to commute between Dunsfold and Blackpool to flight-test the Sea Furies, the trip generally taking David Lockspeiser just over an hour. The first trip was for a local air display, but by January 1958 they were a regular occurrence, which continued until the end of May.

It is frequently stated that G-AMAU was used as a 'chase' aircraft during the early test flights of the Hawker P 1127 (forerunner of the Harrier). The logbook certainly shows many local flights during the period September 1960–October 1961, when the P 1127 was under development and test at Dunsfold, plus some flights to Filton, where the Pegasus engine was manufactured, but unfortunately nothing is logged with regard to the purpose of those flights. By the time of the test flights, the blue and gold colour scheme had given way to grey/green camouflage with the name *The Last of the Many!* reapplied below the cockpit and the civil registration applied in small black letters below the tailplane. During winter maintenance on 11 December 1962, the Merlin 24, which had been fitted in August 1951, was removed and replaced with a Merlin 502, serial number 212473.

By now relegated to airshow displays, and a small amount of air taxi work, G-AMAU continued flying throughout the mid-1960s until early 1968, when it had the C of A renewed as normal but was delivered from Dunsfold to Henlow on 29 March by John Farley. Here, it was repainted in 1940s-style camouflage and markings and joined two other Hurricanes (LF363 and RCAF 5377/G-AWLW) to fly in the epic film *The Battle of Britain*. Initially flown with the 'whip' aerial, this was soon replaced with a rigid 'sword'-type mast that sloped slightly backwards compared with the other Hurricanes – a feature which it retained for several decades after the film and which helped to distinguish it from the other two Hurricanes used in the flying sequences. All of the aircraft carried a multitude of different codes and serials during the filming, and some that are known for PZ865 are 'H3429/KV-M', 'MI-B' and 'MI-G'.

Squadron Leader D.W. Mills delivered it from Henlow to the film set at Debden on 8 May 1968, and he and Flight Lieutenant Curry were its pilots at Debden, North Weald and Duxford until the latter flew it from Duxford to Dunsfold on 7 June. Here, John Farley used PZ865 for an air display the following day, before Flight Lieutenant Curry flew it back to Duxford on 10 June for it to rejoin the film unit at Debden on the 11th. The majority of the flying took place at Debden or Duxford, but Curry flew it to Hawkinge on 2 July, where it filmed some scenes, before he ferried it to Northolt – where it featured as Air Vice-Marshal Sir Keith Park's personal Hurricane 'OK-1' between 5 and 8 July. Another diversion was the Hawker Siddeley Families Day held at Hatfield on 13 July, Curry performing the display, having delivered PZ865 on the 12th from Duxford and returning to Debden on the 15th. Later that week all three Hurricanes were flown to Blackbushe, where they arrived on the 16th and left on the 18th, the nearby forest roads being used for the refugee sequences seen at the opening of the film. Most of August and September was spent filming at Duxford, the final sequences being shot at Sywell between 24 September and 1 October – on which day the Hurricane was ferried to Bovingdon by Squadron Leader Mills.

Simpsons Aeroservices Ltd had moved from Henlow to Bovingdon when the lease on the hangars had expired, and all of the aircraft were gathered there before they were returned or disposed of. Hawker contracted 'Tubby' Simpson to overhaul G-AMAU, and this took place during the winter months. In addition to normal rectification work, the opportunity was taken to strip the fuselage and to recover it with new fabric, four coats of dope being applied before it was repainted in its grey/green delivery camouflage scheme. The work was complete by 17 March 1969, and Flight Lieutenant Curry delivered it to Dunsfold, where John Farley test flew the aeroplane and then carried out a display on 14 June.

G-AMAU/PZ865 then settled down to its last few years with the manufacturer, carrying out its airshow displays in the hands of the Hawker test pilots. Hugh Merewether experienced a tail oleo failure on 26 July 1969 when it sheared whilst taxiing across the grass after landing at Dunsfold following a display at Lee-on-Solent. The regular routine continued until 1971, when the directors of the company decided that it was appropriate to present the Hurricane to the newly formed Royal Air Force Museum at Hendon, along with their Hart G-ABMR and Hawker Cygnet G-EBMB. It would seem that some discussion took place at a high level within the company, and in the event the Hart and Cygnet went to Hendon but PZ865 was presented instead to the BBMF. John Farley carried out a test flight at Dunsfold on 21 March 1972, shortly after which the aircraft was flown from Dunsfold to Coltishall by Duncan Simpson, thus becoming the last Hurricane delivered to the RAF!

Almost immediately the civil registration was cancelled, the colour scheme was changed and PZ865 emerged in the markings of Squadron Leader Bob Stanford-Tuck's 'DT-A' of No 257 Sqn at Debden in late 1940 – markings which it retained

until 1977. As with all of the Flight's aircraft, the colour scheme has been changed at each major overhaul, and the markings carried by PZ865 during its time with the Flight are:

1972–77    'DT-A' of No 257 Sqn, Squadron Leader Bob Stanford-Tuck, 1940

1978–81    'JU-Q' of No 111 Sqn, 1940

1982–88    *The Last of the Many!*, its original colour scheme from 1944

1989–92    'RF-U' of No 303 Sqn, Sergeant Josef Frantisek, 1940

1993–97    'J' of No 261 Sqn, Malta, September 1940 (cannon refitted)

1998–2004    'Q' of No 5 Sqn, South East Asia Command (SEAC), 1944

2005–10    'JX-E' of No 1 Sqn, Flight Lieutenant Karel Kuttelwascher, 1942

2012–16    'EG-S' of No 34 Sqn, SEAC, Flight Lieutenant Jimmy Whalen, 1944

Between October 2004 and March 2005, PZ865 underwent a deep-strip maintenance inspection and a brand new radiator was fitted along with all new control cables, this work being carried out by the Aircraft Restoration Company Ltd at Duxford. When it reappeared, it was in the markings carried by BE581, flown by Flight Lieutenant Karel Kuttelwascher, DFC and named *Night Reaper*. A further in-depth restoration was carried out by the same company between October 2010 and March 2012, in which the fuselage tubing – originally fitted at Langley in 1944 – was replaced with new material. A new centre section, supplied by HRL, was also installed. Up until that time PZ865 was essentially the same aircraft that had rolled out of Langley in July 1944. When it reappeared, the fighter was in the markings carried by Hurricane IIC HW840, coded 'EG-S', of No 34 Sqn, SEAC during 1944. The original aeroplane had been the personal mount of Canadian pilot Flight Lieutenant Jimmy Whalen, DFC.

Stu Goldspink performs a sharp wingover manoeuvre in R4118 before disappearing into the clouds below. This photograph was taken during an air-to-air sortie from Old Warden in September 2016.

# HAWKER RESTORATIONS LTD

Hawker Restorations Ltd (HRL) developed out of an earlier company, AJD Engineering, which had been founded in 1987 by Tony Ditheridge, Graham Self and Richard Watson. Its first commission was to provide a replica Bristol M1C for an airshow to celebrate the first flight over the Andes in 1918. AJD Engineering went on to supply more than 20 replicas of early aircraft types to museums around the world.

It was during the summer of 1987 that Tony Ditheridge obtained the hulks of two Canadian Hurricanes, BW853 and BW881, and AJD conducted a feasibility study into the possibility of restoring them to flying condition. It soon became very clear that the Hurricane's complex structure made it a much more difficult proposition than the moncoque Spitfire or other conventional fighters. With the costs projected to be in the millions, AJD sold the two Hurricanes. This might have been the end of the story had it not been for Sir Tim Wallis, the New Zealand warbird collector, who approached AJD to restore the ex-Soviet Hurricane P3351/DR393.

Now operating as HRL, P3351 was eventually despatched to New Zealand in late 1995, where it was completed by Air New Zealand Engineering Services. Five more years would pass before the fighter took to the air for its first post-restoration flight in January 2000. It was followed by Mk X AE977, formerly of the Fleet Air Arm, which eventually became the first HRL Hurricane to take to British skies in June 2000. HRL completed a further three full Hurricane restorations for Sir Tim and the sixth, and currently last, Hurricane to fly following a full restoration is Peter Teichman's ex-Canadian aircraft, which has been restored as a Mk IIB 'Hurribomber' and given the serial BE505. A further three more HRL restorations are also close to completion. Despite Tony Ditheridge threatening to retire for some time, the future looks bright for HRL. And thanks to their efforts, and the original, crucial support of Sir Tim, six more Hurricanes grace our skies once again.

The tubular-framed fuselage of Hurricane I P3717 (structurally restored as a Mk IIA), complete with engine bearers, cockpit 'dog kennel' and tail unit. The chunky, roll-formed, ten-sided front and rear spars can be seen resting on the yellow jacks. HRL has to date been responsible for restoring 11 of the 14 Hurricanes now airworthy worldwide, and has worked on four other airframes.

ABOVE Tony Ditheridge and his team at HRL have trebled the world's population of airworthy Hurricanes since January 2000, when Mk I P3351 first flew.

RIGHT A closer view of the 'dog kennel', with a contemporary photograph from a Hawker workshop manual showing these structures being built in a Hurricane factory during World War 2.

FAR RIGHT Woodworking tools, templates and manufacturer's drawings – all critical elements in the restoration of airworthy Hurricanes.

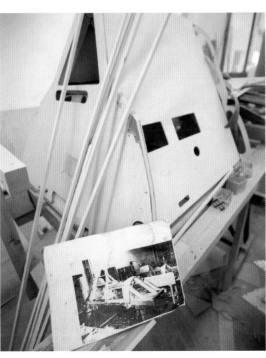

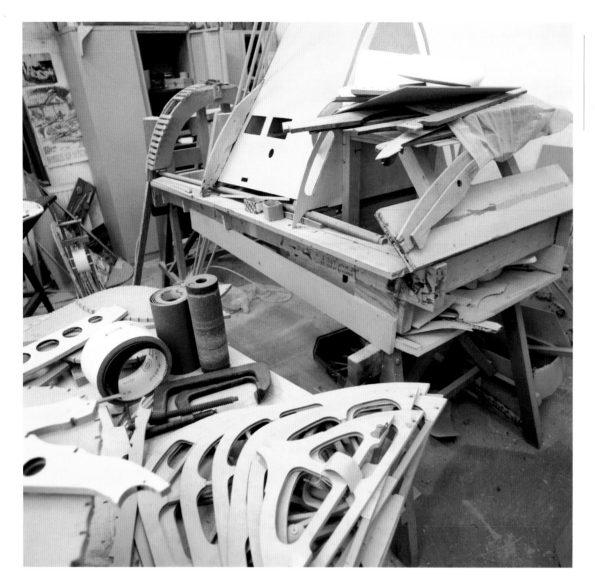

Wooden dorsal section formers and a partially completed plywood 'dog kennel', which forms the cockpit of the Hurricane, dominate this view of the HRL workshop at Milden, in Suffolk.

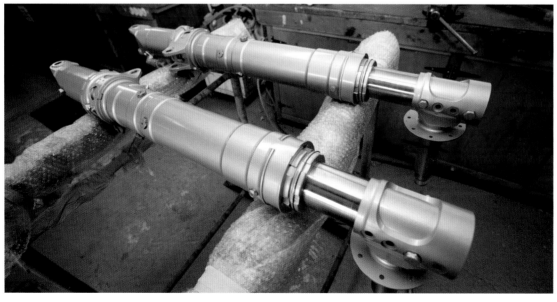

HRL has the capability to fully refurbish Hurricane main undercarriage oleo struts or fabricate new ones.

# BIBLIOGRAPHY

Blackah, Paul, Lowe, Malcolm V. and Blackah, Louise, *Hawker Hurricane – 1935 onwards (all marks) Owners' Workshop Manual*, Haynes Publishing, 2010

Bowyer, Chaz, *Hurricane at War*, Ian Allan, 1974

Brodie, Ian, *The Alpine Fighter Collection's Hurricane Mk IIA*, Reed Books, 2000

Cormack, Andrew, *Men-At-Arms 225 – The Royal Air Force 1939–45*, Osprey Publishing, 1990

Cornwall, Peter D, *The Battle of France – Then and Now*, After The Battle, 2007

Dibbs, John and Holmes, Tony, *Hurricane – A Fighter Legend*, Osprey Publishing, 1995

Dunn, William R., *Fighter Pilot – The First American Ace of World War 2,* The University Press of Kentucky, 1982

Foreman, John, *RAF Fighter Command Victory Claims of World War 2 Part One 1939 – 1940,* Red Kite, 2003

Foster, Wg Cdr R. W. with Franks, Norman, *Tally Ho! From the Battle of Britain to the defence of Darwin,* Grub Street, 2008

Franks, Norman (editor), *The War Diaries of Neville Duke*, Grub Street, 1995

Franks, Norman L. R., *Royal Air Force Fighter Command Losses of the Second World War – Volume 1 Operational Losses: Aircraft and Crews 1939–1941*, Midland Publishing Ltd, 2008

Franks, Norman L. R. *Royal Air Force Fighter Command Losses of the Second World War – Volume 2 Operational Losses: Aircraft and Crews 1942–1943*, Midland Publishing Ltd, 1998

Franks, Norman and O'Connor, Mike, *Number One in War and Peace – The History of No. 1 Squadron 1912–2000*, Grub Street, 2000

Franks, Richard A., *The Hawker Hurricane – A Comprehensive Guide for the Modeller,* SAM Publications, 1999

Gretzyngier, Robert in association with Matusiak, Wojtek, *Poles in Defence of Britain*, Grub Street, 2001

Halley, James J., *Royal Air Force Aircraft L1000–N9999*, Air-Britain (Historians) Ltd, 1993

Halley, James J., *Royal Air Force Aircraft P1000-R9999*, Air-Britain (Historians) Ltd, 1996

Halley, James J., *Royal Air Force Aircraft T1000-V9999*, Air-Britain (Historians) Ltd, 1997

Halley, James J., *Royal Air Force Aircraft W1000–Z9999,* Air-Britain (Historians) Ltd, 1998

Halley, James J, *Royal Air Force Aircraft BA100–BZ999,* Air-Britain (Historians) Ltd, 1986

Halliday, Hugh, *242 Squadron – The Canadian Years*, Canada's Wings, 1981

Holmes, Tony, *Aircraft of the Aces 18 – Hurricane Aces 1939-40,* Osprey Publishing, 1998

Holmes, Tony, *USAAF Colours 1 – American Eagles,* Classic Publications, 2001

Holmes, Tony, *Duel 29 – Hurricane I vs Bf 110: 1940,* Osprey Publishing, 2010

Jefford, Wg Cdr C. G., *RAF Squadrons*, Airlife, 2001

Lucas Laddie, *Flying Colours – The Epic Story of Douglas Bader*, Stanley Paul, 1981

Mason, Francis K., *The Hawker Hurricane*, Aston Publications Ltd, 1987

Minterne, Don, *The History of No 73 Squadron Part 1 – 1917 to November 1940,* Tutor Publications, 1994

Moulson, Tom, *The Millionaires' Squadron – The remarkable story of 601 Squadron and the Flying Sword,* Pen & Sword, 2014

Neil, Wg Cdr Tom, *Gun Button to 'Fire'*, William Kimber, 1987

Neil, Wg Cdr T. F., *Onward to Malta*, Airlife, 1992

Nijboer, Donald, *Cockpit – An illustrated history of World War II aircraft interiors,* Boston Mills Press, 1998

Nohara, Shigeru and Ohsata, Hajima, *Aero Detail 12 – Hawker Hurricane*, Dai Nippon Kaiga, 1994

Page, Geoffrey, *Shot Down in Flames – A World War II Fighter Pilot's Remarkable Tale of Survival*, Grub Street, 1999

Parry, Simon W., *Battle of Britain Combat Archive 1*, Red Kite, 2015

Parry, Simon W., *Battle of Britain Combat Archive 2*, Red Kite, 2016

Parry, Simon W., *Battle of Britain Combat Archive 3*, Red Kite, 2016

Price, Alfred, *Battle of Britain: The Hardest Day – 18 August 1940*, BCA, 1979

Ramsey, Winston G (edited by), *The Battle of Britain – Then and Now Mk IV*, After The Battle, 1987

Rawlings, John, *Fighter Squadrons of the RAF and their Aircraft*, MacDonald, 1969

Richey, Wg Cdr Paul, *Fighter Pilot*, Jane's Publishing Company, 1980

Riley, Gordon, *Hawker Hurricane Survivors,* Grub Street, 2015

Shores, Christopher, Cull, Brian with Malizia, Nicola, *Malta: The Hurricane Years 1940–41,* Grub Street, 1987

Shores, Christopher and Williams, Clive, *Aces High*, Grub Street, 1994

Shores, Christopher, *Those Other Eagles*, Grub Street, 2004

Stowers, Richard, *Cobber Kain – The RAF's First World War II Ace*, Wing Leader, 2012

Thomas, Andrew, *Aircraft of the Aces 57 – Hurricane Aces 1941-45*, Osprey Publishing, 2003

Thomas, Andrew, *Aircraft of the Aces 75 – Royal Navy Aces of World War 2*, Osprey Publishing, 2007

Thomas, Nick, *Hurricane Squadron Ace – The story of Battle of Britain ace Air Commodore Peter Brothers CBE DSO DFC\*,* Pen & Sword, 2014

Townsend, Gp Capt Peter, *Duel of Eagles – The classic account of the Battle of Britain,* Weidenfeld Paperbacks, 1990

Vacher, Peter, *Hurricane R4118,* Grub Street, 2005

Wren, A. H., *Naval Fighter Pilot – Lt Cdr R J Cork DSO, DSC, RN,* Heron Books of Lichfield, 1998

Wynn, Kenneth G., *Men of the Battle of Britain*, Frontline Books, 2015

# INDEX